WORDSWORTH AND THE FIGURINGS OF THE REAL

By the same author

IRONY AND AUTHORITY IN ROMANTIC POETRY

Wordsworth and the Figurings of the Real

DAVID SIMPSON

Hamlet. Do you see yonder cloud that's almost in the shape of a camel?
Polonius. By th'mass and 'tis, like a camel indeed.
Hamlet. Methinks it is like a weasel.
Polonius. It is backed like a weasel.
Hamlet. Or, like a whale?
Polonius. Very like a whale.

(Hamlet, III, 2, 379–84)

As a man is So he Sees

(Blake to Trusler, 23 August 1799)

Humanities Press
Atlantic Highlands, New Jersey

© David E. Simpson 1982

First published in the United States of America in 1982 by
HUMANITIES PRESS, INC.
171 First Avenue, Atlantic Highlands, New Jersey 07716

ISBN 0–391–02450–7

Library of Congress Cataloging in Publication Data

Simpson, David, 1951–
  Wordsworth and the figurings of the real.

  Bibliography: p.
  Includes index.
  1. Wordsworth, William, 1770–1850—Criticism and
interpretation.   I. Title.
PR5888.S53 1982   821'.7   81–7126
ISBN 0–391–02450–7   AACR2

Printed in Hong Kong

For John Barrell

Contents

Abbreviations

PrW: *The Prose Works of William Wordsworth*
PW: *The Poetical Works of William Wordsworth*
CJ: *Kant, The Critique of Judgement*

Acknowledgements

The argument of this book has been greatly assisted by the careful attentions of colleagues who have given precious time to reading over parts of the first draft. I am very grateful to Ross Harrison and Michael Ignatieff, both of whom know a great deal more than I do about the subject matter of parts of what follows. In particular I must thank Penny Wilson, who has read the whole manuscript — some parts of it indeed more than once — and considerably improved it, reading with great concentration while being at the same time very busy with her own work. I have learned a great deal about Wordsworth from John Barrell, and from the students who took part in the courses we taught together. I wish also to thank Paul and Jude Ryan, and Penny Wilson again, real figures of companionship.

D. S.

Introduction

Many of Wordsworth's poems are concerned with the variations, whether momentary or habitual, between how people 'see' things. Mostly it is the meditative subject, the 'I' who speaks the poems, recording the different ways of seeing the world under the pressures of imagination, interest and excitement. The narrators of 'Resolution and Independence', and of the fourth of the 'Poems on the Naming of Places' come to mind here; and the retrospective voice of *The Prelude* offers many examples of fields of vision composed because of, or in spite of, particular preoccupations or extremes of joy or pain. Alternatively, we find reported accounts of how other people see, or have seen, their worlds, in ways not necessarily shared by the narrators of the poems; this applies, for example, in 'The Thorn'. On other occasions a conflict is presented between two ways of seeing, as in 'We Are Seven' and 'Anecdote for Fathers'.

All of these poems discuss and display various ways of 'figuring the real'. It is the mind that sees, not the eye. The mind, if it does not completely 'project' itself into the world, selects and composes such sense data as it receives into particular codes of significance, elements of meaning. And the mind itself is a composite identity open to the refractions of passion and feeling, interest and inclination. The fact that it is possible for two people to 'see' the world in different ways, by selecting different things or qualities for privileged attention and composition into meaning, opens up a series of crucial questions about *consensus*; about what we can and cannot share, and why. How can we agree about what constitutes the world of objects, or about what is important in it, if we are apparently not 'seeing' the same things? What influences determine what we see, and what we fail to notice? Are they historical, or universal? Do all minds share the same mechanism of selection or refraction in their choice of figures? And how can people separated by a perception of different figures communicate with or convince one another?

These are the questions for which I shall try to provide a context in this book, in arguing that the emphasis on the predetermined nature of our seeing, which thus operates in terms of unconsciously chosen or imposed figures, was an urgent concern for Wordsworth, and for other writers of his generation. As soon as representation, which I shall show to be the mechanism of seeing, becomes selective, then the assumption of a commonly available world is threatened. Subsequent consensus will then be based on a choice of figures which will be encoded as the 'real'. That choice, or lack of choice, provides the substance of an important anxiety in the Romantic and post-Romantic mind, and it is reflected and even embodied in its literature.

The point may be made with specific reference to 'The Thorn'. It is a poem about perception and description, and the relationship of interdetermination that subsists between them.[1] The old sea captain's narrative makes frequent reference to sources of avowedly dubious authority; rumour and gossip. In this way, he seems to disavow any responsibility for what he is repeating, and casts frequent aspersion on the reliability of his neighbours' information and suspicions. However, it is clear that his own 'seeing', the supposedly unmotivated perception of the items in his world, is itself determined by the rumours he professes to discredit. We only gradually hear from him the details surrounding Martha Ray's situation, but from the very start of the poem he describes the thorn bush, the pond and the mound, in terms of those details, not yet revealed to us. The landscape is given life by its representation of human attributes and affections; the thorn bush is old, forlorn, as high as a child, about to be buried, and so forth. All these insinuated details, apparently introduced simply to specify which bush is meant, contrive to seed our minds (as the captain's has clearly been already seeded) with an expectation of human significance centred around this bush. The captain, in this way, is *seeing* in terms of what he has been told, even as he consciously avows a disbelief in what he has heard. He is seeing in an impure way, and indeed in an ungenerous way, since a woman's reputation (at the very least) is at stake. He is 'figuring the real'.

We may indeed decide not to follow him in so doing, and Wordsworth makes it very clear that we should not do so in introducing him from the first as a flawed narrator, a person we are not to believe. But is it possible that we all see by figures of one sort or another? At least as early as Hobbes, and perhaps earlier, a concept of the figurative is used to explain how perception makes sense out of matter. These figures are perpetuated in language, and it is this which makes Hobbes' concern for the integrity of language such an urgent one. Without the social discipline it imposes, we would all be blindly groping for things to agree about. The concerns of the writers I am interested in here are not so exclusively with language itself — though that certainly counts — but they do reflect a similar obsession with what can be shared, and how, and what interferes with sharing. How is it that perceived data are not assembled into meaning in the same way by all human beings? Are we all different, or different according to our special societies? Do we see in ways which radically isolate us from all companionship, or do we share ways of seeing with specific subgroups made up of those like ourselves? Would those groups then be social, national, historical? And is there a pure seeing, beyond the limitations of figure, where universality is again possible? Or is meaningful seeing itself only possible because of the fact of those limits, so that partiality becomes the precondition of all intelligibility? The sea captain reports:

> Some say, if to the pond you go,
> And fix on it a steady view,
> The shadow of a babe you trace,
> A baby and a baby's face,
> And that it looks at you;
> Whene'er you look on it, 'tis plain
> The baby looks at you again.
>
> (ll. 214–20)[2]

In such contemplation, we would be alone. But in that "steady view", that fixity of interest, would we perhaps be carrying within us what we are going to see? The progression from shadow to baby to baby's face is interesting, and may suggest a gradual specification of the image brought about, not by a refinement of seeing, but by an intensity of projection. Does this explain the rather trite reflexivity of the captain's last lines (as quoted), whereby for something to be seen there has to be a seer? Tautology is the mode of narcissism. Who's looking at who, kid?

There is a much stranger deviation from what we might call the 'normal' as the captain describes the villagers' one attempt at scientific investigation, or sharpening of perception, to be conducted with spades and trowels. Will there really be a child buried beneath the mound?

> But instantly the hill of moss
> Before their eyes began to stir!
> And, for full fifty yards around,
> The grass — it shook upon the ground!
> Yet all do still aver
> The little Babe lies buried there,
> Beneath that hill of moss so fair.
>
> (ll. 225–31)

How is it that they share what must, barring the hypothesis of some supernatural intervention, be thought of as a kind of hallucination? Is it the product of one person's imaginative seeing, which the rest embrace because it enacts ideas they are themselves unconsciously experiencing? And how is it that this 'sign' seen in nature actually *adds* to their conviction of the existence of the buried child? Wordsworth does not explain this. Perhaps their consciences restrain them from uncovering a truth which they may feel to be less than criminal, and not deserving of the legal punishment which might follow the 'scientific' perception of the real. Or, we can put it the other way round. Perhaps they are embarrassed at the prospect of *not* finding what they expect, and at being thus exposed as credulous and malicious. By stopping short, they contrive to maintain the possibility of a truth for which they never have to accept responsibility; the rumours can then persist without any question of verification. If this is the case, then Martha Ray becomes a scapegoat, a figure on whom is directed all the crueller instincts of the community. Rumour can preserve her in this rôle, whereas 'fact' might clear her name. And even if a body were to be discovered, what would it prove? Not, certainly, that she had murdered her child. But how much 'justice' could she expect from a judge and jury already primed with the details of the rumours surrounding her, thereby perhaps 'seeing' in the same impure way as the old captain sees?

In the two ways of seeing reported by the sea captain, the static reflection of the single observer's face as the face of another (or, the imposition of an alien image upon one's own reflection), and the collective perception of or belief in natural portents, Wordsworth goes to the heart of an important question. For the two are not separate. We are socialized beings even in our singleness, in our private moments, and we reproduce around us the figures of that society. That is why, I think, Wordsworth is so concerned to analyse societies of people, despite his reputation as a lonely eminence, and to distinguish those in the city from those among mountains and lakes.

The same phenomena are described as deviations of the individual mind in the account of the "first poetic Faculty" in *The Prelude* (VIII, 511ff.).[3] They are the result of "wilfulness of fancy and conceit" (l. 521):

> From touch of this new power
> Nothing was safe: the Elder-tree that grew
> Beside the well-known Charnel-house had then
> A dismal look; the Yew-tree had its ghost,
> That took its station there for ornament:
> Then common death was none, common mishap,
> But matter for this humour everywhere,
> The tragic super-tragic, else left short.
>
> (ll. 521–32)

In the same way, Martha Ray was not allowed a common mishap, nor her child a common death. Here, the gallery of the "tragic super-tragic" includes widows obsessively attached to their deceased husbands' graves, vagrant mothers imaged in drooping foxgloves, and a whole crowd of knights and fairies. These "shapes" produced by "wilful fancy" were often, Wordsworth tells us,

> grafted upon feelings
> Of the imagination, and they rose
> In worth accordingly.
>
> (ll. 584–6)

Fancy is a lower power than imagination, and in here consigning it to the production of shapes not necessarily related to the "feelings" of the imagination, Wordsworth appears to be privileging the higher power. But we must then question what the nature of the grafting might be. Could the "shapes" ever come to change the nature of the "feelings", making them less wholesome and creative (imaginative) than they might otherwise be? How exactly are fanciful shapes "wilful", and imaginative feelings not so? And for whom? Wordsworth's continuation of the discussion tells us more:

> I had forms distinct
> To steady me; these thoughts did oft revolve
> About some centre palpable, which at once
> Incited them to motion, and control'd,
> And whatsoever shape the fit might take,
> And whencesoever it might come, I still
> At all times had a real solid world
> Of images about me; did not pine
> As one in cities bred might do; as Thou,
> Beloved Friend! hast told me that thou didst,
> Great Spirit as thou art, in endless dreams
> Of sickliness, disjoining, joining things
> Without the light of knowledge.
>
> (ll. 598–610)

The "forms distinct" are what discipline the "adulterate power" of figurative projection, which might otherwise run wild (l. 592). They constitute a harmony through time of movement and stillness. The *images* derived are thus *real*, and *solid*; they are figured as having substantial existence. The figuring activity here seems to be authentic, and it is emphatic that it is not likely to be available to those living in cities. There, the corresponding activity is not synthetically related to a living agent in the human identity, but is distanced and detached — a joining and disjoining without "the light of knowledge".

In this passage from *The Prelude* Wordsworth seems to suggest a positive alternative to the kind of figuring that takes place in 'The Thorn'. Here, there is a more creative and valuable construction of the 'real', and it is related to environment. That two versions of the 'real' are possible suggests and indeed derives from a division between two communities of seers. Much of this book will be about that division. There is also another important division, not necessarily synonymous with the first, between those who realize that they are seeing by figures, and are therefore open to new figurings and new orderings of objects, and those who passively assimilate (whether by 'choice' or by coercion) what they take to be an immanent world of natural forms, a stable 'reality'. Wordsworth is clearly seeking to expand the community of the former of these classes over the latter. We can locate the famous ambiguity in his use of the word 'nature' here. Shifting as it does between within and without, between denominating the world of outward forms and that of the human identity, it suggests that the 'real' is itself an unstable entity deriving from the relation between self and other. The 'natural', which so often in everyday usage indicates an unargued principle, a first and last resort — what we all have, see or feelingly respond to — is here unstable, open to definition.[4] What does it mean to debate the 'natural'? It means, at least, a stringent inquiry into what we agree to *call* natural. The term is an authoritarian one, whether we restrict it to something for which we are not responsible, an 'outer' world, or to the sum of our contractually agreed figures, things we have made. Here is Bentham:

> That arrangement of the objects of any science may, it should seem, be termed a *natural* one, which takes such properties to characterise them by, as men in general are, by the common constitution of man's nature, independently of any accidental impressions they may have received from the influence of any local or other particular causes, accustomed to attend to: such, in a word, as *naturally*, that is readily and at first sight, engage, and firmly fix, the attention of any one to whom they have once been pointed out.[5]

Bentham goes on to talk of interest, and susceptibility to pleasure and pain, as the most profitable sources for such a concept of the natural. But an examination of Wordsworth's writing questions, I think, whether we can ever be immune from the influences of local and particular causes. What is 'natural' in the country is not so in the city. There may be no such society of "men in general", since all social groups subsist in particular places. Thus, it may be that any consensus sufficiently complete to be called 'universal' would have to be thought of as something *imposed* by a dominant faction or subgroup. This obliges us to examine and ponder the figures through which we see. We must read as well as see the world; and instead of reading for the signature of an omniscient creator, we suspect rather the presence of some among our fellow humans, anxious indeed to conceal rather than announce the evidence of their presence. This is a very important insight, and I believe that it results from Wordsworth's observation of life in the city. In such a context, to judge "readily and at first sight" is the most dangerous thing to do. In many of Wordsworth's poems, the 'first sight' produces either confusion or misreading, and must be corrected by the second look. It becomes important, then, that we live in a society which allows us *time* for the second look.

Wordsworth sets in motion, in this way, an analysis of *denaturing*, in calling attention to the instability of the natural; indeed, as I shall argue, he makes that instability a positive requirement. Here is Comte, who deflects our curiosity about 'objective' origins much as Wordsworth does,[6] and then goes on to challenge the more immediate verification of the real:

> Not only must our Positive researches of all kinds be essentially reduced to the systematic appreciation of what actually exists, by abandoning all attempts to discover their first origin and final destination, but it is further requisite to feel that this study of phenomena, far from being able to become absolute, must always remain relative to our organisation and our circumstances. While recognising, under this double aspect, the necessary imperfection of our speculative resources, we see that far from possessing the power of studying thoroughly any really existing object, we cannot so much as guarantee the possibility of thus establishing, even in the most superficial way, the fact that all really existing objects do exist, for the greater part of them must perhaps altogether elude our notice.[7]

In this way, "real knowledge" for Comte is "necessarily relative" (p. 29). He might have added 'figurative', for that is the mode of producing knowledge he signals in suggesting that many potential objects elude our notice, while others are privileged into 'reality'. This produces no absolute insecurity in Comte, in that phenomena are ordered by a balance of fact and theory which he calls "rational prevision" (p. 54), whose essence is social; and this emphasis on the social determination of the 'real' is very important in the nineteenth century. Emphasis on cultural relativism had always been a commonplace in the liberal tradition in its affirmation of the principle of toleration of other societies; what becomes more prominent after Wordsworth is a sense of division within one's own society. I shall trace the degree to which the aesthetic and philosophical ideas about the place of figured forms relate to the important questions in the analysis of social organization. The 'imagination' is defined in such a way that it can only be thought of as flourishing within particular social contexts and environments. It consequently serves to describe polemically the failures of the contexts immediately observed.

The roundness of that last phrase, 'immediately observed,' calls for at least a moment of hesitation, for it is in the context of the questions raised by such a hesitation that the title of this book is a carefully chosen one. In common terms of reference, the 'real' and the 'figured' would be thought of as mutually exclusive, the one beginning where the other ends. Here, each of these terms is intended to reflect on and destabilize the other. Their conflation, or partial conflation, says something both about the subject matter and the method of what follows.

What I have already said about 'The Thorn' will serve as a rehearsal of the subject matter. The Romantic writers, and Wordsworth among them, worked within the orbit of a crisis in which the figured and the real were coming to be more closely identified. What is regarded as the real has already been figured or processed by the mind. Subjectively, this appears as the process of the modifying imagination; intersubjectively or socially, it becomes what we have come to call 'ideology'. The detailed exposition of this is the point of this book.

Before passing on to such an exposition, I would like to make a few preliminary points about method, some consciousness of which is demanded by the very nature of the subject matter itself. For the juxtaposition of this reading of Wordsworth with the range of different discourses to be invoked (though by no means exhausted) — epistemology, language theory, aesthetics, political economy — as registering the same inquiry into issues of representation, itself insists on a question about the relation of the figured and the real in an immediately contemporary way. Where, it may rightly be asked, does 'real' history fit into this scheme of analogies and correspondences? Did Wordsworth derive his ideas from reading philosophers and economists, or did he, and perhaps those same philosophers and economists, transcribe a process going on before his eyes in the 'real' world of shepherds and farmers among the Lakes? This is the most difficult question to be faced by any literary criticism which aspires to be in some sense 'historical'. Even leaving aside the uncomfortable (or liberating) modern axis of the hermeneutic process whereby we reorder or refigure the past in terms of our immediate priorities and affilliations (the 'Marxist' reading of X, the 'Freudian' reading of Y, though they seem to ruffle the most feathers, are merely the most obvious), there still remain difficult questions to be addressed when the past is conceived faithfully *as* a past. Let me say straight away that I shall not try to adjudicate the balance between faithful transcription and distortion in Wordsworth or any other writer. I would assume that most writing operates in some middle space between reflection and refraction, transcription and modification. This insight actually seems to be one of the leading preoccupations of Wordsworth's poetry, which in this way poses the question of its own coming into being and its own status as a communication. Wordsworth's London, as represented in *The Prelude*, may stand as an example of the critic's predicament. It certainly has a place in an inherited genre or writings about the city. At the same time, the specific order which it composes relates to immediate concerns in Wordsworth's writing which relate both to analogous discourses (political economy, city versus country) and, we assume, to observed events (blind beggars, theatres, and increased accumulation of men in cities). The London passages as a whole are a function of all of these influences and inspirations, and of course they are read in the context of the critic's own priorities.

Again, take the comments Hazlitt offers on the credibility of Wordsworth's case for the strength and integrity of the elementary human passions as evinced by mountain dwellers. Against the tide of Wordsworth's notoriously positive endorsement of the rustic way of life, Hazlitt comes back with the following argument:

> All country people hate each other. They have so little comfort, that they envy their neighbours the smallest pleasure or advantage, and nearly grudge themselves the necessaries of life. From not being accustomed to enjoyment, they become hardened and averse to it — stupid, for want of thought — selfish, for want of society. There is nothing good to be had in the country, or, if there is, they will not let you have it. They had rather injure themselves than oblige any one else.[8]

Who is right, in terms of a fidelity to what is (or was) the case, 'really'? Readers may all too readily decide, as they often do with Crabbe against the writers he purports to satirize, that one writer is in possession of a truth which efficiently unmasks another's self-deception or purposeful mystification. How much did Hazlitt draw from observation and how much from his already prefigured conceptions? Might not the one, indeed, inform the other? We read on:

> Vanity and luxury are the civilisers of the world, and sweeteners of human life. Without objects either of pleasure or action, it grows harsh and crabbed: the mind becomes stagnant, the affections callous, and the eye dull. Man left to himself soon degenerates into a very disagreeable person. Ignorance is always bad enough; but rustic ignorance is intolerable.
>
> (p. 123)

Here, if we are once alerted to the prominence of the eighteenth-century debates about the functions of luxury and the respective intellectual characteristics of town people and country people (both of which I shall touch on later), then we come to suspect that Hazlitt too is 'seeing' in a motivated way, constructing a covert apologia, behind the guise of 'realism', for a system of values which it is one of the functions of Wordsworth's poetry to deny. We have, in this opposition between the two writers, an opposition within discourse, prompted by opposite convictions about the social order, the effects of wealth and commerce, the rôles of town and country, and so forth. Neither can be assumed to be simply recording the 'real', for Wordsworth's position also partakes of an *a priori* perspective emphasizing Spartan self-sufficiency and the absence of surplus production as desiderata for the best kinds of human life.

I have made this point at some length, not to reduce all inquiry to a static scepticism, but to demonstrate the difficulties involved in relating any writing, whether it be explicitly theoretical or apparently a transcription of direct observation, to something we can agree to call in an unthinking way the 'real'. I would not go as far as some do in denying any reference to a reality outside that of discourse,[9] nor would I wish to suggest that the search for it is a secondary or irrelevant task. It is, rather, because of figured orderings, in Wordsworth as in Hazlitt, that it must become a *difficult* task, one requiring careful historiography and scrupulous attention to sources. I have neither competence nor space for such a task, and that is why I have refrained from adjudicating the issue of truth to 'fact', even as it remains the case that what follows will refer to genres of writing which offer themselves as prescriptive and descriptive analyses of an urgent historical crisis. The urgency, I hope, will not seem diminished, nor is my caution intended to encourage any kind of bad faith. Much of the book will be spent showing how and why figures *do* carry all the passions and convictions of reality, and that they are, effectively, real. Thus, if there are no confident references to things as they 'were' in what follows — though I certainly take it for granted that the condition of England gave little cause for satisfaction or approbation in the period under discussion — then there is still much to be said about how things were *seen, felt* and *argued*. Perhaps I may say 'figured', having now made it clear that no loss of intensity or conviction is to be inferred from the use of that word.

Some of the above points may also help to explain why it is that discourses other than literature have been used, with apparent licence, to throw light on Wordsworth's poetry. I have not felt in any sense limited to what Wordsworth actually read, and indeed have often made reference to texts which we may be quite sure that he did *not* read. Once again, a few questions need to be aired here, even if they cannot be resolved. What is the authority for the relevance of connections which go beyond those which can be empirically proven? I shall make a case, for example, for a Kantian argument at work in a poem which Coleridge wrote before we can be sure that he had read much, if any, of Kant.

This habit may be defended on two counts, the first of which is itself empirical. The German philosophers I invoke, especially in Chapter 2, were often not known to the writers they are used to illuminate. However, those same German philosophers were frequently very well read indeed in the writers of the English rationalist tradition, who were widely translated into German in the eighteenth century. In this way they belong to the same tradition as does, for example, Wordsworth, without there being any direct debt or connection. (Of course, when we speak of the empirical, we should never forget the possible importance of word of mouth connections between, for example, Wordsworth and Coleridge.)

The second justification is more elusive, but far more pervasive, and once again it takes us to the very roots of the way in which we write about the past. It is an often unspoken assumption of such writing that there is something which we are entitled to call, in Shelley's (and Hazlitt's) phrase, the 'spirit of the age'. This appears as a set of questions and solutions which different writers address themselves to, whether known or unbeknown to each other. The mechanism by which this operates is often the subject of bitter controversy. Idealist critics tend to think of it as prior to the particular facts through which it appears. As Coleridge put it, if I may use him slightly out of context, "an idea . . . is in order of thought always and of necessity contemplated as antecedent".[10] It is not to be constructed out of partial and contingent manifestations of actual phenomena, out of "any particular state, form, or mode, in which the things may happen to exist at this or that time," but rather from "the knowledge of *its ultimate aim*" (p. 12). As a mode of analysis of the past, this means that deviant or incommensurable facts, forms and modes can be ignored as the prioristically constituted idea is made the essential feature of history and the principle of organization to which empirical data have to conform. We can see this at work in Hegel's account of the past, wherein privileged moments of history (or literature) are boldly made representative of the development of *Geist*, with no attention whatsoever lavished on unincorporated details or events.

A second approach, which we may call materialist, offers a different emphasis, working out by various forms of induction the identity of the 'idea' as it is constituted out of the material bases of life as it is lived. Here, what we have called the 'idea' is but a refracted expression, after the event, of a series of empirical relations. It does still have the power to redetermine experience, so that it continues to have a formative influence on history, at least in periods of stability when the base conditions themselves remain unchanged. The word for this repository of order is now not so much 'idea' as 'ideology'. It is no longer a metaphysical function of a universal mind but an active consequent of and participant in material history.

Of these two approaches, the first was certainly more common among Romantic writers, and it continues to claim its latterday disciples. We shall see, however, in Wordsworth's poetry as well as in the discourses which give it a context, that the second option was not unexplored in the generations before Marx. As I have said before, the proving of real (material) history is beyond the scope of this book. I am convinced of its importance, though I would not accept that it need be passively reflected or embodied in the work of any writer. Thus I am writing about 'ideologies' without trying to offer any determinate thesis for their specific originations.

To return to the main point, there are, then, two justifications for writing about analogies rather than causes, one simply empirical (A and B may both have read C, though not each other), the other more generally historical and heuristic (A and B may respond to similar pressures in their reading of their experience, without knowing it). I hope that this goes some way toward explaining the rather wide scope of the writings I have drawn upon to elucidate a Wordsworthian preoccupation. Quite apart from the historical importance of these analogies, which is what is most important, there is the added advantage that they offer vocabularies for making sense of literature in very precise and insightful ways. They offer, that is to say, a historical aesthetic.

This brings me to another statement of purpose. It will soon become apparent that I have not attempted to construct general definitions for some of the more 'loaded' words I am using; I mean words like 'metaphor' and 'symbol', words which rhetoricians argue about and between. This is because the writers to be discussed do not all use such words in the same way, and I have meant to retain the specificity of those uses. Any implicitly universalist, rhetorical definitions of the various modes of figuring would distract attention from the nature of my curiosity, which is historical and directed to the issues which inform the whole practice of representation at a particular point in time. The key words are thus not those which discriminate between figures in an abstract rhetorical way, but those *behind* the very *constitution* of figures: power, exchange, community, faction, intention, and so forth. Coleridge was worried about the effects of what he called 'metaphor', whilst Shelley, for example (who is not discussed at length here), used the word to signal something radically creative. This difference is not much illuminated, to my mind, by a detached consideration of what metaphor 'is'. Instead, we must attend to the contexts in which the metaphorical mode is positioned, and the purposes for which it is *used*. Thus Coleridge compares it to the 'symbolic' and finds it lacking, whilst Shelley constructs his idea of metaphor to counter the ordinary way of words and things, the predetermined ortho-doxies inhibiting the making of all new relations.

I have said something about what is implied in the words 'figuring' and 'real'. There are two other words which call for a preliminary explanation. First, *intention*, which does not seem to have the sense I invoke for it until the late nineteenth century.[11] I mean by it the direction or motivation of the mind towards certain things (or figures) rather than others; that which determines selection or unconscious decision about what to 'see'. Thus the perceptions of the villagers in 'The Thorn' (of the bush, the pond, the trembling grass, and so forth) are intentional perceptions, and as such they lead us to question the motives behind them. We end up making ethical judgements about those motives, about whether they are charitable or cruel, sharable or exclusive. An extreme viewpoint, like that of Blake, would hold that all perception is intentional; that what we see is a function of who we are, that beholding is becoming.

Second, *desire*. This is not a faculty of the mind, but a principle of energy which fuels and directs the very disposition of the faculties themselves. It is a positive-negative energy. It ensures the continuance of activity, part of which is always potentially creative, but it does so at the expense of any satisfaction with things as they are at any one moment. Desire in fact defines itself as the absence of satisfaction. Adam Smith, as we shall see, understands the positive-negative, seeing (what I call) desire as the source of all human achievements as well as of a great deal of human misery. Desire provides at once the energy to dissolve existing figures (in which sense it is central to Romantic theories of imagination), and also an eventual disappointment with whatever new ones are created. It is thus both a tool of vested interest — we keep on doing, striving, wanting, in ways which are potentially or actually open to manipulation — and at the same time a force threatening the stability of that interest, when it is allowed to breach the limits imposed upon it. It appears in many forms, and under many names; in Fichte's theory of knowledge, Wordsworth's aesthetics, and Smith's economics, to name but three. My use of the word is thus more embracing than the concept as we find it in Hegel (*die Begierde*), which refers to a particularly selfish, almost animal aspect of intentionality whereby we pursue our immediate needs in the material world, uninhibited by conscious reflection. I use the word more abstractly to describe the energy which ensures that one particular intentional configuration will always give way to another, and another. In this sense desire is the true opposite to satisfaction, which it always undercuts in a movement of restlessness which places it at the very heart of the Romantic aesthetic.

This version of 'desire' once again helps to explain why my concepts of the 'figured' and the 'real' are deliberately unstable. Under the aegis of desire, all figurings are a progression to a real which never *is* but is always *about to be*. Of course, it will be clear from what has already been said that this formulation of desire does not preclude a more literal and empirical level of the 'real' out of which desire itself is generated, and by which it may be determined.

Some of the writers to be discussed will themselves offer such explanations. 'Desire' will be positioned as a result of the hegemony of commerce and the existence of the national debt, or, later, as the energy behind the capitalization of the economy, from which it indeed also derives. But at this point, the dragon is eating its own tail. Marx's 'real' is itself unstable: change the economic base of social life, and you change also what is seen as the world. What governs life and fuels ideology is itself a figure, one endowed with a horrifying power to reproduce itself into efficient reality by controlling our modes of representation. It is a figure which has *real power*, a figure whose reality *consists* in power, but it is not of itself immanent, metaphysically unarguable, or beyond the reach of our energies. Wordsworth too, I shall be arguing, is an important analyst of the figures of power, and the power of figures.

One final point. There are many 'Wordsworths', and no book of literary criticism that I know of has yet done justice to them all. It may be that his writings, and the historical pressures operative upon them during the fifty or so years of his career, are diverse enough to make it impossible, or at least very difficult, for any critic to present a complete reading, one establishing absolute coherence among all his public and private statements. Traditionally, for example, one may write a book on Wordsworth which ignores much or all of what was written after 1815. Whether the ultimately coherent Wordsworth be thought possible or not, I should say that such an ambition is no part of the purpose of this book. The kinds of meanings of poetry discussed here are not simply to be adjudicated by reference to a biographical entity called 'Wordsworth', helpful and important though such reference may be. They relate to 'discourse', to something which is rather loosely under the control of the independent subject, conscious and unconscious, inevitable as it is that they are announced through and refracted by that subject. Even within a single poem, a statement or conjunction of statements may encourage more questions than subsequent conclusions can resolve in any summary way. In this way, meanings are to be sought as much in the interrelations of the language of poetry with the languages of contemporary argument and expression as in the corporate identity 'Wordsworth'. I assume and try to demonstrate, therefore, an essentially social aspect to poetic statement. I quite accept that some poems may allow specific relations more than others, and that other poems may even demand entirely different relations. My argument does not pre-empt the case for an 'orthodox' Wordsworth, but it does try to bring forth one of the 'Wordsworths' who has not hitherto been much appreciated.

This also partly answers, by anticipation, the question of whether Wordsworth should be deemed to have been conscious of the contexts and implications of his writings as here adduced. How, it might be asked, can one reconcile the apparently radical aesthetic implicit and explicit in the poetry with the famous 'conformity' of the mature poet? The beginnings of an answer to this question are to be found in the insistence, prominent in Wordsworth's writings, that his ideal community of independent owner-occupiers is now part of a lost world, or at best a world disappearing fast. This makes it available as a model for criticizing the inadequacies of the incumbent present, without at the same time committing Wordsworth to a revolutionary programme aimed at its reestablishment. Hence the mixture of moral urgency and historical despair and, perhaps, the strange, self-implicating anxiety about the poet's own position as an outsider on the inside; a concerned intelligence already deprived of crucial influence, and obliged to chronicle not only the epiphanies but also the transgressions and impositions of its own figuring. The owl of Minerva may indeed, as Hegel said, take wing only at dusk, and be afflicted thereby with the moral imperative to ponder the conditions of its own survival and the medium of its locomotion.

1 Companionable Forms

Methinks, its motion in this hush of nature
Gives it dim sympathies with me who live,
Making it a companionable form,
Whose puny flaps and freaks the idling Spirit
By its own moods interprets, every where
Echo or mirror seeking of itself,
And makes a toy of Thought.

Coleridge, 'Frost at Midnight'

1 COLERIDGE: THE BROTHER POET

Coleridge's so-called 'conversation' poems project, in various ways and to varying degrees, assertions of control. Out of the silence of meditation there comes the poet's voice, and out of the private figurations of the imagination there emerges a predication of consensus and shared experience. The receiving spirits of the conversational gestures are themselves created, within this silence, by the poet. The "pensive Sara" of the poem usually called 'The Eolian Harp', the sleeping babe in 'Frost at Midnight', and the "gentle-hearted Charles" to whom 'This Lime-Tree Bower my Prison' is especially directed have no answering voices in these poems. Their 'replies' are constructed by the meditative mind of the single speaker; their figurative presence depends on their actual absence, or silence, as they thus contribute to the tale of special significance which the speaker wishes to adorn.

I shall begin with an account of a poem of 1797, 'This Lime-Tree Bower my Prison'. Because I shall discuss it at some length, and because it provides a statement of the issues which will be repeatedly referred to in the rest of the book, it is worth quoting entire:

Well, they are gone, and here must I remain,
This lime-tree bower my prison! I have lost
Beauties and feelings, such as would have been
Most sweet to my remembrance even when age
Had dimm'd mine eyes to blindness! They, meanwhile, 5

Friends, whom I never more may meet again,
On springy heath, along the hill-top edge,
Wander in gladness, and wind down, perchance,
To that still roaring dell, of which I told;
The roaring dell, o'erwooded, narrow, deep,   10
And only speckled by the mid-day sun;
Where its slim trunk the ash from rock to rock
Flings arching like a bridge; — that branchless ash,
Unsunn'd and damp, whose few poor yellow leaves
Ne'er tremble in the gale, yet tremble still,   15
Fann'd by the water-fall! and there my friends
Behold the dark green file of long lank weeds,
That all at once (a most fantastic sight!)
Still nod and drip beneath the dripping edge
Of the blue clay-stone.

                  Now, my friends emerge   20
Beneath the wide wide Heaven — and view again
The many-steepled tract magnificent
Of hilly fields and meadows, and the sea,
With some fair bark, perhaps, whose sails light up
The slip of smooth clear blue betwixt two Isles   25
Of purple shadow! Yes! they wander on
In gladness all; but thou, methinks, most glad,
My gentle-hearted Charles! for thou hast pined
And hunger'd after Nature, many a year,
In the great City pent, winning thy way   30
With sad yet patient soul, through evil and pain
And strange calamity! Ah! slowly sink
Behind the western ridge, thou glorious Sun!
Shine in the slant beams of the sinking orb,
Ye purple heath-flowers! richlier burn, ye clouds!   35
Live in the yellow light, ye distant groves!·
And kindle, thou blue Ocean! So my friend
Struck with deep joy may stand, as I have stood,
Silent with swimming sense; yea, gazing round
On the wide landscape, gaze till all doth seem   40
Less gross than bodily; and of such hues
As veil the Almighty Spirit, when yet he makes
Spirits perceive his presence.

                                     A delight
Comes sudden on my heart, and I am glad
As I myself were there! Nor in this bower,   45
This little lime-tree bower, have I not mark'd
Much that has sooth'd me. Pale beneath the blaze
Hung the transparent foliage; and I watch'd
Some broad and sunny leaf, and lov'd to see
The shadow of the leaf and stem above   50
Dappling its sunshine! And that walnut-tree
Was richly ting'd, and a deep radiance lay
Full on the ancient ivy, which usurps
Those fronting elms, and now, with blackest mass
Makes their dark branches gleam a lighter hue   55
Through the late twilight: and though now the bat
Wheels silent by, and not a swallow twitters,
Yet still the solitary humble-bee
Sings in the bean-flower! Henceforth I shall know
That Nature ne'er deserts the wise and pure;   60
No plot so narrow, be but Nature there,
No waste so vacant, but may well employ
Each faculty of sense, and keep the heart
Awake to Love and Beauty! and sometimes
'Tis well to be bereft of promis'd good,   65
That we may lift the soul, and contemplate
With lively joy the joys we cannot share.
My gentle-hearted Charles! when the last rook
Beat its straight path along the dusky air
Homewards, I blest it! deeming its black wing   70
(Now a dim speck, now vanishing in light)
Had cross'd the mighty Orb's dilated glory,
While thou stood'st gazing; or, when all was still,
Flew creeking o'er thy head, and had a charm
For thee, my gentle-hearted Charles, to whom   75
No sound is dissonant which tells of Life.[1]

As so often, Coleridge here seems to be attempting to construct a
theology of perception, an assurance of the validity of a personal,
imaginative configuration of experience within a community
composed of all sympathetic human beings and their God. The
poem moves from a statement of deprivation and isolation, a lament

over the loss of materials for future restoration by memory, to an incremental awareness of the positive and enlivening consequences of being thoughtfully and feelingly alone. It seems to reach a crescendo of conviction around l. 60, and dies down thereafter to a quiet assurance of achieved spiritual community with the "gentle-hearted Charles". The absence of apparent stimulation in the immediate environment has turned out to be a blessing, as the solitude which had at first seemed so unprofitable turns out to have a value. Necessity turns to virtue, and being left behind turns out not to be such bad luck after all.

It is the process by which this conversion of vacancy to completion takes place that interests me here. As he recounts, by drawing upon his own memory, the highly specific details of the landscape which he imagines Charles Lamb to be experiencing, Coleridge also builds himself a place within it, creating an imaginative present "As I myself were there" (l. 45). The key point in this self-incorporation involves the invocation of "joy". The "swimming sense" (l. 39) which is proffered for Charles (forecasting, by the way, the "swimming book" of 'Frost at Midnight', a poem I shall shortly discuss) seems to dissolve any posture of division between self and landscape, subject and world, just as it permits the participation of the absent speaker. This synthesis is produced by "joy", which further licenses the inclusion of the "Almighty Spirit" and his chosen communicants as both sources and sharers of the experience. Again, as the moral is drawn later in the poem, it is "joy" which seals the covenant:

> and sometimes
> 'Tis well to be bereft of promis'd good,
> That we may lift the soul, and contemplate
> With lively joy the joys we cannot share.
>
> (ll. 64–7)

If Coleridge had written, say, 'the *things* we cannot share', there would be nothing arresting in the line. As it is, however, the same word seems to specify both what is and what is not experienced by the speaker. Thanks to the energies of contemplation, there is joy in joys *not* shared. It is of course a commonplace of language theory that the same words have to be used for different experiences or objects having something in common, even as they also involve differences. But I think that Coleridge can be taken to refer to more than this, and that he is in fact addressing a problem which is at the heart of the 'conversation' poems. It is also central to the argument of this book, and is thus worth examining at some length.

The same word is here used to describe what is for Charles the product of direct experience ("the joys we cannot share") and what is the consequence of a meditation upon that experience ("lively joy") by another, at a distance. It is implied that the speaker's joy is the same *emotion* as that which is produced in the ramblers by the contemplation of different objects. That part of experience which belongs to mind and heart alone, independent of whatever objects might happen to call it forth or act as its vehicle, is shareable, even as those empirically given objects are not. Thus the joys are both shared and not shared, as the word is poised between first person and third person experience. It invokes a whole of which they hold only part in common, that part which belongs to the mind alone, strictly considered. This allows for the movement intimated by the poem's narrative whereby Coleridge's own joy is compounded out of his recollections and associations of the wider landscape together with his private perceptions of the bower.

This expression of joy in what is around him, itself first activated by associations from elsewhere, is the point at which Coleridge's priorities take on a Kantian appearance. The images held in the memory have enhanced the immediate context by a carrying over of *delight*. It is not the images themselves, or the images alone, which continue to matter, so much as the faculty of the *mind* which they have wakened into action, and which now determines how new items of empirical observation are *seen*. In this way the speaker shares the emotion which he imagines Charles Lamb to feel, but it is related to different objects. The things around him are now seen in a new light.

Coleridge sees the activating energies of the aroused mind as having in themselves a redetermining effect on what is 'seen'. Kant had produced an epistemology based on the presence of 'categories', or mental dispositions for perceiving data and constructing experience in an organized way. We share, for example, the categories of unity, plurality, causality, and so forth (given to us in terms of space and time), which are transcendental, although they are not always active upon or called forth by the same objects. Roughly speaking, and leaving aside the question of synthetic *a priori* propositions, these categories become available as objects of attention by way of the sensible intuitions which they themselves must be thought to make possible; we are obliged to posit their existence, says Kant, as soon as we ask the question of how connected experience is possible. This is not the place, nor do I have the competence to enter into a detailed estimation of the arguments of the *Critique of Pure Reason*. Suffice it to say that in that work Kant both assumes and argues for a necessary consensus among human subjects in the interaction of the categories with contingent phenomena. It will be clear that such an argument or assumption must be made if a scientific method, one dealing with things which are as good as 'facts', is to be maintained. And it will be equally clear that within the famous distinction between *noumena* and *phenomena*, things as they are in themselves and things as they appear to us, the control of what is variable by what is shareable must be asserted if we are to avoid the threat of a radical subjectivism unsettling that very normative model of experience whose existence the whole theory is designed to explain.

Kant operates with an epistemology very close to that which we may find at work in Coleridge's poem. There are two parts to the whole which is experience: one relates to material objects in the world, the other belongs to the mind strictly considered, in isolation from sense data. There is a real instability in Romantic philosophy which Kant is inevitably broaching even as he solves it. If experience is indeed this synthesis of concept and intuition, of that which is 'in' the mind with that which is 'outside' it, and given that the same concepts cannot always appear in conjunction with the same intuitions, just how much of experience *is* shareable with other people, and how will we *know* it when it is? One person may experience what he calls 'joy' in the contemplation of a sunset, another in the sight of an aeroplane taking off. How can either be sure that the other shares his *emotion*, when he has only the contingent signs or vehicles of language or gesture to depend upon? Kant certainly explains how it is possible that two people *can* communicate successfully, but this does not determine that they will always do so. This may indeed be why Kant is more concerned with scientific method than with language, which he notoriously never discusses. Scepticism is easier to displace in experimental science, where proof 'happens' if it has properly been made to happen.

Before placing Coleridge's argument in the context of the *Critique of Judgement*, which is where Kant squarely faces the status of the aesthetic, it is worth pointing out a more 'conventional' solution to the question of consensus, that found in Thomas Reid's *Essays on the*

Intellectual Powers of Man (1785). Reid addresses the problem of beauty, asking whether it belongs in objects or in the mind which perceives them. His view is that it is original to the "moral and intellectual powers of mind", which is the "fountain" through which what we perceive in the "visible world" appears beautiful.[2] He quotes approvingly a passage from Akenside which is interesting in the context of Coleridge's poem:

> Mind, mind alone! bear witness earth and heav'n,
> The living fountains in itself contains
> Of beauteous and sublime. Here hand in hand
> Sit paramount the graces. Here enthron'd,
> Celestial Venus, with divinest airs,
> Invites the soul to never fading joy.
>
> (qu. p. 793)

This is a more pagan and earthly idea of 'joy' than that which Coleridge seems to wish us to suspect in his own poem.[3] But, for Reid, the question is one of recognition. We may think we know our own mind well enough, but others "we perceive only through the medium of material objects, on which their signatures are impressed" (p. 793). How is it that falsification is avoided? What produces a reliable accord between minds and signatures? The answer, as so often, is God. God has given us faculties, and objects to perceive by means of them. It would be impious to suggest that in so doing he has left large areas of incoherence or confusion between the two. The tension between object and subject is resolved by regarding beauty as properly belonging to both, albeit original to mind:

> To say that there is in reality no beauty in those objects in which all men perceive beauty, is to attribute to man fallacious senses. But we have no ground to think so disrespectfully of the Author of our being; the faculties he has given us are not fallacious; nor is that beauty, which he has so liberally diffused over all the works of his hands, a mere fancy in us, but a real excellence in his works, which express the perfection of their Divine Author.
>
> (p. 783)

There is, however, one major difference between Reid's argument and Coleridge's poem: the latter is written in implicit consciousness of the fall. The mythology of loss, isolation, exclusion from paradise seems to at least taint the opening of the poem, emphatically so in the second line of a manuscript version which refers rather histrionically to Coleridge's accident with the boiling milk as leaving him "Lam'd by the scathe of fire, lonely and faint" (*Poetical Works*, p. 178). The fall is rendered fortunate at the end, when being "bereft of promis'd good" has been turned to advantage by an enlivening of the expelled (that is, imprisoned) consciousness. But it still insists that any consensus or communication must be created out of an original state of division by means of earnest activity and work. It is this which makes Coleridge's version of the theological argument (ll. 37–43) a somewhat troubled and ambiguous gesture, compared with what we find in Reid. The "hues" which "veil the Almighty Spirit" may be thought both to reveal and to conceal, demanding effort and decipherment precisely in that they render necessary the application of that precious faculty of will and consciousness. In a poem of 1795 not discussed here, 'The Eolian Harp' (*Poetical Works*, pp. 100–2), Coleridge had already administered to himself a quite spectacular rebuke for forgetting the state of sin and the consequent need for Christ's assistance. Here nothing as dramatic is intimated, but it is nevertheless emphatic that the sense of peace and communion which ends the poem has been worked for, not merely received. The efficiency of that work seems to be authenticated in two ways. The "Almighty Spirit" may be invoked as the ultimate presence, which may be what gives Coleridge the power and permission to bless (l. 70), though it is invoked ambiguously; and, second, there is a shared capacity in human minds to experience (joy) in the same way, even as the objects of attention differ.

Something of the tentativeness of Coleridge's formulation may be appreciated by further comparison with Kant, specifically the description of the aesthetic in the *Critique of Judgement*.[4] Kant argues that the experience of "the beautiful" operates through a judgement of taste, one essentially not concerned with the real existence of any object as a focus of need or inclination. There is no element of intention in the properly aesthetic response:

> All one wants to know is whether the mere representation [die bloße Vorstellung] of the object is to my liking, no matter how indifferent I may be to the real existence of the object of this representation.[5]

Moreover, such a judgement would become impure if it were "tinged with the slightest interest [Interesse]", for judgements of taste depend precisely on a freedom which would be compromised by attention to material reality. This is by definition what separates the beautiful from the agreeable and the good:

> An object of inclination [Neigung], and one which a law of reason imposes upon our desire [Begehren], leaves us no freedom to turn anything into an object of pleasure. All interest [Interesse] presupposes a want [Bedürfnis], or calls one forth; and, being a ground determining approval, deprives the judgement on the object of its freedom.
>
> (I, 49; *Werke*, V, 279)

At the same time as judgements of taste have nothing to do with the real existences of objects, they are — and here is the crux — made at the same time on the *assumption* of universality. This is possible in part because the subject recognizes the judgement as interest-free; "he can find as reason for his delight no personal conditions to which his own subjective self might alone be party", and therefore assumes that it rests upon "what he may also presuppose in every other person" (I, 51). Kant insists that this is *only* an assumption, and that there can be "no rule according to which anyone is to be compelled to recognize anything as beautiful" (I, 56). This being the case, the process for reaching agreement about the beautiful can only be performance, and never prescription. No universality is proveable, even as it is always assumed.

Remove the theological inscription from the argument of Coleridge's poem, and one has here something very close to the passage describing the joyful contemplation of joys not shared. Kant's more secularized theory offers a way of reading the poem as an assumption rather than a conviction or experience of sharing. As Coleridge cannot 'prove' that the feelings he has had about the landscape are necessarily to be shared by Charles, yet derives comfort and energy from the assumption that they are, so Kant allows for nothing scientific in the communication of the beautiful. There are no unarguably necessary *a priori* convictions, nor is there a complete adequacy of general theory to particular instance. This means that communication (here, education) must proceed by ostension, on the spot, and not by inference, at a distance:

The master must illustrate what the pupil is to achieve, and how achievement is to be attained, and the proper function of the universal rules to which he ultimately reduces his treatment is rather that of supplying a convenient text for recalling its chief moments to the pupil's mind, than of prescribing them to him . . .

(I, 266)

Kant goes on to show how this generates a problem for the pupil arising from the temptation to concentrate upon particular, limiting examples, thus mistaking the vehicle (the contingent) for the spirit (the *a priori*, in the mind):

Only by exciting the pupil's imagination to conformity with a given concept [Begriff], by pointing out how the expression falls short of the idea to which, as aesthetic, the concept itself fails to attain, and by means of severe criticism, is it possible to prevent his promptly looking upon the examples set before him as the prototypes of excellence, and as models for him to imitate, without submission to any higher standard or to his own critical judgement.

(I, 226)

This was to become a familiar Romantic concern, as we shall see. Once the focus of attention lapses into a concentration on the contingent, then the material usurps the mental, and no amiable communities or viable theories of knowledge can be generated out of that.

The qualification made above by Kant indicates the besetting threat to a model of mind which locates what is most important as least open to incontrovertible demonstration. Nevertheless, the assumption of universality is unavoidable, and we posit "a common sense [Gemeinsinn] as the necessary condition of the the universal communicability of our knowledge", as is presupposed by "every logic and every principle of knowledge that is not one of scepticism" (I, 84; *Werke*, V, 309). We do this

by weighing the judgement, not so much with actual, as rather with the merely possible, judgements of others, and by putting ourselves in the position of everyone else, as the result of a mere abstraction from the limitations which contingently affect our own estimate. This, in turn, is effected by so far as possible letting go the element of matter, i.e. sensation [Empfindung], in our general state of representative activity, and confining attention to the formal peculiarities of our representation or general state of representative activity.

(I, 151; Werke, V, 368)

Coleridge's "joy" is clearly posited as a shared one by means of a similarly presupposed common faculty, and one similarly explained by making a distinction between the element of matter and the element of mind, which Kant calls the "formal peculiarities" of the experience. At the same time, such a sharing can *only* be *assumed*. I shall be suggesting that this feature of aesthetic perception, which isolates the perceiving subject from any assured contact with a wider community, except as it is assumed or continually reconstructed, is a crucial issue for Wordsworth as he constitutes the aesthetic into the most creative and important kind of perception. Further, it may be that what pertains to the aesthetic mode as here explained by Kant is also a feature of the whole of perception. This is certainly one of the questions to which Wordsworth's poetry addresses itself. In either case, in part or in whole, we can see that if the assumption of shared experiences and values is questioned or removed, then we lose any sure sense of our own meanings and of their effects upon others. If consensus is continually being constructed and reconstructed, at the same time as it is implicitly only partial, excluding as much as it includes, then the idea of universality in perception and communication must give way to one founded in what we now call 'ideology'. As this shift begins to take place, we shall see that the part of the mind held sacred by Kant here, and used as the rationale for Coleridge's gesture of sharing, i.e. the *a priori*, comes to be vulnerable to the determining effects of the contingent and the external. In particular, those who came after Coleridge were often obliged to be more aware of all the things which can inhibit the experience of "joy".

But this is to anticipate a pattern of development which we see happening only incipiently in Coleridge's poem, and between a small group of friends, though friends he "never more may meet again" (l. 6). His joy, as I say, partakes of the features of a judgement of taste; he assumes the universality of the formal, subjective part of the experience, separated out from the material circumstances which occasion it. Thus it is a joy which he can, and cannot, share. Shared humanity is not dependent on items of sensible intuition, nor even on the physical presence of other people. This recognition converts what might otherwise be an experience of loss and complaint into one of integration and benediction.

Bearing in mind Kant's insistence on universality as an assumption, and only an assumption, in aesthetic judgements, we might register the conditionals in Coleridge's poem as of special importance. The assertive declaration of achieved insight, "Henceforth I shall know" (l. 59), follows on from a series of qualifiers — "perchance" (l. 8), "perhaps" (l. 24), "methinks" (l. 27) — which it cannot in fact negate or supplant, unless the idea of "Nature" itself be deemed to include a lively element of sympathetic mind (again, the theological option). This implicit retraction of confidence is important, serving as a reminder that the speaker's gesture of sharing is actually one of self-sufficiency prompted by the absence of actual human contact. Such contact has to be thought about rather than enacted; or at least *enacted* by *being* thought about. Moreover, being left behind may be a critical loss should he never meet his friends again.

Thus it is absence or isolation which provides the speaker with the opportunity for educative meditation, and that meditation cannot but be qualified, however gently, by a sense of its private and partial status. Silence produces articulation, which then passes back into silence with no assured declaration of reply, except that supplied of course by the alerted and sympathetic reader. It is absence which calls forth the voice, and the speaking forth is a quest for completion.

Turning to 'The Nightingale', a poem which Coleridge first published in *Lyrical Ballads*, we find the same preoccupations present, and this time much more openly. The meditation begins in silence and near-darkness, a situation which is itself being moralized as "A pleasure in the dimness of the stars" (*Poems*, p. 264), at the moment when the nightingale begins its song. This song is at once defined by the speaker as part of the joyous continuum of nature, and an enacted refutation of that tradition which casts it as the voice of pain and melancholy. This received interpretation is, we are told, a mystification, a reading of the world based upon an intentional reconstruction and distortion of an otherwise pure phenomenon:

> In Nature there is nothing melancholy.
> But some night-wandering man whose heart was pierced
> With the remembrance of a grievous wrong,

Or slow distemper, or neglected love,
(And so, poor wretch! filled all things with himself,
And made all gentle sounds tell back the tale
Of his own sorrow) he, and such as he,
First named these notes a melancholy strain.

(ll. 15–22)

Coleridge adds a footnote to make clear that no adverse criticism of Milton is intended; for Milton's attribution has "a *dramatic* propriety", being "spoken in the character of the melancholy Man". Regrettably it has insinuated itself into the literary tradition thanks to those poets who are content to borrow rather than experience nature for themselves, and they are supported by that class of readers which spends its time in "ball-rooms and hot theatres" (l. 37), and consequently never challenges these borrowings.

The speaker's gesture is an extraordinary one, not because it purports to reconstruct the inherited literary tradition — which it indeed turns on its head — but because it declares that the authority for this reinterpretation will be acknowledged by all who take the trouble to walk out into the night and listen to the nightingale's song. The speaker thus appears to declare his immunity from the 'dramatic' perception already invoked as an excuse for Milton's poem, as if he and he alone is able for the first time to describe the 'thing in itself', unrefracted by his own besetting mood. Why does he not, for example, apply the same logic to himself as he has applied to Milton's melancholy man, and entertain the possibility that what he 'hears' is a function of his own state of being? This point is not raised, and instead we are invited to subscribe to something closely akin to an aesthetic judgement of taste. For the speaker of the poem clearly assumes a universality for his perception, and very obviously so because the poem recognizes what it means to displace, the prior judgements of others upon the same 'object', the nightingale's song.

Reading on through the poem, however, something happens which works to unsettle this assumption of universality. The poet or reader who has in fact subscribed to the tradition of the "melancholy bird"

had better far have stretched his limbs
Beside a brook in mossy forest-dell,
By sun or moon-light, to the influxes

Of shapes and sounds and shifting elements
Surrendering his whole spirit, of his song
And of his fame forgetful! so his fame
Should share in Nature's immortality,
A venerable thing! and so his song
Should make all Nature lovelier, and itself
Be loved like Nature!

(ll. 25–34)

The speaker, it is implied, has done those things, and had others done so then there would be no arguments about the import of the sounds now being heard. What is interesting about this passage is that limiting conditions are admitted. We are, implicitly, no longer dealing with an assumption about the status of a pure perception, but with an insight into the influence of external and contextual factors upon that perception. The speaker has in fact been 'educated' into hearing the song of the nightingale in the way that he does. There are two versions of the song, and each is heard by a different class of person. It is possible that only those who have surrendered their spirits in the way described above will authenticate the "Nature" which the speaker purports to reflect and intensify. Such "Nature", indeed, is perhaps to be perceived only as a consequent of that state of mind which, according to the speaker, it offers to produce. The production would then be a reproduction, operative only upon those who have already experienced it; 'passive' reception is possible only if prior activity has taken place.

We deduce, then, that the speaker's judgement cannot be properly free of limiting conditions. As soon as he has described the inadequacy of the judgements of others as related to certain predispositions and circumstances, like residence in ballrooms or besetting melancholia, then he has implicitly circumscribed the universality of his own. Of course, Coleridge (or his speaker) is not to be upbraided for failing to carry through a convincing judgement of taste. Rather, the comparison with Kant's formulation is interesting because of the way in which it points the specific attitude to the aesthetic in the poem, which, we can now see, posits or admits a division within the society of listeners. Membership of both factions, moreover, is still open, because the very strength of the speaker's special pleading is compelled to publicize the alternative it wishes to displace.

The poem moves on through two paragraphs of evidence

strenuously adduced by the speaker — "*And* I know a grove . . . "
(l. 49, my italics) — to the moment of parting from the scene. The
song begins, suddenly, again, and at this point we are directed to the
child in the party:

> My dear babe,
> Who, capable of no articulate sound,
> Mars all things with his imitative lisp,
> How he would place his hand behind his ear,
> His little hand, the small forefinger up,
> And bid us listen!
>
> (ll. 91–5)

Not yet old enough to be brought within the language contract, the
child can only strive for some approximate utterance in sound.
Presumably he seeks to imitate both the arbitrary phonemes of adult
language, which belong to mature mental operations and not to
unmediated nature, and the pure sounds of that nature, by some
form of onomatopoeia. As yet unconscious of the distinction, *all*
sounds exist to him within a continuum to be imitated, and
consequently (for the integrity of language is recognized only with
the fall into consciousness) all are travestied, all marred. Incipiently
adult, and therefore conscious, he cannot be completely a part of
any natural harmony, and yet he has not yet reached the moment of
human language properly defined. His 'meaning' is conveyed
ostensively, by gesture, and not by articulation; and the holding up
of the forefinger reminds his father of another instance of silent
communion when the child's sobbing was quieted at once by
contemplation of the moon.

The speaker's interpretative mind relates to his child much as it
does to the song of the nightingale. He describes in language things
which happen outside language, and can only be transposed into it
by 'interpretation'. Both the bird's song and the child's gestures are
brought within a frame of meaning acceptable to the adult
consciousness and communicable by language; both are used to
insinuate the speaker's control over the process of signification.
Whatever private companionship the child may have with
nature — and we can know nothing of this — is at once brought
within the conventional figurations of adult exchange.

That these incidents belong to "a father's tale" (l. 106) may be
taken to indicate once again the speaker's awareness of a special

context in which they will be seen to have a certain significance, and one perhaps closed to other people. This accords with the hint of a conditional in l. 94, "How he would place his hand beside his ear" (though this might also suggest a habitual action), as if the child cannot yet control his gestures with sureness, so that the father interprets what he would be doing, if he could. The conditionals resound again in the concluding lines of the poem, which look to a prospective future, and emphasize that element of willed or intended coherence which has been present in the meditation all along. Here one of the deepest of human relationships, that of father to son, is brought within the spectrum of the same problem of representation as we often see the Romantics exercising in the sphere of external objects.

In another poem of the same year, 'Frost at Midnight' (*Poems*, pp. 240–2), these themes appear yet more frontally and more critically. Once again, the poem is built around the play of silence and articulation, and articulation of two different and incommensurable kinds, the "gentle breathings" (l. 45) of the sleeping child and the verbal meditations of the speaker. Here, the question of authority is much more apparent than before as the adult affirms even more assertively a happy future for his child — "Therefore all seasons shall be sweet to thee" (l. 65) — based on an apparent intuition of the language God speaks to his chosen. In fact, we can suspect that the verifiability of such a language would depend exactly on the adult's *not* being able to hear it intelligibly for himself:

> But *thou*, my babe! shalt wander like a breeze
> By lakes and sandy shores, beneath the crags
> Of ancient mountain, and beneath the clouds,
> Which image in their bulk both lakes and shores
> And mountain crags: so shalt thou see and hear
> The lovely shapes and sounds intelligible
> Of that eternal language, which thy God
> Utters, who from eternity doth teach
> Himself in all, and all things in himself.
>
> (ll. 54–62)

Does that vocabulary of strenuous, biblical predication, "shalt wander . . . so shalt thou see . . .", serve as a recourse, indeed, to an *authorized* language, one which reciprocally inscribes its speaker's own exclusion from the society of eternal language? Is it another result of his attempt to punctuate the silence by which the meditation is vexed into action, and to which it returns? The child, it is said, will wander "like a breeze". Not only is this motion antithetical to the present vexing vacuum ("unhelped by any wind"), but it is located in a realm of natural determination, outside the sphere of *consciousness*. In this respect, it is strictly 'inhuman', in so far as being human presupposes the exercise of consciousness. In 'The Eolian Harp' (*Poems*, pp. 100–2), Coleridge voices a rebuke, through the "belovéd Woman", to his urge to belong to the "intellectual breeze" (l. 47) of Pantheist totality, exactly because it displaces the "family of Christ" (l. 53), the need for the intervention of the Saviour in the predicament of a "sinful and most miserable man" (l. 62), and for the cultivation of those faculties which might make that intervention deserved, the " Faith that inly *feels*" (l. 60). Wordsworth too, in *The Prelude*, is compelled to alternate the feelings of freedom and half-conscious enjoyment which the opening images of the breeze seem to promise, with the more strenuous and narrowing demands of going in particular directions.

We should register, then, a discomfort in the choice of companions Coleridge predicts for his child, "like a breeze". It echoes and unsettles the initial act of tentative determination which the parent has encoded in the name itself. Writing to Thomas Poole in September 1796, Coleridge thus announced the birth of his child:

It's name is DAVID HARTLEY COLERIDGE. — I hope, that ere he be a man, if God destine him for continuance in this life, his head will be convinced of, & his heart saturated with, the truths so ably supported by that great master of *Christian* Philosophy. —
(*Letters*, I, 236)

The child has been 'figured' into an ideal relation to his as yet latent future; the parent's ambitions, however natural and generous they might be, are in the giving of the name an imposition of a conscious prospectus.

In fact it is the faculty which creates figured form, not through the name but through the visual or mental image, which is analysed more openly than ever in this poem, and it is this analysis which is most important to my argument. The part of the mind which establishes patterns and relations in the world is figurative because it cannot pretend to record in any passive way any sequence of pre-established correspondences put before it. On the contrary, it

actively creates such correspondences by operating imaginatively
upon the given elements of things. It is, further, an antithetical
faculty which is actually 'vexed' into activity, and perhaps into
over-activity, by an external peacefulness and silence. Only the film
on the grate is moving before the speaker's eye:

> Methinks, its motion in this hush of nature
> Gives it dim sympathies with me who live,
> Making it a companionable form,
> Whose puny flaps and freaks the idling Spirit
> By its own moods interprets, every where
> Echo or mirror seeking of itself,
> And makes a toy of Thought.
>
> (ll. 17–23)

There is a peculiar coactivity of mind and nature presented here.
The motion of the film creates the sympathies, as if without human
influence ("Gives it dim sympathies"), but the presence of that film,
now called "form", is at once interpreted according to the moods of
the "idling Spirit", a faculty which belongs strictly to the human
mind. It is difficult not to suspect, however, that the attribution of
prior activity on nature's part, the making of the "form" with which
the mind apparently has nothing to do, is in fact a fallacy. The
'sympathies' are much more likely to reside in the mind than in
nature, because the mind is the locus of their being perceived.
Coleridge may mean to signal just this by writing the word
"Methinks", as if the experience of passive reception is an illusion.
The "idling Spirit", in other words, or some similar faculty, may
actually create the thing it then pretends to respond to. Similarly in
'The Nightingale', something like a choice of self, or a particular
series of events, has created the 'nature' which is then heard again in
the bird's song.

This is familiar Romantic doctrine, whether it be poets creating
the tastes by which they would be enjoyed, or mountain shepherds
seeing glories around their heads; and there is nothing essentially
problematic so long as the 'seeing creatively' is endorsed by
reference either to a divine sanction or to an achieved human
consensus within which we will all 'see creatively' the same way, or
at least in such a way as we can communicate successfully to others.
Human exchange is then saved from the threat of indecipherable
idiosyncrasy. It seems to me, however, that Coleridge chooses in this

poem to complicate and trouble the availability of either of the above options. The spirit is an idle one, and thought becomes a "toy", as if what is full of noble possibilities is converted to a mere plaything threatening to turn the world into a narcissistic facsimile of one person's inner life, neither divine nor sharable.

The variants on this important passage give us clues about Coleridge's uncertainty on the subject. The quarto pamphlet version of 1798 describes a faculty

That loves not to behold a lifeless thing,
Transfuses into all its own delights,
Its own volition, sometimes with deep faith
And sometimes with fantastic playfulness.

(ll. 21–4)

This faculty contains, then, the possibility of figurative activity at both ends of the ethical spectrum, faith and playfulness, nor is there any apparent rule of thumb for telling the difference. In the *Poetical Register* version of 1809 the word "volition", usually related by Coleridge to the lower, material aspects of our needs and desires, those which we share with the animal world, has been replaced by the more dignified, human and capitalized "Will", which in Coleridge's later writings was insistently glossed as the obscure but essential centre of our moral being.[6] In what seems another slight retraction, the capital is absent in the 1828 edition of *Sibylline Leaves*.

Further, in the early versions of the poem, the definition of the activity of the figurative faculty is related to the "self-watching subtilizing mind" (1798) or the "self-watching mind" (1808–9); it is a problem not felt by the superstitious schoolboy, but one experienced by the adult mind as it has learned the demands of mature moral and intellectual activity.

We have in this poem, I would maintain, all the essential elements of a crisis in perception and representation which recurs throughout the nineteenth century in various and important ways. Firstly, we find the implication that all perception may be 'figurative', both the part which is confessed as such, the function of the "idling Spirit", and the part which is presented as objective, the making of sympathies. In so being, it cannot with any certainty be endorsed as true to things either as they 'are' or as they are seen by others. To use Kant's vocabulary, universality cannot be predicated of forms which are themselves recognized as shifting and personal.

Secondly, as a consequence of the above, we can suspect from the evidence of this poem and the others discussed that the mode of perceiving and representing other people obeys the same rules and risks the same misattributions as the perception of objects in the world. In other words, what might otherwise be seen as a limited and abstractly philosophical problem relating to whether we share our companionable forms with others, is thus from the start related to a searching ethical question bearing upon social life at the most fundamental level. If our perception of other people as well as of objects is intentional, and is directly a function of our needs, our dispositions, and even of our idleness, what possibility is there for charitable interchange and for the social contract which we might hope to base upon it? And are there any potentially corrective moments in experience which might disrupt the intentionally created patterns we (separately) create around us, and which would open the possibility of something more generous than the blind clash of vested interests, interests which might moreover even be voiced in mutually exclusive and unintelligible languages? How many of us see the sun, how many see hosts of heavenly angels, and how many see a disc the size of a golden guinea? If there are moments of correction and consensus, do they involve a recognition of some pure world of 'things in themselves', beyond the struggles of secondarily figured forms, or do they simply *appear* as such, while remaining in fact the products of other, superior, and more successfully mystified vested interests? Might not the very idea of a 'pure' perception be itself the imposition of someone else's way of seeing, as Blake saw the consensus of Newtonian scientific method to be?

II WORDSWORTH: THE NAMER OF PLACES

Standing very much at the head of this nineteenth-century investigation into the figurative — one which I cannot fully explore here — and standing, it might be said, like a giant, is Wordsworth. The drama of a poem like 'The Thorn' devolves very obviously around the question of the nature of perception and its relation to the disposition of the perceiver, and it directs us urgently to the place of human beings within such a drama. Is there really a woman on the mountain, or just a thorn bush? Did Martha Ray really bury an illegitimate child, and if she did, who is to blame? What is the exact credibility of the old sea captain's narration, and how can we separate fact from fiction given that we have only his account to work with — an account, moreover, which is interpretative from the very beginning in its choice of descriptive vocabulary? If we were to look for ourselves, would our perception be any more innocent? These questions, very clear in the context of this important poem, are repeated in various ways all over Wordsworth's writings, and it would be an encyclopaedic ambition to seek to describe every instance of their occurrence. Wordsworth's protagonists, many of them rural architects of one kind or another, are frequently engaged in an exploration of the tensions between an "unappropriated earth"[7] and the types and emblems which the human mind seeks to derive from or erect upon it. Nor is this seeking simply culpable, or to be avoided by pious decision. The mind, in communicating either with itself (via objects in the world) or with other minds, may be obliged to operate through a process of symbolic or figurative attribution as it works through the inescapable fact of division, of having 'fallen'. At best, such confirmed emblems are creative and synthetic, binding together a particular community; at worst they are triflings of the renegade mind and monuments to invasion and interference. Wordsworth can often be seen to be trying to establish some kind of working distinction between those two extremes of the figurative activity which Coleridge called "deep faith" and "fantastic playfulness". The question always remains, however, whether these extremes are different in kind or merely in degree. If the former, what is the yardstick for distinguishing the two? If the latter, how can the two be kept safely apart? My own sense of the situation is that Wordsworth is more concerned to perpetuate the question than to solve it, and that he recognizes a kind of 'solution' in the exploration itself, conceived as life process rather than as achieved insight or product.

Part of this process is undoubtedly the assertion, which is not rare among the protagonists of the poems, that the ideally responsive mind can be comfortably positioned outside the whole problem. We can thus find a recurring curiosity about (and at the strongest a 'faith in') the existence of a pure perception, one which is simultaneously and completely a reception, a message unrefracted by the operations of an intentional faculty, whether benevolent or destructive. For example, the interchange between 'Expostulation and Reply' and 'The Tables Turned' (*PW*, IV, 56–7) suggests that

there are powers "Which of themselves our minds impress", and
which can be set off against the products of the misdirecting mind by
a simple binary distinction of kind:

> Sweet is the law which Nature brings;
> Our meddling intellect
> Mis-shapes the beauteous forms of things: —
> We murder to dissect.

Pausing only to register the disturbing double reading of the last
line, which suggests not only that we murder *when* we dissect, but
also that we are *prepared* to murder in order to do so (this is an
interpretation which anticipates certain nineteenth-century concerns about empire and expansion), the suggestion that
Wordsworth's speaker puts forward is that it is sufficient to maintain
a heart "That watches and receives" in order to register a 'truth'
and to stay out of trouble. Only a minimal activity, watching and
wise passiveness, is required, if indeed it is activity at all. In his
optimistic declaration of equal opportunity in *The Excursion* (IX,
214–20), the Wanderer seems to imply the same possibility:

> Throughout the world of sense,
> Even as an object is sublime or fair,
> That object is laid open to the view
> Without reserve or veil; and as a power
> Is salutary, or an influence sweet,
> Are each and all enabled to perceive
> That power, that influence, by impartial law.
>
> > (*PW*, V, 293)

He goes on to list other things which are "vouchsafed alike to all";
reason, imagination, freedom of will and conscience. But Wordsworth
well knew, as indeed did Coleridge, that these faculties belong
to a postlapsarian state, a fortunate fall wherein knowledge of value,
meaning and self-experience only accrues through the accumulation of acts of trangression and moments of loss, both large and
small. In the preface to *Poems, 1815* Wordsworth in fact tells us that
the ability to observe "things as they are in themselves, and with
fidelity to describe them, unmodified by any passion or feeling
existing in the mind of the describer", is an activity only to be
carried through under the yoke of compulsion, for "its exercise

supposes all the higher qualities of the mind to be passive, and in a state of subjection to external objects".[8] The absolute integration of man in nature involved in such passive reception may be conventionally 'paradisal' in that it precludes any problem of selection or figuration, and therefore any risk of misappropriation or misattribution. We cannot mistake part for whole, or the figurative for the real, as long as we are immersed in an identity wherein no merely subjective perspective is possible. In this condition, however, it would be impossible to deploy consciousness, for consciousness in Romantic theory is based precisely in the dialectic of self and other, and in the moments of synthesis which that dialectic continually creates and destroys. Hence, if we could regain and maintain a state of absolute oneness, we would not apprehend or experience its *value*; and we should not seek to do so lest we turn traitors to our own "higher qualities". The misfortune of the fall into division is thus, as I have said, inextricably fortunate. Wordsworth entertains again the prospect of complete self-forgetfulness in *Home at Grasmere*:

> What if I floated down a pleasant stream
> And now am landed and the motion gone —
> Shall I reprove myself? Ah no, the stream
> Is flowing and will never cease to flow,
> And I shall float upon that stream again.
> By such forgetfulness the soul becomes —
> Words cannot say how beautiful. Then hail!
> Hail to the visible Presence! Hail to thee,
> Delightful Valley, habitation fair!
> And to whatever else of outward form
> Can give us inward help, can purify
> And elevate and harmonize and soothe,
> And steal away and for a while deceive
> And lap in pleasing rest, and bear us on
> Without desire in full complacency,
> Contemplating perfection absolute
> And entertained as in a placid sleep.[9]

The image is that of Lethe, or something very close to it, but experienced in life instead of in death. It is a state outside language ("Words cannot say"), and a state involving deception. The satisfaction of desire is thus presented as improper even as it is lovingly described. But Wordsworth does not have to approve of "full complacency", in any final way, because it is here experienced as part of a cycle, something to be lost and found again. It can co-exist, then, with that other essential human obligation to struggle, to desire and to choose; to engage, in other words, with figurative attribution and communication, back in the world of language and form.

This passage has a context among other Romantic views on the subject of self-forgetfulness, especially as they stress the factors inhibiting the repetition of the cycle which alone prevents either part of it from becoming fixed and authoritative. It certainly intimates something of the complexity of Wordsworth's sense of the place of figuring, its alternate presence and absence in the ideal mind in an ideal world. But for the moment I wish to concentrate on small beginnings, and to suggest the range of Wordsworth's reactions to figurative activity.

In the poem 'A Morning Exercise' (*PW*, II, 124–5), written in 1828 and then chosen to open that group of poems which Wordsworth had collected under the title 'Poems of the Fancy', we find this specified fancy occupying itself in

> Sending sad shadows after things not sad,
> Peopling the harmless fields with signs of woe:
> Beneath her sway, a simple forest cry
> Becomes an echo of man's misery.
>
> (ll. 3–6)

Thus ravens are made the prophets of death, owls the harbingers of misfortune, and so forth:

> Fancy, intent to harass and annoy,
> Can thus pervert the evidence of joy
>
> (ll. 11–12)

Only the lark, says Wordsworth, addressing himself to the status of birdsong much as Coleridge had done in 'The Nightingale', has never been made an emblem of gloom and misery.

Again, in the second of the two poems 'To the Daisy' (*PW*, II, 138–9), both written much earlier but gathered under the same editorial rubric, Wordsworth upbraids the distorting effects of those minds — his own, specifically — which rifle nature for emblems of themselves:

Oft on the dappled turf at ease
I sit, and play with similes,
Loose types of things through all degrees,
Thoughts of thy raising:
And many a fond and idle name
I give to thee, for praise or blame,
As is the humour of the game,
While I am gazing.

(ll. 9–16)

In a succession of stanzas which might seem prophetic of Shelley's
'To a Skylark', Wordsworth goes on to enumerate all the images
which come to mind as ways of 'seeing' the daisy — a nun, a
sprightly maiden, a queen, a star, and so on. The poem ends with a
rebuke, and a faith in the simple, unrefracted reality and claim to
attention of the daisy 'in itself':

Bright *Flower*! for by that name at last,
When all my reveries are past,
I call thee, and to that cleave fast,
Sweet silent creature!
That breath'st with me in sun and air,
Do thou, as thou art wont, repair
My heart with gladness, and a share
Of thy meek nature!

(ll. 41–8)

The meekness includes, we assume, an education out of the habit of
making similes, seen here to detract from the free-standing integrity
of the simple flower. Such similes might well belong to that "gaudy
and inane phraseology" (*PrW*, I, 116) which Wordsworth found in
the standard poetic diction as it substituted linguistic ornament and
effect for the simple reference to simple things. Hence, perhaps, the
flatness of the word "Flower" — Wordsworth does not even give
the daisy its specific name — which may be taken to signal the
intuition that we may as well give up trying to find the *word* which
does ample justice to the *thing*, and points us back to the immediacy
of an experience outside language, which language even at its most
efficient can only tentatively indicate. A proper appreciation of
nature must then involve a recognition of the value of the grain of

sand quite apart from the chain of associations suggested by it, whether in language or in the mind's eye.

In these two poems Wordsworth details both figurative transgressions and achieved realities beyond the figurative. Both poems are, as I have said, part of the collection of 'Poems of the Fancy', and in a fine book on Wordsworth's attitude to language and representation, Frances Ferguson has argued that we are to take the poet's editorial categories seriously.[10] She suggests that this group of poems analyses a faculty which

> reconciles art with nature by imposing upon nature — but with a confidence that nature will feel no real wound from its impositions . . . The interchange between the human fancy and natural objects appears as a natural structure of desire . . . that very disruption simultaneously seems to afford man's disordered fortunes a measure of nature's stability.
>
> (pp. 62, 63)

I find this case for the 'Poems of the Fancy' very convincing and, as Ferguson goes on to argue, it represents one aspect or variant of an ongoing investigation into representation and the mind-nature relationship. This relationship, I think, is based on figurative attribution, and if there seems to be in the 'Poems of the Fancy' a portrayal of an ultimate education into a pure perception which by-passes the otherwise misappropriating activities of the mind,[11] then we can see in other poems a speaker who is much less certain of the ethical implications of various ways of seeing, and indeed of the possibility of making distinctions between them.

To point a contrast, we may take two assessments of clouds in the sky. In a sonnet published in 1807 (*PW*, III, 26) Wordsworth writes:

> Nor will I praise a cloud, however bright,
> Disparaging Man's gifts, and proper food.
> Grove, isle, with every shape of sky-built dome,
> Though clad in colours beautiful and pure,
> Find in the heart of man no natural home:
> The immortal Mind craves objects that endure:
> These cleave to it; from these it cannot roam,
> Nor they from it: their fellowship is secure.

Here the evanescence of shapes and figures in the sky as they continually self-create and dissolve is contrasted with man's need for a world of fixed forms upon which to base his identity and, contributing to that identity in an ongoing way, for a stable pattern of relations perceived among things outside him.

Conversely, in 'To the Clouds', composed in 1808 but not published until 1842 among the 'Poems of the Imagination' (*PW*, II, 316–20), exactly the opposite evaluation of fluidity is announced. Working through all the similes and analogies construed by the "Fancy" in the shapes of clouds, the speaker describes their subsumption into a state of vacancy and blankness:

> a calm descent of sky conducting
> Down to the unapproachable abyss,
> Down from that hidden gulf from which they rose
> To vanish —
>
> (ll. 34–7)

only to record immediately the appearance of a new train of clouds, perhaps to be as numerous as before:

> From a fount of life
> Invisible, the long procession moves
> Luminous or gloomy, welcome to the vale
> Which they are entering, welcome to mine eye
> That sees them, to my soul that owns in them,
> And in the bosom of the firmament
> O'er which they move, wherein they are contained,
> A type of her capacious self and all
> Her restless progeny.
>
> (ll. 45–53)

The clouds are welcome whether luminous or gloomy, for in their oscillation between those two extremes they typify the inclusiveness and flexibility of the observing mind and eye. Here it is the 'rising to vanish' that is enjoyed, not the fixed form. The poem develops into a meditation too complex to be paraphrased here, but which has the result that even if the memory cannot retain the details of such transient visions, there is still no cause for despair:

> Yet why repine, created as we are
> For joy and rest, albeit to find them only
> Lodged in the bosom of eternal things?
>
> (ll. 92–4)

The "eternal things" here invoked are in fact to be found in transience: the clouds, the sun, and the host of fluid forms they produce between them. Not even the forms produced along the way, held in the memory, are as important as the fact of process itself.

I take the relation between these two poems to be one of 'both/ and' rather than 'either/or'. They cannot both be entertained at the same time, but they can be contained by the same mind at different times, each continually replacing the other. Wordsworth's idea of the mind, looked at as a whole, allows for the interplay of antithetical drives and dispositions, discouraging the ultimate replacement of any one by any other. There are, then, two versions of world-construction or figurative attribution, or rather two poles of a coherent process, one of which aims at fluidity and the other at fixity. Within this process the mind is indefatigably active, and there is little room for a comfortably inert assimilation of a posited 'reality'. The third of the sonnets in 'The River Duddon' series (*PW*, III, 247) explores the relation between the two drives, and I quote the poem entire:

> How shall I paint thee? — Be this naked stone
> My seat, while I give way to such intent;
> Pleased could my verse, a speaking monument,
> Make to the eyes of men thy features known.
> But as of all those tripping lambs not one
> Outruns his fellows, so hath Nature lent
> To thy beginning nought that doth present
> Peculiar ground for hope to build upon.
> To dignify the spot that gives thee birth
> No sign of hoar Antiquity's esteem
> Appears, and none of modern Fortune's care;
> Yet thou thyself hast round thee shed a gleam
> Of brilliant moss, instinct with freshness rare;
> Prompt offering to thy Foster-mother, Earth!

The quest is for the "beginning" of the stream, and for the exemplary emblem or monument which ought, according to human habits and values, to mark that moment of origination. It does not exist, of course, and its absence is recorded in several ways. The stream is self-begotten and continually self-begetting, the earth being only a foster parent. It is a kinetic whole indivisible into parts, and it casts around it not an objective material emblem but a phenomenal variable, a fall of light and colour, a "gleam" of moss. We are reminded of the film flickering on the grate in 'Frost at Midnight'; the 'thing' which attracts the attention of the observing eye is not properly a thing at all, but appears as it does only as a result of the interaction of other things, here the stream, the moss, the light, and the position of the eye. The moss, presumably of itself inert and dull, takes on movement and colour because of the stream, which also of itself offers no material for selection and representation. The observation that the moss is "instinct with freshness" further immaterializes the nature of the emblem, and it points us back to a paradox in the speaker's own opening ambition to create a "speaking monument". Speech does not take solid form, just as freshness remains an abstract and unrepresentable quality.

The vocabulary of the opening lines, moreover, suggests that the speaker may not extend entire good faith to his own efforts. If the idea of 'painting' registers something of the sense of gaudy decoration and deceitful representation, as we shall see that it does in the 'London' passages of *The Prelude*, then the 'giving way' has to be read as a succumbing to temptation. Nevertheless, the human eye is validated in a particular way, even though it is a way which runs counter to the speaker's monumental ambitions. The natural emblem of the gleaming moss has nothing to do with monumentality or with the works of man; it cannot be 'built' into objective form, because its existence for the mind as an idea is not dependent upon that idea being a resemblance of something which is 'in' an object. Locke's distinction between primary and secondary qualities comes to mind here, and is worth explaining now, as I shall refer to it again. For Locke, all "ideas" are in the mind, as all "qualities" are in objects; and qualities are "powers" producing ideas. Primary and secondary qualities are distinguished according to whether or not the ideas caused by them are "resemblances" of what is in the object itself. Primary qualities are bulk, figure, texture, motion of parts; secondary qualities are such as colour, taste, sound. The ideas we have of the former are resemblances of what is 'real', those of the latter are not. They still have a material *origin* — "And what is Sweet, Blue, or Warm in *Idea*, is but the certain Bulk, Figure, and Motion of the insensible Parts in the Bodies themselves, which we call so"[12] — but the way they *appear* to us, as ideas, is incipiently subjectivized, as the examples Locke gives go on to show. The fire which warms us at a distance pains us at close quarters; and hands which are themselves at different temperatures will feel respectively hot and cold when plunged into a bucket of water which is at some intermediate temperature. The ideas in the mind are not resemblances *of* qualities in the object (fire, water), although they are caused *by* qualities in the object. These qualities are therefore secondary, and exist in objects only as powers to produce sensations.

Wordsworth in this way emblematizes a secondary quality in his perception of the gleaming moss. In being discouraged, for lack of materials, from selecting out graspable things, the mind is also being introduced to the pleasures of phenomena which depend upon its own unstable dominion. The instability comes from the interaction of its own interior fluctuations (mood, disposition, whether or not it takes the time to look for the fall of light) with the changes wrought in nature (climate, sun or shower, and so forth). No *separation* between mind and world is sanctioned here, with the result that the eye never achieves a position of difference from which it might invade or dominate. Because nothing "peculiar" is provided for the eye to fix upon at first glance (and that word "peculiar" is interesting, given what I shall be saying about Wordsworth's polemic against the ornamental and metonymic), it relaxes, takes second place, and finds a pleasure different from that which it set out to "build".

The gleaming moss thus provides an experience of emblem-seeing for the mind, without the mind having to leave *traces* of its presence on the natural landscape. There is satisfaction without despoilation. Nothing is *required* of the 'real' in utilitarian terms, and there is nothing to tempt the adverting eye to repose within a fixed perspective. The stream has provided the emblem most suitably analogous to speech itself — something which, like the clouds, rises to vanish, and yet is always rising. *Writing* has tendencies toward the monumental, as Wordsworth recognized in some among the 'Poems on the Naming of Places', but *speech* prescribes its own disappearance as part of its very content.

Building, of course, is one of the most obviously available images of the fixing of form, and given the central Romantic concern to preserve the play of innering and outering and to inhibit the mind's tendency to fix itself either at the objective or at the subjective pole, we need not be surprised to discover that 'building' is often discouraged by Wordsworth. He sees it, moreover, not just as a definite philosophical threat to the single mind, but as having problematic consequences for society at large. Thus he is particularly critical of such buildings as are the figured forms of certain people's possessive control, whether over the land itself or over a language of special and generally unavailable significance. These emblems work to separate one part of humanity from the prospective wholeness of an appreciative community. Thus we find, for example, an "Admonition" directed at those who "may have happened to be enamoured of some beautiful place of Retreat, in the Country of the Lakes" (*PW*, III, 2), and Wordsworth implicitly directs a similar admonition at himself, in the first of the 'Poems on the Naming of Places'. Emma's Dell must remain unmarked, and most particularly so because it already functions within someone else's subsistence economy. The shepherd's hut intimates that the land is needed for life itself, and not just for pleasant diversion.[13]

These are instances of the miscreative functions of the figuring imagination; miscreative, because they divide man from man in seeking, however covertly, to establish an exclusive possession based on personal experience or private languages. But what keeps Wordsworth away from a bombastic denunciation of such activities, and from the poetry of outrage, is the intuition that we cannot *but* embark on similar or closely related gestures to achieve communication at the deepest and most necessary levels. This must now be demonstrated.

In the sixth of the 'Poems on the Naming of Places' (*PW*, II, 118–23), finished by 1802 but not published until 1815, Wordsworth describes his relationship to a "stately Fir-grove" (l. 9) within which he was in the habit of seeking shelter during harsh winter weather. He remains something of an intruder, watched suspiciously by the sheep, but finally breaks the habit because the trees grow together so densely that he cannot move around comfortably under their canopies. He then tells of returning to the grove in the month of April and discovering a pathway under and between the trees, not noticed before. He infers that this must have been created by the pacings of his brother during his spell home from the sea; the grove is therefore associated with and named after the brother, Wordsworth himself now esteeming it with "a perfect love" (l. 87).

Thus the rediscovery of the modified landscape becomes for the poet a way of relating, in mind and heart, to his absent brother. It may well be, in fact, his only way of so doing:

> Year followed year, my Brother! and we two,
> Conversing not, knew little in what mould
> Each other's mind was fashioned; and at length,
> When once again we met in Grasmere Vale,
> Between us there was little other bond
> Than common feelings of fraternal love.
>
> (ll. 70–5)

As there appears to have been no direct discourse between the brothers, the pathway has become a means for William to identify with some otherwise uncommunicated part of his brother's life. As with Coleridge's 'This Lime-Tree Bower my Prison', such 'communication' is predicated upon the absence of the person to whom it is related. The irony becomes almost unbearable, indeed, when we recall that Wordsworth's brother John was to lose his life at sea in 1805. The silence and absence which intimates the presence of death in the so-called 'Lucy poems' was here to play out its cycle in the biography of the poet.

Because the fraternal passion is not spoken out to the brother himself, and is thus not verified in a social context, we even have to question the details of its coming into being on this occasion. The passion itself, of course, has a truth of its own; but it may be that that truth is actually achieved through a *constructed* causal sequence of events rather than through an observed factual situation:

> Pleasant conviction flashed upon my mind
> That, to this opportune recess allured,
> He had surveyed it with a finer eye,
> A heart more watchful; and had worn the track
> By pacing here, unwearied and alone,
> In that habitual restlessness of foot
> That haunts the Sailor measuring o'er and o'er
> His short domain upon the vessel's deck,
> While she pursues her course through the dreary sea.
>
> (ll. 58–66)

If this really describes the way things happened, then we register the peculiar, insentient trance within which the brother has figured his experience on dry land, constructing it as a facsimile of what he is used to elsewhere. He would not be seeing what most of us would recognize in the landscape; he would be 'seeing as'. If, however, this is not what happened, then we must examine the speaker's own construction of events as a hypothesis, and relate it to an intentional element or preoccupation in his own mind. Does he seek to cast his brother as a self-absorbed solipsist in order to assuage his own discomfort (and perhaps guilt) at the awkwardness of their relationship? Perhaps the brother was "alone" because he, the speaker, left him unattended and ignored? Was the fir-grove a 'companionable form' for the brother, as it now is for the poet? Or is the brother himself a figment of the poet's interior strife? There is no way of making this decision, I think; the point is to recognize the complexity of the figurative process enacted by the narrator, a complexity which includes the question of whether a similar process had been earlier enacted by the now absent brother. We appreciate the urgency of the need, given that the speaker now has no other opportunity of expressing fraternal love; but we sense also its insufficiency when we wonder for whom this communication is really taking place. The final passage of the poem brings us into a present wherein the poet now frequents the grove in all weathers to think upon his brother, who is perhaps — "if I rightly guess" (l. 98)—at these very moments reciting his (the speaker's) own poems on board his ship in another version of affection expressed through mediated, figured forms. Narcissistic self-projection and seemingly heartfelt affection are inextricably entwined. Each seems to be the mode most naturally and feelingly available to the other. Meanwhile

> At every impulse of the moving breeze,
> The fir-grove murmurs with a sea-like sound,
> Alone I tread this path; — for aught I know,
> Timing my steps to thine; and, with a store
> Of undistinguishable sympathies,
> Mingling most earnest wishes for the day
> When we, and others whom we love, shall meet
> A second time, in Grasmere's happy Vale.
>
> (ll. 103–10)

The conditionals resound again, even more forcefully than they have done in Coleridge's so-called 'conversations', as the narrator

finishes by having removed himself from an uncontingently observed landscape to one determined by 'seeing as'. It is not a
'universal' which is being assumed here, but a fragile moment of
sharing with one other, special person, as the "sea-like" sound of the
grove unites the two brothers kept apart, not just by the elements,
but by the human heart and the difficulty of its relation to direct
discourse, unfigured form.

Another of Wordsworth's finest poems, and Coleridge's
favourite, 'The Brothers' (*PW*, II, 1–13), devolves again around the
fraternal relationship. It is a poem whose ramifications far exceed
those I shall try to describe here, but it does focus very directly on
the process of figurative attribution and its necessity and tragic
insufficiency for the deeper kinds of human communion.

I shall concentrate on Leonard's reading of the landscape as he
returns from the sea to his native locality

> With a determined purpose to resume
> The life he had lived there; both for the sake
> Of many darling pleasures, and the love
> Which to an only brother he has borne
> In all his hardships, since that happy time
> When, whether it blew foul or fair, they two
> Were brother-shepherds on their native hills.
>
> (ll. 69–75)

He goes straight to the family graveyard, and finds — the tombs are
all unmarked — that one more grave has been added to the plot
since he saw it last. As he stands before it, his memory begins to
construct the possibility that he *has* seen this grave before, and
merely forgotten it. There then follows a striking passage wherein he
remembers his journey to the village some hours before:

> He had lost his path,
> As up the vale, that afternoon, he walked
> Through fields which once had been well known to him:
> And oh what joy this recollection now
> Sent to his heart! he lifted up his eyes,
> And, looking round, imagined that he saw
> Strange alteration wrought on every side
> Among the woods and fields, and that the rocks,
> And everlasting hills themselves were changed.
>
> (ll. 91–9)

The experience of having lost his way, which must at the time have been troubling rather than joyful, is now intentionally proffered as evidence for the fallibility of his memory. He is trying hard to imagine a world in which his brother is not dead, and if he could thus lose his way in a landscape which ought to be familiar to him,[14] then he could also have misremembered the number of graves in the plot, or perhaps even have guided himself to the wrong graveyard. The immediate context is reconstructed at the demands of an aspiration to be elsewhere; the very hills themselves seem changed. For a moment, perception here is at the service of intention, and in a much less culpable and destructive way than it is, for example, for the old sea captain of 'The Thorn'.

Leonard is then engaged in conversation by the vicar, and he begins again to observe and question the elements of landscape around him:

> —I remember,
> (For many years ago I passed this road)
> There was a foot-way all along the fields
> By the brook-side — 'tis gone — and that dark cleft!
> To me it does not seem to wear the face
> Which then it had!
>
> (ll. 131–6)

Receiving this as vague and uninformed commentary, the vicar replies that in fact things are much the same as ever, but when forced to recognize that Leonard is indeed hyper-observative he admits that the two neighbouring springs on "that tall pile" have been disturbed by a flash of lightning striking "Close to those brother fountains" (this phrase was omitted from the poem after 1820); only one now remains. Leonard has thus selected from the landscape the one detail which is overtly emblematic of the change he fears has come about. Indirect discourse is here a way of keeping off the unbearable truth whilst at the same time intimating its presence. The emblem introduces what is otherwise at first unbearable.

After some conversation about unmarked graves, Leonard gradually draws from the vicar the story of the death of his brother James, who had one day left his companions and, it is assumed, fallen asleep on the top of a rock,

> one particular rock
> That rises like a column from the vale,
> Whence by our shepherds it is called, THE PILLAR.
>
> (ll. 366–8)

From here the vicar conjectures that he had fallen to his death while sleepwalking, a habit he had developed out of "disquietude and grief" (l. 394) at the assumed death of his brother Leonard, the very Leonard who has now returned.

James too, in other words, had 'selected' part of the landscape, the single rock, as the emblem of his own standing alone; as with brother and brother, the part is disjoined from the whole. Receiving this news, Leonard departs without telling the vicar who he is:

> his long absence, cherished hopes,
> And thoughts which had been his an hour before,
> All pressed on him with such a weight, that now,
> This vale, where he had been so happy, seemed
> A place in which he could not bear to live.
>
> (ll. 422–6)

He returns to the sea, from whence he came.

The above is a sketch of the main elements in the poem which refer to figurative and intentional attribution. Leonard has recognized the priest, but has throughout been unrecognized by him. More than this, he has actually been seen as a "tourist", an urban idling spirit who has nothing better to do than to ransack the countryside for gratuitous experiences of sentimental melancholy (ll. 105–12). The vicar is boastful of not needing names and epitaphs to remember the dead, but he has no eye for the living presence before him. This is an anguished and paradoxical misunderstanding, for there is a sense in which Leonard really is an outsider; he has left the valley, he has not enacted all the living rituals which go along with belonging to a dear perpetual place, and it may thus seem itself emblematic that he has been taken for dead by the villagers. It is often implicit in the structures and insights of Wordsworth's poems that such loss *must* occur with the accession to consciousness, and thus it may be significant that Leonard leaves the "vale" (veil) and a condition wherein the brothers are compared to natural presences devoid of the faculty of reflection; where they are seen as birds and flowers (ll. 276–8).

The process of loss in this poem, however, is specified with a sharpness quite absent in the drama of the fir-grove. There is no sense of there having been any self-experienced insufficiency in the brothers' relations with each other. Quite the opposite, and in this case Leonard's leaving his native hills has nothing to do with a freely taken decision. He was forced into it by the death of his grandfather and the ensuing sale of all his possessions:

> The estate and house were sold; and all their sheep,
> A pretty flock, and which, for aught I know,
> Had clothed the Ewbanks for a thousand years: —
> Well — all was gone, and they were destitute,
> And Leonard, chiefly for his Brother's sake
> Resolved to try his fortune on the seas.
>
> (ll. 301–6)

The background is one of bonds, interests and mortgages which drove old Walter Ewbank to a grave "before his time" (ll. 214–16). The marginal rural economy based on owner-occupiers held together by communal feeling and tradition — a model of social organization Wordsworth undoubtedly felt to be disappearing, if it had not already disappeared — is here threatened by the growth of monopoly and the commercial and financial relations of a new age, or a different place.

Looking back to the other poem of fraternal affection, discussed above, we may indeed wonder whether the economic factor is, as I have just said, "quite absent" from its narrative. If William and John are unable to communicate directly with each other, could that be because the nature of their occupations renders them closed to shared experiences? John's pacings are an indication that the ordering of the grove is produced by obsessive behaviour; the conversion of wild nature,[15] in other words, into a condition where William the poet can *use* it as a place to meditate and create, is enacted by the brother in a state of distraction. Work is done upon the grove; and that it has faintly negative implications of invasion we may infer from the reference to the thrush's nest built so close to the ground

> As gave sure sign that they, who in that house
> Of nature and of love had made their home
> Amid the fir-trees, all the summer long
> Dwelt in a tranquil spot.
>
> (ll. 23–6)

as well as from the fearful sheep (l. 31). Thrushes will now build more cautiously, and sheep appear less often. John's 'work' is a consequence of his being unable to break the habits of a seafaring life; in terms more familiar to the later nineteenth century, he is alienated to the extent that he cannot make a distinction between work and leisure, or between one kind of experience and another, in a radically different environment. And what of the poet William? He has come to the vale in the first place because he prefers "studious leisure" to "the attractions of the busy world" (ll. 1–2), but in fact the work done upon the grove could be said to reintroduce the element of interference he might think he is avoiding. Before its modification, his desire to frequent the grove (l. 41) is inhibited by its refusal of a place where "My feet might move without concern or care" (l. 38). John's modifications provide that place of convenience (not an unambiguous quality for Wordsworth), in that sense contributing to William's own form of obsessive behaviour, poetic meditation (l. 88ff.). It is this obsession which must be thought to contribute to the impossibility of direct discourse between the brothers, and it helps to explain also his insistence that John be cast as a *"silent* Poet" (l. 80) on a "joyless Ocean" (l. 84), one repeating, moreover, his own verses. The figuring of the landscape which produces a form of silent communication between the brothers is thus at all levels predicated in alienation. The path is made by alienation, it produces (at least mildly suggests) alienation of nature in the eviction of sheep and thrushes, and it is recorded and perhaps 'invented' by one alienated within the poet's vision. Who is to say, out of this complexity, what is to be attributed to personal election, and what is the result of enforced habits? Each tends to appear as the other, of course, and much of what I have to say later will be filling in the terms of that problem.

In 'The Brothers', as I have said, the emphasis on the pressure of a historical and economic situation is much less ambiguous. There are two reasons why Leonard should leave the valley again at the end of the poem. One is crudely contingent; there is no more place for him there now than there was before, in fact less. That Leonard is taken for a tourist indicates that the vicar is all too familiar with the type — prophetic indeed of the modern economy of the English Lakes. We would infer, however, that Leonard is much more strongly affected by the reasons of the heart, and indeed the two pressures act together rather than in any way conflicting. The landscape which had previously been made the emblem of his affection for his brother has now become an icon of pain and loss. The "brother fountains" have been reduced to one, and the prevailing presence is now that of the "one particular rock" where James met his death. We are indeed in a context where "the feeling therein developed gives importance to the action and situation and not the action and situation to the feeling" (*PrW*, I, 128). The mind 'makes' or selects its world at the service of its particular preoccupations. This is a central Romantic intuition. What is further prophetic about Wordsworth's poem is his sense that the 'making' goes on in conjunction with and at least partly because of certain undeniable pressures from the historical and social situation within which the figuring mind is positioned, and over which it has no control.

Leonard returns to the sea, which had during his earlier voyages been the passive repository of his created images. Here he had gazed over the vessel's side

> And, while the broad blue wave and sparkling foam
> Flashed round him images and hues that wrought
> In union with the employment of his heart,
> He, thus by feverish passion overcome,
> Even with the organs of his bodily eye,
> Below him, in the bosom of the deep,
> Saw mountains; saw the forms of sheep that grazed
> On verdant hills — with dwellings among trees,
> And shepherds clad in the same country grey
> Which he himself had worn.
>
> (ll. 56–64)

The sea is shapeless, and thus infinitely shapeable by the imaginative eye. It reflects both the self and the self's desires. Water is the medium within which the tension of part and whole is least evident. Wordsworth's speaker had discovered that fact as a problem of representation in the sonnet 'How shall I paint thee?' already discussed. Here, the sea offers Leonard no disruption of the *totality* of his imagined landscape, no separation of self from community, brother from brother, particular rock from happy vale.

This experience of wholeness, now tactile rather than optical, also informs Hegel's account of the rite of baptism:

John's habit (nothing similar is known to have been done by Jesus) of baptizing by immersion in water those drawn to his spirit is an important and symbolical one. No feeling is so homogeneous with the desire for the infinite, the longing to merge into the infinite, as the desire to immerse one's self in the sea. To plunge into it is to be confronted by an alien element which at once flows round us on every side and which is felt at every point of the body. We are taken away from the world and the world from us. We are nothing but felt water which touches us where we are, and we are only where we feel it. In the sea there is no gap, no restriction, no multiplicity, nothing specific. The feeling of it is the simplest, the least broken up.[16]

Leonard does not immerse himself in the sea, of course, but the passage in Wordsworth's poem is drawn from a description of the calenture, which all too often ended in the observer falling to his death from the masthead. The loss of the self in the mirror of the sea, whether by optical or tactile means, is a death wish. The fact that there is no gap, restriction, multiplicity, nothing specific, precludes any anxiety about the process of selecting and representing, but it does so by a displacement of consciousness, which is the essential element of *life* for the Protestant mind. Thus, for Hegel, baptism inducts us into "a new world in which reality floats before the new spirit in a form in which there is no distinction between reality and dream", but that world cannot be of *this* world. It partakes of a "forgetfulness", a "solitude which has repelled everything, withdrawn itself from everything". In Wordsworth's pattern of experience it may be an earned or even unavoidable respite, but it will never exclusively satisfy the mind that has experienced also the euphoria of anxiety, of striving. The Wordsworthian protagonist must survive the temptation to synthesize the figured image of completion, the sea and all it is made to contain, with the actuality of what it intimates, the fact of death.[17] In the following passage from *The Prelude*, it is the isolation of preconsciousness, of a condition wherein the mind's activities have no social context and therefore bring with them no acute moral dilemmas, which is imaged in the contemplation of the sea:

> Hitherto I had stood
> In my own mind remote from human life,
> At least from what we commonly so name,

Even as a shepherd on a promontory,
Who, lacking occupation, looks far forth
Into the endless sea, and rather makes
Than finds what he beholds.

(III, 543–9)

The "lacking occupation" is always a crime to the Protestant consciousness, even as that apparent freedom from direction and desire is felt to provide the mind's most valuable insights. Thus the lack of occupation itself generates a "making", a disturbing of silence and emptiness by the mind's own provision of form and meaning, perhaps themselves the relics of other preoccupations and desires. But this whole passage is put across as a description of what is, so to speak, 'corrected' by the residence in Cambridge. It is an image of what the young poet *cannot* maintain.

What comes out of Wordsworth's two poems about brotherhood is that the mind's figurative faculty has more dignified and essential functions than would be the case if it were limited to the idle play of fancy. It exists to make bearable the experience of loss, and the aspiration toward completion, toward a full 'integration' of the self into the world. This must always *remain* at the level of aspiration; the attempt to have it otherwise must result either in the death-in-life of fetishism (fixation on one exclusive object, to which all mental energies are directed) or a complete loss of all object-focus, and consequently of all self-identity, in a pantheistic oneness wherein there is no function for consciousness. In Wordsworth's poems the insistence on aspiration is often maintained by the superimposition upon it of an unarguable loss. Thus, in the sixth of the 'Poems on the Naming of Places', it is suggested that the brothers achieve no actual communication, being limited to that imaginative projection instanced by Wordsworth himself through the emblems of modified landscape and printed poetry.

In 'The Brothers' the nature of that loss is yet more final (imaged in death) and, moreover, overdetermined. It is clearly stated, as I have already said, that Leonard is forced to leave his native valley by economic pressures. But it is also implicit that some sort of separation from his brother is inevitable with time. The period of their lives during which Leonard and James had no need of the figuring faculty and its emblems rooted in loss and absence is described thus by the vicar:

> Leonard and James! I warrant, every corner
> Among these rocks, and every hollow place
> That venturous foot could reach, to one or both
> Was known as well as to the flowers that grow there.
> Like roe-bucks they went bounding o'er the hills;
> They played like two young ravens on the crags.
>
> (ll. 273–8)

The vicar's narration is not authoritative, of course, far from it, but it is hard not to take the hint here that the kind of oneness with nature and each other that the brothers felt could not have been carried through into their adult lives. This in no way 'excuses' the economic forces at work in their lives, for had there been continued contact then there would have been opportunity for renegotiated communications. The point is rather, I think, that it complicates the estimation of the figurative activity in the poem. The situation is overdetermined in that what the displaced brother experiences as a result of direct empirical pressures is also suggested as a natural consequence of growing older. The incipiently dialectical presentation of this incident allows us, as it does in the other poem about the fraternal affections, to speculate about the possible mutuality of the economic and the psychological. There is nothing in the poem to authorize us to answer the question one way or the other, but it is not impossible that the historical context specified in the economic cause of Leonard's leaving itself goes some way toward explaining why it is that the psyche also behaves as it does. As we have seen and shall see again, there is much in Wordsworth's writing to suggest the presence of an intuition of the effects of external forces upon the spontaneous activities of the mind. The mythology of necessary loss, appearing elsewhere and more famously in the 'There was a boy' poem on the poet's own childhood, might have been different in a different historical context.

To return, however, to questions we can hope to answer: emblems are licensed by Wordsworth most readily when they operate at the service of the deepest human needs. It is because they are necessary to the expression and satisfaction of these needs, and because they are at the same time always open to terrible misuse, that they give rise to a problem. When properly oriented to their environment, their users recognize that the satisfaction derived from emblems is incomplete, and therefore not to be dwelt upon to the exclusion of alternative experiences. At the end of 'Michael' the pile of stones remains, the emblem of the broken family (and again, the leaving of the land and the invasion of the country by the habits and demands of the town are involved), although other and more obvious signs of human presence, like the light which is seen within the cottage and which serves as a "public symbol" (*PW*, II, 84) of the life of the inmates, have long since disappeared under the plough. It survives, perhaps, because it is incomplete; only minimally 'present' and therefore unnoticed by the new owners of the land as they erase the emblems of their predecessors in the cause of efficiency.

Traditional and long-established connection with a particular landscape is indeed admitted by Wordsworth as sufficient to obtain 'planning permission'. In a poem which appeared in the second volume of *Lyrical Ballads* (*PW*, IV, 200–1), "old Sir William" is not taken to task even for having contemplated building a folly on an island in the lake. Wordsworth is glad that he abandoned the project, but nevertheless Sir William was

> a gentle Knight,
> Bred in this vale, to which he appertained
> With all his ancestry. Then peace to him,
> And for the outrage which he had devised
> Entire forgiveness! — But if thou art one
> On fire with thy impatience to become
> An inmate of these mountains, — if, disturbed
> By beautiful conceptions, thou hast hewn
> Out of the quiet rock the elements
> Of thy trim Mansion destined soon to blaze
> In snow-white splendour, — think again; and, taught
> By old Sir William and his quarry, leave
> Thy fragments to the bramble and the rose;
> There let the vernal slow-worm sun himself,
> And let the redbreast hop from stone to stone.
>
> (ll. 21–35)

Wordsworth's poetic persona is, I think, often structured around the uncertainty about whether 'he' is a gentle knight or an intrusive builder of mansions, and much of the ambivalence to be found in the poetry of building and naming relates to this uncertainty. Emblems of authentic human occupation are however allowed, like the dramatically presented church tower in *The Excursion* (*PW*, V, 305),

> In majesty presiding over fields
> And habitations seemingly preserved
> From all intrusions of the restless world
> By rocks impassable and mountains huge.
>
> (IX, 576–9)

The most famous instance of this kind, presented very obviously as a case for special exemption, is the convent of Chartreuse described in *The Prelude*. It stands as a striking departure from the prevalent pleasure of making all things new which the young itinerant has experienced journeying through France in the period immediately following the Revolution. Manuscript A^2 explains this exemption in a passage which was substantially repeated in the 1850 text:

>   — 'Stay your impious hands,'
> Such was the vain injunction of that hour
> By Nature uttered from her Alpine Throne,
> 'Oh leave in quiet this transcendent frame
> Of social Being, this embodied dream
> This substance by which mortal men have clothed,
> Humanly clothed, the ghostliness of things
> In silence visible and perpetual calm.
> Let this one Temple last; be this one spot
> Of earth devoted to Eternity.'
>
> (p. 198)

Nature is here made to conspire with and endorse the required clothing of ghostly things by substance, and the evolution of the social unit which is consequent upon or implicit in that act of clothing. This monastery, like the church tower, is presented as a working emblem, and valued as such. And it is often the working emblems and the ruins which Wordsworth endorses, the former because their functions are still actively recreated and the latter because they have begun to lose their nudity as assertions of particular human ownership or claim. Thus Sir William's half-built folly is now enjoyed by the robin and the slow-worm. Similarly, in the first of the two sonnets 'At Furness Abbey' (*PW*, III, 62–3), the abandonment of the building has allowed nature to work on it by "counter-work", intermingling her own natural growths of flower and ivy with the mouldering walls, either "to prevent or beautify decay". The present form of this structure is thus a product of both

man and nature, and announces a different ownership from that of
any particular individual:

> Even as I speak the rising Sun's first smile
> Gleams on the grass-crowned top of yon tall Tower
> Whose cawing occupants with joy proclaim
> Prescriptive title to the shattered pile,
> Where, Cavendish, *thine* seems nothing but a name!

Perhaps the most explicit account of the emblem-making process
at work on the landscape occurs in *Home at Grasmere*. The passage is
a long one, but worth quoting entire:

> No, we are not alone; we do not stand,
> My Emma, here misplaced and desolate,
> Loving what no one cares for but ourselves.
> We shall not scatter through the plains and rocks
> Of this fair Vale and o'er its spacious heights
> Unprofitable kindliness, bestowed
> On Objects unaccustomed to the gifts
> Of feeling, that were cheerless and forlorn
> But few weeks past, and would be so again
> If we were not. We do not tend a lamp
> Whose lustre we alone participate,
> Which is dependent upon us alone,
> Mortal though bright, a dying, dying flame.
> Look where we will, some human heart has been
> Before us with its offering; not a tree
> Sprinkles these little pastures, but the same
> Hath furnished matter for a thought, perchance
> To someone is as a familiar friend.
> Joy spreads and sorrow spreads; and this whole Vale,
> Home of untutored Shepherds as it is,
> Swarms with sensation, as with gleams of sunshine,
> Shadows or breezes, scents or sounds. Nor deem
> These feelings — though subservient more than ours
> To every day's demand for daily bread,
> And borrowing more their spirit and their shape
> From self-respecting interests — deem them not
> Unworthy therefore and unhallowed. No,
> They lift the animal being, do themselves

By nature's kind and ever present aid
Refine the selfishness from which they spring,
Redeem by love the individual sense
Of anxiousness with which they are combined.
Many are pure, the best of them are pure;
The best, and these, remember, most abound,
Are fit associates of the [   ] joy,
Joy of the highest and the purest minds;
They blend with it congenially; meanwhile,
Calmly they breathe their own undying life,
Lowly and unassuming as it is,
Through this, their mountain sanctuary (long,
Oh long may it remain inviolate!),
Diffusing health and sober chearfulness,
And giving to the moments as they pass
Their little boons of animating thought,
That sweeten labour, make it seem and feel
To be no arbitrary weight imposed,
But a glad function natural to Man.

(p. 78–80; Ms. B, ll. 646–92)

Several arguments are to be observed here. It is stressed that the validation of a community is necessary if figurative attribution is to be something more than merely self-regarding idiosyncrasy. Objects are not appropriated and endowed with meaning by two people alone, but are used by a working society to integrate its own emotions with the landscape on which it depends, and within itself. We can certainly sense an uneasiness on the speaker's part about his own relationship to those who work, as well as a definite condescension in paraphrasing the nature of such people's lives; but this does not unsettle what is being commended here. The habit of endowing passive objects with feelings and associations, though it may begin in "self-respecting interests", is not simply a miscreative activity; it refines the selfishness from which it springs by giving people a direct emotional connection to objects, and to each other by means of those objects. Once 'outered' by the anxious or appreciative individual, these figured forms become part of a language with which he can discourse with himself, and which is also at best available to others, redeeming selfishness by love. Most of these feelings are "pure", and as such they are as good as 'things in themselves' — "Calmly they breathe their own undying life" —

fulfilling the functions of a substantial reality never to be located in objects taken alone, apart from feelings.

The last lines of the passage are particularly interesting. Such figured natural objects reciprocally feed back an animating function to thought, one which serves to "sweeten labour" and make it seem a natural function rather than an arbitrary imposition. This touches on a profound and controversial subject. It suggests that man's natural capacity for endowing objects with life serves to naturalize labour and make it almost pleasurable. Having been cast out of Eden into a world where work is essential to survival (most of all in the marginal subsistence economy of the Lake District), man redeems himself and heals his divided condition by the activities of the figurative mind. Work, consciousness and the creative mind here evolve together, each a cause of the others. The activity of figuring offers to establish connections between otherwise disparate things, thus insinuating a level of control and reintegration over things cast as separate from mankind at the moment of the fall. Man (and we are right to use the masculine) reads himself into a world designed once more for his happiness, but that happiness is now inseparable from the presence of labour. That this process is something of a rite of propitiation is suggested by the use of the word "offering" at l. 660. The forms thus created by being endowed with life and human aspiration are potentially dangerous ones, in that they may threaten to turn into fetishes, obsessive images of externalized human attributes. If these were the kinds of figures operating to "sweeten labour" then the social order would be of a highly suspicious sort. Such a prospect is not however invoked here. Sensations are not fixed and repeated but in flux — there is joy *and* sorrow—and different people have different objects of attention. In addition, the inhabitants of the valley are self-employed. The status and effects of figuring will become a much more urgent question when the provision of objects for the making of companionable forms is in the hands of someone else, who may also control and channel the native energies of the individual mind.

But this is to anticipate. Let me summarize some suggested conclusions about the case for Wordsworth's view of the figurative as it stands so far.

Whether the process of figurative attribution be metaphoric or metonymic/synecdochic — whether, in other words, it involves the comparison of two otherwise disparate things in terms of common qualities or the making of a part or attribute of a thing to stand for the whole — it would seem that there must always remain a risk of misattribution and misdemeanour. The perceiver of parts and relations is in a position of power; choices are being made by selection and comparison. The world is all before us, and some things are ignored as others are privileged, or despoiled, by attention. What matters, I think, is not whether such activity be deemed 'incorrect' in any limited epistemological sense. If we have no grasp upon a 'real' outside what is figured — and I shall argue that this is being postulated by philosophers in a way analogous to its position here within the mythology of fallen man — then the important distinctions have to be made between the different *kinds* of figurings as they affect human beings and the objects of the environment. These distinctions are to be made in performance; they depend not on abstract rhetorical classifications but on *how* emblems are created, on what the *motives* behind them are, and on how they are subsequently *used*.

Thus, as I have said, figurative attribution is often endorsed not because it is in any abstract sense 'right', but because there is no living or communicating without it. Even where reordering or building is involved, as with Michael and his pile of stones or the Derbyshire brothers and their trees, necessity makes virtue. But the mind which operates with things which already exist, and leaves them as they are *except* in the mind, seems least of all prone to accusations of bad faith. Wordsworth praises the speaking monuments more than those of bricks and mortar, and among the latter class prefers those which are half-built, or half-decayed and being reassimilated into a natural landscape. This most tolerated species of 'seeing as', where the mind operates on given objects without physically transforming them, is the least materialized version of figuring. It does not alter the condition of things in the world — the landscape of 'The Brothers' is not changed by the 'use' made of it by Leonard and James — and therefore does not inflict modified or secondarily created forms on other people. It is not, in other words, a gesture of power, though it may have limiting effects on individual minds. At the same time, it has the advantage of alerting the mind to that part of itself which is most valuable; the *things* it has figured are not perpetuated as distractions from the *faculty* of figuring itself, the *act* of making meaning. In the same way, Coleridge suggested that the joys shared are more important than those unshared, that it is the strictly mental component in the experience of joy which matters most, and may most properly be assumed to be universal.

This process of mental attribution may incur problems of its own, of course. At one extreme, the mind may lapse into a relation with the chosen object which is one of fixation or fetishism. Martha Ray in 'The Thorn', at least according to the narrator's construction of her, transfers her affections from the living man, Stephen Hill, to the mountain; the dead object is selected via linguistic contiguity (hill —> mountain) as an obsessional attachment re-establishing control over an otherwise inchoate experience. Martha's behaviour is simultaneously misattributive and self-inflicting, but we cannot view it as a 'crime' given the deep trauma which apparently affects her. It is typical of Wordsworth that he should present the range of lived possibilities intimated by any critical or theoretical position we might take up as a way of approaching his poetry, and what is most prophetic of the future in his treatment of the variations open to the figuring mind is his sense of the social and communal references and causes operating on that mind. Coleridge articulated a division in the society of those who listen to the nightingale. I must now try to make clear Wordsworth's sense of the threat of externally prefigured forms as they compromise even further what can never be in the first place a simply innocent or 'open' mind.

III CAMBRIDGE AND LONDON: PLACES ALREADY NAMED

When we would talk about a theory of knowledge or a theory of perception in Wordsworth's writings, then we are at the same time talking about a context for that theory, a *place* where we might expect to find it verified in experience. The mind is inescapably social even when it is most convincingly solitary, and Wordsworth is always concerned to assert the social function and value of solitude. We may approach a sense of what it was that for him constituted the best possible context, the 'chosen vale', and the reasons for that choice, by examining those parts of *The Prelude* which show the mind under siege from a hostile environment. This hostility turns out to be educative, indeed, but only because he can escape from it.

Cambridge inclined the young poet into a condition wherein "Imagination slept", albeit "yet not utterly" (III, 260–1). It appealed seductively to that part of him which loved "idleness and joy" (l. 236), and made joy out of idleness. It is not so much "wilful alienation" as "loose indifference" (ll. 330, 332), but nevertheless it is a world where the young man wears his badges of difference and distinction, his cap and gown, with shallow pride and self-esteem:

> Up-shouldering in a dislocated lump,
> With shallow ostentatious carelessness,
> My Surplice, gloried in, and yet despised,
> I clove in pride through the inferior throng
> Of the plain Burghers, who in audience stood
> On the last skirts of their permitted ground,
> Beneath the pealing Organ.
>
> (III, 316–22)

The alienation, if not wilful, is nevertheless reciprocal, as the syntax suggests: "gloried in, and yet despised" is an adjectival phrase which can describe either the surplice or the subject, "I". The poet both glories in and despises his surplice, the badge (or metonym) denoting difference, as he is himself gloried in and despised by the community around him (as an emblem of social distinction). The separation of part from whole is enacted at two analogous and indeed causally related levels. The young man *bears* an emblem of division, to which his own attitude is ambivalent, and he *himself* is such a figure for the unprivileged beholders. That the surplice is not boldly worn, but carried, indicates exactly the unsureness he feels about it, and the alienation from self which is here inscribed within the alienation from the community.

This little incident is an exact symptom of the society which Wordsworth did not want, and it is crucial that the alienation effected by the imposition of the metonym (he would have been obliged by the 'rules' to wear his gown to chapel) is reciprocally divisive both of the inner self and of the social self. This is a 'class' society based on the figurative expression of difference, dividing man from man and therefore from himself. It is thus a community where

> the inner heart
> Is trivial, and the impresses without
> Are of a gaudy region.
>
> (III, 457–9)[18]

It encourages and rewards a mode of 'seeing as' which is very closely akin to that upbraided in the two from among the 'Poems of the Fancy' already discussed:

> Meanwhile, amid this gaudy Congress, fram'd
> Of things, by nature, most unneighbourly,
> The head turns round, and cannot right itself.
>
> (III, 661–3)

In those other poems, which showed the mind operating in the presence of nature, there was space and time for a potential correction of the mind's worst habits. Here there is less chance for the head to right itself, for there is no example of right-headedness to stand as context and support. Individuals here constitute a society which then redetermines them *as* individuals, and spoils also those who come into it from outside. Even the young Wordsworth, with his unusual alternative experience, is affected by what he hates, and the fact that from these experiences "profit may be drawn in time to come" (l. 668) is made possible only by the strength of that alternative.

In the account of the Cambridge experience in general, as well as in the passages already cited, we can see clear connections between this improper society of alienated figures and the famous polemic elsewhere in Wordsworth against what he called "poetic diction". What is the "intervenient imagery" (l. 555) of Cambridge if not a monumental incarnation of poetic diction as social practice and human environment? Here are the "surfaces of artifical life", with their "wily interchange of snaky hues" (ll. 590, 594), equivalent to (and productive of, in fact) the "motley masquerade of tricks, quaintnesses, hieroglyphics, and enigmas" (*PrW*, I, 162) of poetic diction. And, like poetic diction in its insinuation of the myth of the "peculiarity and exaltation of the Poet's character" (*ibid.*), they too separate man from man. As poetic diction employs figures of speech to describe "feelings and thoughts with which they had no natural connection whatsoever" (*PrW*, I, 160), so Cambridge inspires the relation of "things, by nature, most unneighbourly" (l. 662); metaphor gone awry.

Wordsworth's reaction to this, whether immediate or recollected, is a recourse to the virtues of plainness, implicitly a validation of the society of the "plain Burghers" from which he was at the time divided. He asks for

> a healthy, sound simplicity,
> A seemly plainness, name it as you will,
> Republican or pious.

(ll. 405–7)

In this respect, Puritan and radical are at one. That Cambridge does not provide "A habitation sober and demure" (l. 448) drives him at first into self-sufficient solitude, wherein he can live on the images recollected from elsewhere, but then, with the passage of time, into idleness and minor dissipation, "Rotted as by a charm" (l. 339). For the single subject cannot remain invulnerable to the pressures and pleasures of society if an alternative to that society is consistently unavailable. Habit determines experience, so that when Wordsworth returns to his native hills for the vacation he takes with him the habits learned in the town, habits which cause him to 'see' in a new and lesser way: "There was an inner falling-off" (IV, 270). This is the state of mind which is 'corrected' by the famous meeting with the soldier in the dark (IV, 360ff.). Conversely, after the passage of more time at home, he is able to build up a new set of habits and consequently a defence against Cambridge second time around (VI, 19ff.).

But Cambridge is not merely negative, for it provides the young poet with a prevision of London; it contains "in dwarf proportions . . . The limbs of the great world" (III, 615–16). It inoculates him, so to speak, against the graver threats apparently posed by the urban inferno. London is much more complicated than Cambridge, and is much more than an oasis of idleness and privilege, but again the young poet confronts the analogues of poetic diction in the "motley imagery" and "string of dazzling Wares" (VII, 150, 173) before his eyes. With the emblem of the surplice we saw how the metonym or figure served to place the individual and the community in mutual isolation, inner and outer; in the city, however, the profusion of symbols and emblems of one sort or another is much greater, and the passage of the eye from one to another much more rapid. Everything is in motion, and every individual or interest is 'represented' by something. The city is a shifting assemblage of incoherent significations. There is an overbalance of signifiers over potential things signified, and the one is often at odds with the other. Thus the famous passage on the blind beggar (VII, 611ff.), so often quoted in discussions of Wordsworth, describes a man who cannot see the message he holds up to others;

he is divorced from his own social 'identity'. More comically, Jack the giant-killer appears on stage dressed in black, with the word "INVISIBLE" written on his chest (VII, 309); there is a clear relation of negation between signifier and signified. The theatre in fact provides Wordsworth with a useful image of the city as a whole as it introduces discordance and deceit into the process of representation. Everywhere, things are not what they seem, as tradesmen's signs, shop fronts and human beings all flow together with "no law, no meaning, and no end" (l. 704). This is a prefiguring of the world of Dickens, which will require a special providence, and one uncomfortably akin to fictional artifice, to produce such laws, meanings and ends. The following passage specifies some of the versions of misrepresentation which particularly concern the poet:

> At leisure let us view, from day to day,
> As they present themselves, the Spectacles
> Within doors, troops of wild Beasts, birds and beasts
> Of every nature, from all Climes conven'd;
> And, next to these, those mimic sights that ape
> The absolute presence of reality,
> Expressing, as in a mirror, sea and land,
> And what earth is, and what she has to shew;
> I do not here allude to subtlest craft,
> By means refin'd attaining purest ends,
> But imitations fondly made in plain
> Confession of Man's weakness, and his loves.
> Whether the Painter fashioning a work
> To Nature's circumnambient scenery,
> And with his greedy pencil taking in
> A whole horizon on all sides with power,
> Like that of Angels or commission'd Spirits,
> Plant us upon some lofty Pinnacle,
> Or in a Ship on Waters, with a world
> Of life, and life-like mockery, to East,
> To West, behind us, and before;
> Or more mechanic Artist represent
> By scale exact, in Model, wood or clay,
> From shading colours also borrowing help,
> Some miniature of famous spots and things
> Domestic, or the boast of foreign Realms;

The Firth of Forth, and Edinburgh throned
On crags, fit empress of that mountain Land;
St. Peter's Church; or, more aspiring aim,
In microscopic vision, Rome itself;
Or else perhaps, some rural haunt, the Falls
Of Tivoli, and high upon that steep
The Temple of the Sibyl, every tree
Through all the landscape, tuft, stone, scratch minute,
And every Cottage, lurking in the rocks,
All that the Traveller sees when he is there.

(VII, 244–79)

It is the invocation of an "absolute presence of reality" (l. 249), one
which is not there, which seems to disturb Wordsworth here. This
process of aping is set apart from the mode of representation which
has in mind the "purest ends"; for he knows that such figurations are
necessary to the deepest kinds of communication. Here, however,
man's more shallow weaknesses and fancies are responsible for what
he sees. Wordsworth is alarmed at the possibility of bringing the
rural landscape inside the city by means of the facsimile, and also by
the posture of "power" adopted before it. The facsimile pretends to
provide "absolute presence" but of course cannot do so; in reducing
an "whole horizon" to an organized spectacle for the complacent
beholder, it invites that beholder into a position of gratuitous
"power", implicit in the thrill of control which comes from standing
on the "lofty Pinnacle". The aggrandisement of self which comes
with standing thus erect is bought at the expense of the objects
represented in the picture, which are diminished to exactly the same
degree as the self is elevated. As always in Wordsworth, self and
world posit each other simultaneously at the moment of seeing, and
this is why the environment of London is so threatening to those
contained within it. London provides, in its multitude of emblems
and signs, too much 'outside', too many objects demanding
assimilation by the mind. The mind therefore cannot keep up the
steady pace of giving out and receiving back; there is not the
necessary space and time to draw back for the 'second look' which
has to happen if this cycle is to be maintained. We can see this
'second look' at work in another passage from *The Prelude*:

As when a Traveller hath from open day
With torches pass'd into some Vault of Earth,

The Grotto of Antiparos, or the Den
Of Yordas among Craven's mountain tracts;
He looks and sees the cavern spread and grow,
Widening itself on all sides, sees, or thinks
He sees, erelong, the roof above his head,
Which instantly unsettles and recedes
Substance and shadow, light and darkness, all
Commingled, making up a Canopy
Of Shapes and Forms and Tendencies to Shape
That shift and vanish, change and interchange
Like Spectres, ferment quiet and sublime;
Which, after a short space, works less and less,
Till every effort, every motion gone,
The scene before him lies in perfect view,
Exposed and lifeless, as a written book.
But let him pause awhile, and look again
And a new quickening shall succeed, at first
Beginning timidly, then creeping fast
Through all which he beholds; the senseless mass,
In its projections, wrinkles, cavities,
Through all its surface, with all colours streaming,
Like a magician's airy pageant, parts,
Unites, embodying everywhere some pressure
Or image, recognis'd or new, some type
Or picture of the world; forests and lakes,
Ships, Rivers, Towers, the Warrior clad in Mail,
The prancing Steed, the Pilgrim with his Staff,
The mitred Bishop and the throned King,
A Spectacle to which there is no end.

                                    (VIII, 711–41)

There is a great deal to be said about this passage, and I cannot
pretend to offer an exhaustive account of it here. We notice, for
example, that the process of making meaning takes place in a cave, a
contained context wherein the perceiver has withdrawn from the challenges of a larger and perhaps unassimilable landscape. But the
point at issue is that the reaction to the cavern, and consequently the
'vision' of it, passes through a first stage of hyperactivity and flux
which offers no stability of perspective and therefore no meaning, to
a second stage of deadness and fixity where the absence of life and
movement again fail to provide a meaning. There follows a third

stage, that of the 'second look', which reconciles the fluid and the fixed, more determinate than the one and more lively than the other; this produces a steadily *developing* succession of types and pictures. There is enough of form to provide 'meaning', in the shape of a reading of the figures, and enough of life and movement to prevent such readings from becoming fixed and thus authoritative, at which point further activity of the mind would be rendered impossible. Thus the spectacle has "no end", and the shaping mind goes on shaping, avoiding the Scylla of fetishism and the Charybdis of formlessness.

The walls of the cavern offer two crucial things, two co-ordinates of space and time, which the immediate experience of London cannot offer. Firstly, there is a limited field of vision, or *space*, which can be processed by the mind in isolation from other stimulants and distractions. Secondly, there is enough *time* for the second look to take place without any demand for attention from other objects. The two go together, of course, and they intimate that perception best takes place in certain contexts rather than others. London, for example, corresponds to the first stage of 'seeing' in the cave, where the eye has not had time to adapt to the shade and sees merely an overactive and formless space within which it cannot stabilize. This feature of life in the metropolis can be causally related to the incidence of the theatre and the spectacle, and what they speak for; this is why the account of the 'second look' is so illuminating. Because there is no proper balance of innering and outering, and because that balance tips so heavily toward a dominance of external signs and objects succeeding each other in rapid and unmanageable sequence, art in the metropolis functions to provide the opposite extreme and to offer the mind some momentary relief. Thus, to offset the experience of reiterated *passivity*, the inhabitants of the city require interludes of equally extreme *activity*. Hence the spectacles and the products of greedy pencils, which invite the beholder into briefly maintained postures of mastery. At these moments, the world becomes as passive before the perceiver as the perceiver habitually is before the world.

This violent oscillation of mastery and slavery becomes even more sinister when we recognize that the compensatory experience of power happens only in facsimile, and in a way divorced from any "absolute presence". Wordsworth's objections to tourism take on a new significance here. This confounding of the figured and the real, the facsimile with the "absolute presence" (which is yet itself a

different species of figure, as we have shown), means that the
capacity for telling the difference is blunted, or never cultivated.
Such people will never be able to experience the urgency of the
'second look' wherever they are, because nothing in their habitual
experience prepares them for it. Thus any visits to the country must
remain embedded within the cycle of mastery and slavery imposed
by urban life; they will see only facsimiles, and react to them only as
diversions from a 'reality' elsewhere. They have, as Wordsworth
says elsewhere, been rendered unfit for "all voluntary exertion" and
reduced to a state "of almost savage torpor" (*PrW*, I, 128).

Returning to the account of perception inside the cave, we must
register the fact that Wordsworth describes this mode of ideal
figuring as a "Spectacle". Why does he use the same word to
describe both what he censures and what he recommends? In fact,
astonishingly, he tells us that the whole passage is an account
(through simile) of his experience of London itself. He passed, in
other words, through a state of frenetic confusion to "a blank sense
of greatness pass'd away" (VIII, 744), and thence to a mediated
quickening, between the two. The rest of Book VIII in fact
rehabilitates London as a place where the imagination can indeed
work to perceive "the unity of man" (l. 827) and the immanence of
"unutterable love" (l. 859). But the image of the cave yet remains,
in spite of its introduction in this surprising context, suggestive of a
privileged perception which cannot tend to flourish in the city. It
depends upon criteria which are almost never satisfied there, and
whatever reconciliation Wordsworth effects with his experience of
the metropolis asks to be taken in the light of the fact that he chose
not to live there. It is worth mentioning, moreover, that that
reconciliation appeals to a side of his mind which responds to things
of which his writings in general do not approve:

> that vast Metropolis,
> The Fountain of my Country's destiny
> And of the destiny of Earth itself,
> That great Emporium, Chronicle at once
> And Burial-place of passions and their home
> Imperial and chief living residence.
>
> (ll. 746–51)

Commerce as the means for the conquering of the earth is a
controversial institution, as we shall see. It may be taken as a mark

of Wordsworth's honesty or ambivalence that he incorporates into his autobiography those feelings and experiences which do not, I would argue, accord with the social and ethical priorities which his writings generally endorse.

We can now begin to see why life in the country has for Wordsworth a status beyond that which would be the product of mere pastoral inclination, and we can see at the same time why he might have been so deeply unsure of his own position within the rural economy. The country differs from the city in two essential ways: it is less densely populated by people, and less densely circumscribed by objects and potential signs. The Lake District satisfies these demands more fully than most landscapes, being very sparsely populated by both people and objects. There are, and were, few natural or human monuments, few trees and few habitations. There are of course mountains, but these too are few and stand in identifiable singleness one from another. In the chosen vale, then, the geographical counterpart to the cave, the mind has the maximum opportunity to carry through the 'second look', and for extending the looking through time. This is how the "passions of men are incorporated with the beautiful and permanent forms of nature" (*PrW*, I, 124), and this is why Wordsworth can use the vocabulary of incorporation rather than that of causality, either version of which would be a mode belonging to the city.

The fact that the Lake District is very lightly populated by people suggests that there is there the best possible chance of sharing meanings with others, or of exploring the consequences of *not* sharing (which for Wordsworth is undoubtedly a fact of life). It is not often that "joy of one/Is joy of tens of millions" (*The Prelude*, VI, 359–60), as the young poet had found it to be in the brief prime of post-Revolutionary France. More often the sharing of joys is tentative and difficult, itself the subject of meditations whose genesis is owing to the fact of absence or loss. Wordsworth is a poet of alienation, one whose ideal communities are constructed out of the negative, and there are certainly personal and temperamental factors implicated in this. But his poems do permit the tracing of a coherent polemic against a historical crisis, both in theory and, at some definite level, in the world-as-observed. In this sense, if there is to be any prospect of an achieved community between man, nature and other men, then it is in environments like that of the Lakes that the opportunity may be most profitably explored.

The relation between the description of London and the account of poetic diction, to which I have pointed already, suggests that Wordsworth's idea of language is also to be related to context in a specific way. Wordsworth contends that the language of country people is language at its best, because such people "hourly communicate with the best objects from which the best part of language is originally derived" (*PrW*, I, 124). We should not be led into any realist hypothesis by reading this vocabulary of original derivation as one of simple or direct causality. The word should ideally be "an incarnation of the thought" (*PrW*, II, 84), not of the thing. Rural language users do not 'embody' the mountains in their words; it is rather that the presence of the mountains, and (what is at least as important) the absence of other things, exercises a discipline over thought and emotion, which then is manifested in language:

> because, from their rank in society and the sameness and narrow circle of their intercourse, being less under the action of social vanity they convey their feelings and notions in simple and unelaborated expressions.
>
> (*PrW*, I, 124)

This simplicity and unelaboration is often a direct intimation of what, being most important, cannot be 'said', but it is not explicitly used to mark out man from man, as the figuratively overelaborate sign systems of Cambridge and London, and their literary language, are used. This authentic rural language makes use only of the essential kinds of figurative attribution, that which "native passion dictates" (*The Prelude*, XII, 264) and which Wordsworth calls the "original figurative language of passion" (*PrW*, I, 161).

At this minimal level of operation, the use of the figurative stands most chance of avoiding the posture of power which all such activity must risk, as it works by inscribing the subject into a particular way of seeing. At least when power is thus courted, the rural context offers most chance for its being corrected. Reciprocally it avoids also the posture of alienated passivity of the kind which is typical of life in London, and where the subject is cast as the consumer of an already prefigured way of seeing. There, to respond to a sign is to accede to someone else's possession of power.

One paradigm of this approved level of figurative activity is the epitaph. By the seriousness of its coming-into-being it dissuades us from the capricious and unmeditated, reproaching the "transports of mind" and "quick turns of conflicting passion" (*PrW*, II, 60) which might otherwise go into the creation of a companionable form.

Man will be less disposed in this case than in any other to

> avail himself of the liberty given by metre to adopt phrases of fancy, or to enter into the more remote regions of illustrative imagery. For the occasion of writing an Epitaph is matter of fact in its intensity, and forbids more authoritatively than any other species of composition all modes of fiction, except those which the very strength of passion has created; which have been acknowledged by the human heart, and have become so familiar that they have been converted into substantial realities.
>
> *(PrW*, II, 76)

Here is the confirmation of that passage from *Home at Grasmere* which suggested the necessity of fiction to sweeten the labour of life. Our 'realities' may be fictions, properly speaking, but they are all we have and all we need so long as we do not infringe certain rules in creating them. We should attend to what connects, and not what separates man from man, and we should test out the products or fictions so figured against time, against continuing confirmation by strength of feeling.

IV THE SPOTS OF TIME: SPACES FOR REFIGURING

If space is the theatre of figurative representation, then time is the measure of its continuance or disappearance, and the oxymoron at the heart of Wordsworth's famous phrase gives us a clue to the nature and resolution of such representations. Because the spots are of *time*, they are not to be held within any stable perspective, not to be visualized or fixed by the look. They are identities whose very definition supposes *process*, monuments of creative instability.

One of the most frequently reiterated aspects of the poet's youth and early maturity in *The Prelude* is its antithetical or oxymoronic experience of nature. "Foster'd alike by beauty and by fear" (I, 306), there is from the first a sense that what nature teaches the child is not any simple harmony with the world, but a continually evolving oscillation between extremes of identity and difference, synthesis and opposition. These "Severer interventions" (I, 370) produce a personality based on the capacity to hold together through time experiences of radically different kinds. Here "fear and love" (XIII, 143) will be equally at home,

> With the adverse principles of pain and joy,
> Evil as one is rashly named by those
> Who know not what they say.
>
> (XIII, 147–9)

The "soothing influences of nature" are thus derived not only from rebirth but also from passing away, from the "types of renovation and decay" (*PrW*, II, 54). Only in this way can pleasure itself be prevented from solidifying into fixed form, subservient to

> The tendency, too potent in itself,
> Of habit to enslave the mind, I mean
> Oppress it by the laws of vulgar sense,
> And substitute a universe of death,
> The falsest of all worlds, in place of that
> Which is divine and true.
>
> (XIII, 138–43)

The insistence on the assimilation of the different aspects of nature through time also involves the mind's active response to what it is given; the mind must 'figure' the materials which are to hand into redisposed forms, providing whatever degree of activity or passivity nature seems not to provide. This is exactly how Wordsworth describes the imagination, a faculty inescapably figurative in that it does not seek to reflect but to refract or reconstruct what is before it. In the preface to *Poems, 1815*, Wordsworth thus describes the imagination as it operates on "images independent of each other":

> These processes of imagination are carried on either by conferring additional properties upon an object, or abstracting from it some of those which it actually possesses, and thus enabling it to re-act upon the mind which hath performed the process, like a new existence.
>
> (*PrW*, III, 32)

He then specifies a second activity of the imagination, that "upon images in conjunction by which they modify each other", wherein

the conferring, the abstracting, and the modifying powers of the
Imagination, immediately and mediately acting, are all brought
into conjunction.

(ibid., p. 33)

Clearly, these two operations correspond to two types of figure. The
former, working on images in isolation, involves the metonym or
synecdoche; hence Wordsworth's example of the cuckoo being
represented by means of its song, in a way which "dispossesses the
creature almost of a corporeal existence" (p. 32). The second
activity of the imagination, working on images in conjunction, is
exemplified by the famous example of the stanza from 'Resolution
and Independence', the one beginning "As a huge stone is
sometimes seen to lie". Here the three images, the stone, the sea-
beast and the old man, are indeed brought into conjunction, but by
a process which involves ignoring some of the qualities of each in
order to stress those which are held in common:

> The stone is endowed with something of the power of life to
> approximate it to the sea-beast; and the sea-beast stripped of
> some of its vital qualities to assimilate it to the stone; which
> intermediate image is thus treated for the purpose of bringing the
> original image, that of the stone, to a nearer resemblance to the
> figure and condition of the aged Man; who is divested of so much
> of the indications of life and motion as to bring him to the point
> where the two objects unite and coalesce in just comparison.

(p. 33)

The clarity in Wordsworth's discourse, as it intimates the negative
implications in what it is celebrating, is astonishing. The imagination has "no reference to images that are merely a faithful copy",
and the "operations of the mind" (p. 31) which it thus involves
invoke the mind's highest faculty. But the price of that exalted status
may be very high if it is not scrupulously restrained. In both the
above detailed kinds of imaginative activity, the metonymic and the
metaphoric, Wordsworth makes it clear that there is a 'taking away'
of vital qualities. The cuckoo almost loses "corporeal existence"
(and there is no easy metaphysic of a transcendent spiritual identity
put in its place), and the old man loses the signs of life and motion. If
the rhetorical effect of poetry be to insinuate a particular 'way of
seeing', then there are obvious risks in encouraging this kind

of selectivity among the imaginative; that is why the doings of
Wordsworth's speakers are so often implicitly or explicitly qualified,
and why the after effect of the figurative experience is often an
education *into* generosity.

Thus the "consolidating numbers into unity, and dissolving and
separating unity into number" (p. 33) which constitutes the highest
pleasure of imagination, inescapably invokes the possibility of the
freak of power. Given that this activity is also necessary and
healthful, we can see the importance of that discipline in nature
which 'fights back' and refuses to allow such moments of control to
endure through *time*. This cycle of experience, involving the correction of the interpretations held at one moment by the
perceptions of another, is exactly what we find exemplified in the
passages illustrating the "spots of time".

The threat is intimated from the start as the poet defines such
moments as those wherein we have the "deepest feeling" that the
mind

> Is lord and master, and that outward sense
> Is but the obedient servant of her will.
>
> (*The Prelude*, XI, 272–3)

This lordship and mastery, which would seem to admit all the
negative functions of the figurative imagination, is however qualified by the examples which follow. There are two of them, the
experience of the pond and gibbet (l. 279 ff.) and that of the father's
death (l. 346 ff.).

The first of these passages describes the poet coming upon the
gibbet in early childhood, and the sense of "visionary dreariness"
(l. 311) which invested the whole landscape as a consequence of this
sighting. Later in life, the adult poet comes to live in "daily presence
of this very scene" (l. 320); familiarity and the society of those he
loves now render it acceptable and even a place of joy, informed by
"The spirit of pleasure and youth's golden gleam" (l. 323). What is
most significant here is the suggestion that the later experiences are
more pleasurable *because* of the force of those earlier, antithetical
memories. The mind endows the landscape with excess value
precisely because it had formerly seemed (or been made to seem) so
threatening. Through time, therefore, two extremes of negative and
positive evaluation combine to produce a kind of balance. The pain
of one perception is answered by subsequent pleasure, and the

pleasure itself is tempered by the memory of pain. The figuring mind has, implicitly, been made wary of wholehearted investment in the figurings of any one moment. It has been made to, or has made itself understand that mastery must be seen together with slavery as two extremes of an ongoing and mediating process.

In the second example, the poet describes how, as a schoolboy, he had been so anxious for the holidays to begin, that he climbed to the top of a crag to try to spy out the approach of the horses which were to carry him home. Then we are told, simply, that his father died ten days after he did arrive home,

> And I and my two Brothers, Orphans then,
> Followed his body to the Grave. The event
> With all the sorrow which it brought appear'd
> A chastisement; and when I call'd to mind
> That day so lately pass'd, when from the crag
> I look'd in such anxiety of hope,
> With trite reflections of morality,
> Yet in the deepest passion, I bow'd low
> To God, who thus corrected my desires.
>
> (ll. 367–75)

The juxtaposition of these events is not explained, but we may infer that the death of the father, happening as it does at an irrevocable moment in time, stands in the poet's mind as an answer to that earlier desire to speed up the passing of time. The wish for the earlier arrival of the horses then comes to seem as if it involved also a wish that the moment of the bereavement should come sooner. It is as if the prior dissatisfaction with what had been given is punished by having something taken away. It is a strange, though not at all unconvincing gesture which has the child read himself into a position of responsibility for the father's death, and the subsequently informed adult voice of the narrative may mean to signal as much in making reference to the "trite reflections of morality" which were part of the "deepest passion"; as if the course of events in the world could really be that coherent! The syntax expressing this conjunction of triteness and passion, moreover, allows it to be referred both to the moment of chastisement and to the initial "anxiety of hope". This is appropriate, for the two moments are not different in kind — they both belong to the ongoing figuring of experience outside which Wordsworth offers himself no authoritative position.

This particular antithesis, which may be seen to involve a reminder of the objectivity of time after a wishful attempt to speed it up, is itself assimilated in later life. The images and events which are associated with the top of the crag come to seem

> spectacles and sounds to which
> I often would repair and thence would drink,
> As at a fountain; and I do not doubt
> That in this later time, when storm and rain
> Beat on my roof at midnight, or by day
> When I am in the woods, unknown to me
> The workings of my spirit thence are brought.
>
> (ll. 383–9)

The whole cycle of 'transgression' and punishment now becomes restorative, and continually restorative, as the fountain both quenches the thirst of the moment and yet continues to flow. The confidence which accrues from this seems to consist in the insight that the mind can contain and survive such antithetical events, and put them to the service of a continually evolving identity.

Both examples of the operations of "spots of time" then seem to involve a recognition and acceptance of the notion that the figurings of the moment are always displaced, often painfully, into subsequent and ongoing refigurings. This is to be distinguished from mere repetition, an oscillation between mastery and slavery, activity and passivity, in that the passage of time makes simple repetition impossible — at least for the ideally imaginative mind, if not for Martha Ray as she is described to us. It is also quite different from the experience of the city, in that here the individual mind itself is at all times co-operative in administering such adjustments and corrections as occur. The forms which come into being are not prefigured by others, and are integrally educative rather than merely habit-forming.

This acceptance of antithesis helps to explain the presence of what is often felt to be a confusion in Wordsworth's epistemology. *The Prelude* presents a whole range of formulations of the mind-world relation, varying from active mind (and passive nature) to active nature (and passive mind), with consequent variations in the attribution of the 'real'. Thus the poet is unsure whether he has "transferr'd/His own enjoyments" to nature in a process of anthropomorphism, or whether he really has "convers'd/With

things that really are" (II, 410 f.). At one moment his figured forms
are the products of "deep analogies by thought supplied" (III, 122),
at another they result from "Nature", which "Thrusts forth upon
the senses" (XIII, 86) what is to be seen. At other times,
correspondingly, some kind of mediation between these two
positions is proposed. Outward form is "to the pleasure of the
human mind/What passion makes it", but outward things have at
the same time a "passion in themselves" which "intermingles" with
man's activities (XII, 286–93). Thus there is produced

> A balance, an ennobling interchange
> Of action from within and from without,
> The excellence, pure spirit, and best power
> Both of the object seen, and eye that sees.
>
> (XII, 376–9)

These various positions, and the various permutations possible
between them, would clearly make no sense as an attempt to
propose a stable theoretical description of perception, one true for
all places and at all times, and indeed for all people. All Romantic
epistemology is basically synthetic, positing the co-operation of
mind and world in the act of seeing and knowing; but it must be
stressed that Wordsworth's version of the balance is actually an
interchange through time, a process of which no one extrapolated
moment or incident is properly representative. There is no
privileged figuring of the real, which becomes an objective standard
of normalcy; there is only a *series* of figurings, wherein a whole set of
positions will be taken up from time to time, rising to vanish like
clouds in the sky, and living on in the modified figures of the
imaginative memory.

This formulation sheds new light on the problem with which this
chapter began, that of how communication can take place, and
consensus be established, in a world which may be composed of
unstable personal configurations, companionable forms only of the
isolated single mind and the projected receiver of its messages. We
might infer from the Wordsworthian model, as I have described it,
that if a series of positions are occupied at different times by the same
mind, then all other minds (readers) might be expected to occupy
similar positions at some time in the cycle of their experiences. Thus
we might come to understand the transcendental structure of our
minds as held in common with that of the poet, irrespective of the

particular objects which we happen to relate to the particular dispositions of the mind within that structure. If we all go through the cycle of activity and passivity in our relations to the environment, then we hold that cycle in common even as no two people need be at the same point at the same time. We can thus contemplate the joys we cannot share, with something which may not improperly be called 'joy'. Further, as long as the process itself continues to occur, the particular deviations toward the extremes of mastery and slavery which it must include have no critical significance. They cannot solidify into a mystification of the 'real' as long as they are consistently dispersed by the figures which succeed them, and are never controlled by a single person or faction.

The above explanation, if it were applicable, would solve both the question of what different minds may hold in common (given that they cannot be assumed to 'see' the same 'objects'), and the ethical predicament of how we should respond to our world and to each other. What is fascinating about Wordsworth, however, is that at the same time as he affords us the materials to come up with explanatory models such as the above, he incorporates an insistence on the contextual considerations which must qualify or even spoil the prospect of such a model ever being adopted as practicable. He is in fact both prophetic and descriptive; he senses the urgent import of the ideally imaginative vision because he is so critically aware of what there is to threaten it, both in the world at large *and* in the aspiring individual mind, for they go together. The young man with his surplice performs the alienation whose effects he learns to deplore. A moral consensus is being sought in the mind of the sympathetic reader even as the very condition of that consensus is shown to be an empirical experience based in disturbance and disjunction. I think that there are two ways in which Wordsworth's discourse refuses its reader any position of acquiescent comfort. Firstly, there is the evidence that the insights of the poet as narrator will be felt to the full only by those sharers of a specific locale; a small community, a marginal economy, in a landscape sparse in its potential for being figured. Secondly, the whole model of adequation which the poet creates for himself out of the hard-won insights accompanying the experiences of consciousness, loss and transgression, is itself a figuring of the individual mind as it seeks to reflect on its own operation. This matters especially in Wordsworth since we are often shown that the dramatic speaker, the 'I', often functions by misapprehension and in solitude. There is thus no moment of perpetuated self-consciousness, no taking up of a position of authority, for the same reason that there is no 'spot' or fixed place which is not in fact defined in time. There is no perspective for commenting upon figures which is not itself a figure, and here we can suspect a source for the anxiety with which the Wordsworthian narrator sometimes turns to the brother poet, or to Dorothy. Kant had set himself a philosopher's task, and he had explained how experience is possible by reference to the tools the mind has to work with, the categories. The unspoken assumption behind this is that experience is *normal*. Wordsworth sets out from the other end, so to speak, and might have been happy to have been able to come to that conclusion. What troubles him is the suspicion that different minds are in fact operating with different tools, and tools either of their own mysterious making, or given them at second hand to be used at the service of their inventors. Wordsworth's urgent concern is certainly with the empirical. The sharing of the capacity to structure experience by space and time matters less to him than the use of that capacity in generous ways.

2 The Figures of Desire

For there is no such thing as perpetuall Tranquillity of mind, while we live here; because Life it selfe is but Motion, and can never be without Desire, nor without Feare, no more than without Sense.

Hobbes, *Leviathan*, I, 6

There is more reason in your body than in your best wisdom. And who knows for what purpose your body requires precisely your best wisdom?

Nietzsche, *Thus Spake Zarathustra*

I SEEING THE FIGURE

The rest of this book will be given over to an attempt to place the questions I have highlighted in Coleridge and at greater length in Wordsworth into a wider (but I hope precise) historical context. This context is intended to make clear the importance of the complexity of personal and social interactions and perceptions presented in Wordsworth's writings as they examine the genesis and consequences of figured forms. I have explained already, in the second section of my introduction, the case for the acceptance of a logic of historical reference which is not limited to what Wordsworth can be proved to have read. To begin with, I shall try to establish a context for the Romantic crisis in configuration, or representation, as it relates to the terms then available for the articulation of a theory of knowledge.

We can help to make this clear by an appreciation of the revitalized rôle of metaphor in Romantic theory. In his remarks on language, Wordsworth famously privileges authentic metaphor and the natural passion which it speaks forth over the excessive and merely derived tropes and figures of the popular poetic diction. Those trapped among the theatres and street signs of London are condemned to experience the social analogues or consequences of such a diction, in contrast to those who are offered the prospect of the companionship of self-originated figures in the rural landscape.

Wherever one lives, however, the presence of the figure is not to be avoided; it is a feature of all perception and communication, and at best it is indeed the result of the activity of the mind's highest faculty.

This does represent a radical departure from one of the basic assumptions underlying the traditional acceptance of the place of the figurative in poetic discourse: that the process of relation and redirection which it encourages should exist at a level strictly secondary to the communication of prior meanings. Metaphor, the most often discussed of all figures, is there to decorate the realities on which it depends, and not to constitute a world of its own making. The reader or hearer must be able to separate what is *meant* by a statement from the effects of *how* it is said, and to infer from the figure the 'thing' which gave rise to it, and to which it must be reapplied. Further, the distractions which metaphor always does occasion tended to be allowed only by being limited to certain *kinds* of language. Even Hobbes, who was notoriously censorious of metaphor in the public language whose necessary features he discusses in *Leviathan*, was thus able to enjoy the effects of well-wrought figures and tropes in poetry, for poetry is consciously concerned with pleasure and persuasion; it does not claim to be the rational language in which the most important kinds of social interchange must be carried on. Here is a passage from *The Whole Art of Rhetoric* on the qualities of grace and delight in oratory:

> But *metaphors* please; for they beget in us, by the *genus*, or by some *common* thing to that with another, a kind of *science*. As when an *old man* is called *stubble*; a man suddenly learns that he grows up, flourisheth, and withers like grass, being put in mind of it by the qualities common to *stubble* and to *old men*.[1]

Hobbes clearly recognizes the persuasive power of metaphors, but given that the very function of rhetoric is persuasion, they are not out of place:

> He that will make the best of a thing, let him draw his *metaphor* from somewhat that is better. As for example, let him call a *crime* an *error*. On the other side, when he would make the worst of it, let him draw his *metaphor* from somewhat worse; as, calling *error, crime*.

(p. 489)

In a language which does not draw attention to itself as persuasive, but which insinuates itself as the 'real' — which in Hobbes' case means the language of an agreed consensus — metaphor becomes improper. Thus, in *Leviathan*, which concerns itself with the language on which public contract is to be founded, those who use words metaphorically, that is "in other sense than that they are ordained for", are said to "deceive others" (*Works*, III, 20).

This limitation upon the province of the figurative corresponded to an emphasis on the efficiency of nouns, names of 'things', as stable signifiers either expressing, or in Hobbes' case at least partly substituting for, reality. In this spirit Monboddo identified a barbarous language as one which found itself driven to an excess of metaphor:

> not being able to express a thing by its proper name, they are naturally driven to tell what it is like. The most perfect language is, therefore, that which has proper names for every thing, and uses figurative words only by way of ornament.[2]

Such a "perfect language" would hardly be possible as an object of admiration for, for example, Wordsworth. The question of having "proper names for every thing" does not for Wordsworth constitute success or failure in the realm of authentic meaning; what matters is how words are used to signal forth the important 'realities' behind them, the human passions. These are the agents which select from or even constitute the world of things, figuring them into companionable form, which we may estimate positively or not according to its capacity for creative exchange, whether with the self through time or with other selves. Figures are inevitable; what matters is that they be "dictated by real passion" and not mechanically adopted (*PrW*, I, 161). Reference to things, and the denotative function of language in general, is less important than this relation to the truth of feelings, which the best poetry is derived from and should consequently encourage in others.

This redirection of concern, appearing so dramatically and urgently in Wordsworth, relates to a series of preoccupations in psychology, language theory and in the theory of knowledge, all of which contributed to bring forward the place of the figurative in explaining the operations of the human mind. Firstly, and in the context of what we would now call 'psychology', there was the commonplace of the 'association of ideas', which was a standard

element in eighteenth-century philosophical inquiry. Treated in
important ways by Hume and by Hartley, its most significant source
was Bk. II, ch. 33 of Locke's *Essay*. Of the association of ideas, Locke
says that "perhaps, there is not any one thing that deserves more to
be looked after" (p. 397). Its effects and operations partake exactly
of "the Nature of Madness", but Locke's concern is strictly with the
universal incidence of the syndrome in everyday, normal life; he
speaks of man not "when he is under the power of an unruly Passion,
but in the steady calm course of his life" (p. 395). The method by
which ideas come to be associated is, as is well known, highly
idiosyncratic, depending largely on custom, habit and past
experience. As such these associations contrive to keep people apart,
whether individually or in factions; having naturalized different
associations, they do not 'understand' each other. Significantly, the
account of association relates precisely to the standard account of
the operation of metaphor:

> *Ideas*, of no alliance to one another, are by Education, Custom,
> and the constant din of their Party, so coupled in their Minds,
> that they always appear there together, and they can no more
> separate them in their Thoughts, than if they were but one *Idea*,
> and they operate as if they were so. This gives Sence to *Jargon*,
> Demonstration to Absurdities, and Consistency to Nonsense, and
> is the foundation of the greatest, I had almost said, of all the
> Errors in the World; or if it does not reach so far, it is at least the
> most dangerous one, since so far as it obtains, it hinders Men from
> seeing and examining. When two things in themselves disjoin'd,
> appear to the sight constantly united; if the Eye sees these things
> rivetted which are loose, where will you begin to rectify the
> mistakes that follow in two *Ideas*, that they have been accustom'd
> so to join in their Minds, as to substitute one for the other, and, as
> I am apt to think, often without perceiving it themselves?
>
> (pp. 400–1)

Locke is talking about what the eye sees; things which in themselves
are distinct but are always *seen* in conjunction gradually produce an
improper conjunction or confusion of the *ideas* (in the mind) by
association. In a similar way, if the eye sees *words* conjoined in a
metaphor, it will gradually come to infer a like connection among
things. This is Locke's process working backwards, and producing
the same confusions; in this way, Coleridge was to say, the mind

comes to worship its own creations (or, in the case of an inherited metaphor, those of another mind) as 'objective'.

In his discussion of "method", Coleridge asserts that some perception of "mental relations" is essential to all organized thinking and expression. This will tend to proceed by observation of affinities, which may include perception of contiguities and associations. To preclude the despotism of the senses, Coleridge is at pains to stress that these relations are *mental*, and even then they must never become obsessive:

> where the habit of Method is present and effective, things the most remote and diverse in time, place, and outward circumstance, are brought into mental contiguity and succession, the more striking as the less expected. But while we would impress the necessity of this habit, the illustrations adduced give proof that in undue preponderance, and when the prerogative of the mind is stretched into despotism, the discourse may degenerate into the grotesque or the fantastical.[3]

Method, again, is judged as one judges a metaphor; it is "the more striking as the less expected", but there must be something in the conjunction which allows us to validate it for ourselves, so that it is not merely freakish. It results from the standard Romantic mediation, from "the due mean or balance between our passive impressions and the mind's own re-action on the same" (p. 453), and it is maintained only "when the objects thus connected are proportionate to the connecting energy, relatively to the real, or at least to the desirable sympathies of mankind" (p. 455). Coleridge is well aware of the figurative element in the association of ideas as central to the mind's highest activities, as he is aware also of its potential usurpation of the means of communication, turning it into a private language of madness and fixation. The difference between the two resides in a consensus about the "real" or the "desirable" sympathies of mankind.

How might such a consensus come about? This leads us to the other ways in which seeing figuratively was held to be important in explaining the workings of mind and language. It is difficult, indeed, to make any clear or absolute separation between the theory of language and the theory of mind in the context of the eighteenth century; the two interpenetrate to such a degree. The dominant cast of eighteenth-century language theory was nominalistic, in ascribing to language a central rôle in any perception of 'reality'. Language depends for its efficiency on universals or abstract concepts; we have the class term 'table' by which we identify a series of things with certain qualities and use-values in common, and the efficiency of the term depends exactly on its generality, its holding together these qualities into a unity. The class term does not describe exhaustively any specific member of the class. To do this we have to introduce qualifiers (wooden, with short legs, under the window, etc.). It is the very generality of the class term on which its efficiency depends, a fact which gave rise to the following comment on the situation from an American writer, A. B. Johnson:

> The generality of language is an irremediable defect in its structure; for were we to invent a separate name for every sight which we now denominate white, language would be too voluminous for utility, and perhaps for our memory. The same remarks apply to every word.[4]

This is only a defect, of course, if we expect language to provide a new noun for every item in the created world. It might also be a problem if there were the prospect of an argument about what constitutes the authenticity of a general term, and it is this possibility which relates to the present case for the importance of the figurative or relational element in the medium of language. An extreme nominalist position would accord no existence to universals (class terms) except as *names*. If we use a language which thus has no verifiable relation to a 'real' world of things, it will tend to follow that that language becomes our principle of order and coherence in perception and communication. Elements of the language have a strictly arbitrary relation to what they signify, so that authority for signification must be sought not in nature but in human contract. The extreme position taken by Hobbes suggests that language not only derives from contract, but is of absolute importance in upholding it:

> But the most noble and profitable invention of all other, was that of SPEECH, consisting of *names* or *appellations*, and their connexions; whereby men register their thoughts; recall them when they are past; and also declare them one to another for mutual utility and conversation; without which, there had been

amongst men, neither commonwealth, nor society, nor contract, nor peace, no more than amongst lions, bears, and wolves.

(*Works*, III, 18)

In Hobbes' account, God gave Adam the first words, and the rest was up to him and his fellow humans.[5] In this way general terms came into use based on perceptions of likeness, "there being nothing in the world universal but names; for the things named are every one of them individual and singular" (p. 21). Perceptions of shared qualities are relational perceptions; we ask ourselves, as we look at different things, whether they have qualities in common to a sufficient degree to entitle them to incorporation within the same class term. This is not strictly a 'metaphoric' perception, in that metaphor is usually thought to involve crossing the borders of class terms as they have been habitually observed, prompted by the perception of some newly observed property held in common; Achilles is a lion because of his bravery, perhaps, but not for his showing the four-footed, hairy, carnivorous qualities which are the established qualifications for membership of the lion class. It is, however, a perception of likenesses, and my example makes clear that there is a good deal of potential for argument or uncertainty about the authority of the class term. An alternative taxonomy might establish bravery among the essential qualities for membership of the 'lion' class, in which case anomalously cowardly representatives of *Felis leo* would no longer be admitted, but Achilles might be (as long as there are no other qualities, such as four-footedness, debarring him).

There is then a necessary tendency to instability in the metaphoric mode, and this helps to explain why its application was so urgently restrained by many commentators on language. Dugald Stewart stresses that the user of metaphor must "keep steadily in view the habitual associations of those upon whom they are destined to operate".[6] As long as metaphor signals the presence of the class terms it is momentarily subverting, then the stability of those terms is not threatened. In the same spirit, Blair comments that

particular care should be taken that the resemblance, which is the foundation of the Metaphor, be clear and perspicuous, not far-fetched, nor difficult to discover. The transgression of this rule makes, what are called harsh or forced Metaphors, which are always displeasing, because they puzzle the reader, and instead of illustrating the thought, render it perplexed and intricate.[7]

Again, if the metaphor does not make the new resemblance clear, it at the same time calls into question the whole principle of resemblance upon which class terms as a whole are generally based. To say that Achilles is a saucer, or a giraffe, or a cigarette, is the more subversive for the fact that there is almost no relation we cannot justify, if we think hard enough.

To return to the main point: the conventional strictures about the use of metaphor are the more urgent because the perception of relations between things is central to language, in so far as it does not and cannot employ a new noun for every object. Blair makes exactly this point in his conjecture about the development of language from whatever origin it might have had:

> According as men's ideas multiplied, and their acquaintance with objects increased, their stock of names and words would increase also. But to the infinite variety of objects and ideas, no language is adequate. No language is so copious, as to have a separate word for every separate idea. Men naturally sought to abridge this labour of multiplying words *in infinitum*; and in order to lay less burden on their memories, made one word, which they had already appropriated to a certain idea or object, stand also for some other idea or object, between which and the primary one, they found, or fancied some relation.
>
> (I, 269–70)

Names must serve to refer to a whole range of specific ideas, specific things, infinitely open to minute differentiation yet having enough qualities in common to earn them the common name. Moreover, there is an ongoing place in language for relational apprehension, for the perception of common qualities, as new descriptive compounds are required to serve as names for new things. I take this insight to inform what might otherwise appear as outright conservatism in Samuel Johnson's famous reservations about neologism as they are found in the preface to the *English Dictionary*. Johnson opines that a selection of the best authors in different disciplines writing in the Elizabethan age would produce a speech which "might be formed adequate to all the purposes of use and elegance", through the use of which "few ideas would be lost to mankind, for want of *English* words, in which they might be expressed".[8] In other words, whatever new items and experiences accrue to mankind, as they must so accrue, there exists in Elizabethan English a range of class terms already sufficiently varied to include almost all imaginable novelties. If I may risk an example, Johnson might thus have preferred the word 'skytrain' to 'aeroplane'. The first defines a new idea or thing by metaphorically conflating two class terms which already exist, whereas the second option involves the invention of a new word. If this is indeed Johnson's argument, then it has a democratic function. In an age where universal literacy was not at all assumed, the first option would clearly have afforded the average language user a greater chance of comprehending its denotation than the second (allowing me, please, the anachronism of having trains and aeroplanes in the eighteenth century!). Vocabularies depending on neologism, on the contrary, tend to function efficiently at first only for those who have participated in their creation, remaining a mystery to those outside.

The recognition of the necessity of relational perception was a common one,[9] but I should like to quote it again in the impeccable formulation of John Stuart Mill's *System of Logic* (1843):

> in the simplest description of an observation, there is, and must always be, much more asserted than is contained in the perception itself. We cannot describe a fact, without implying more than the fact. The perception is only of one individual thing; but to describe it is to affirm a connexion between it and every other thing which is either denoted or connoted by any of the terms used. To begin with an example, than which none can be conceived more elementary: I have a sensation of sight, and I endeavour to describe it by saying that I see something white. In saying this, I do not solely affirm my sensation; I also class it. I assert a resemblance between the thing I see, and all things which I and others are accustomed to call white . . . It is inherent in a description, to be the statement of a resemblance, or resemblances.[10]

All descriptive language is based on the perception of relations, and may indeed perhaps even determine perceptions. One thinks of the stories of the societies who 'see' only two colours in the world around them; do they 'see' more than their language allows them to communicate? I shall not try to answer that one; but Mill's observation clearly allows for the inference that arguments about what is white, or cream, or magnolia, relate not just to things in themselves but to the habits and experiences of the observers, and to the language elements they happen, individually or severally, to possess. Description proceeds by association, and association, as we have seen, may be insinuated by nothing more authoritative than habit.

Before leaving this consideration of the theory of language proper, it is worth saying that there were other pressures requiring an assessment of the place of the figurative besides those emphasizing the importance of the perception of relations. Rousseau, for example, had made the figurative the original element of language, from which the literal or 'proper' use of words must be seen to have emerged:

> As man's first motives for speaking were of the passions, his first expressions were tropes. Figurative language was the first to be born. Proper meaning was discovered last.[11]

Bodily reactions to immediate experience, the gesture and the cry, must be supposed to have generated the original components of language. As communication became more specific, less motivated by immediate sensibility and passion, so language became more stable, "more exact and clearer, but more prolix, duller, and colder" (p. 16). It is hard to know how much of a 'theory' Rousseau saw himself to be advancing in his essay on the origin of language; the work was never published in his lifetime, and must be set in tension with other arguments in his major writings.[12] It certainly has a polemical force, however, and as such emphasizes the importance of the figurative potential which remains in language in its developed state. The names of affective states, of things which "please and displease us", could never for Hobbes form the "true grounds of any ratiocination", because they do not denote things about which we can agree by ostension; such words, "besides the signification of what we imagine of their nature, have a signification also of the nature, disposition, and interest of the speaker' (*Works*, III, 28–9). The drift of Rousseau's argument would tend to make such words into the best rather than the worst elements of language, and it is this verdict which is closer to the spirit of the Romantic writers. Coleridge writes that "language is framed to convey not the object alone, but likewise the character, mood and intentions of the person who is representing it",[13] and for Wordsworth it is exactly such characters, moods and intentions (the human passions), which it is the primary purpose of language to communicate. It is the attempt to find a shared language of the feelings, making itself public as it does by *reference* to things, which takes Wordsworth into the stringent analysis of intention and mood, and their relation to environmental influences, which has already been described. Hobbes is right to stress the difficulty involved in reaching agreement about what is referred to by words of such *"inconstant signification"* (p. 28), and Wordsworth faces exactly this question in making inconstancy the very principle of authenticity in his account of the emotions and their choice of things for figured representation.

Blair in fact endorses by anticipation Wordsworth's criteria for proper figurative language:

> For it is, in truth, the sentiment or passion, which lies under the figured expression, that gives it any merit. The Figure is only the dress; the Sentiment is the body and the substance.
>
> (*Lectures*, I, 267)

Such "ornaments" contribute to "the embellishment of discourse, only when there is a basis of solid thought and natural sentiment; when they are inserted in their proper place; and when they rise, of themselves, from the subject, without being sought after" (p. 269). As with Wordsworth, the figure must have an essential rather than an accidental or contingent relation to the emotion which we infer as giving rise to it; and it is the emotion which is being judged, of course, since a poor figure or a misplaced ornament does indeed efficiently represent what lies behind it, and it is *that* which we are to reject. In fact, besides the standard explanation for the presence of figurative language as devolving from "the barrenness of language, and the want of words", Blair also gives a place, and perhaps the prominent place, to "the influence which Imagination possesses over language" (p. 271). His case depends on the associations and passions which accompany and perhaps even determine the perception of every object or idea:

> By this means, every idea or object carries in its train some other ideas which may be considered as its accessories. These accessories often strike the imagination more than the principal idea itself. They are, perhaps, more agreeable ideas, or they are

more familiar to our conceptions; or they recall to our memory a greater variety of important circumstances. The imagination is more disposed to rest upon some of them; and therefore, instead of using the proper name of the principal idea which it means to express, it employs, in its place, the name of the accessory or correspondent idea; although the principal have a proper and well-known name of its own. Hence, a vast variety of tropical or figurative words obtain currency in all languages, through choice, not necessity; and men of lively imaginations are every day adding to their number.

(pp. 271–2)

All language is thus persuasive and affective, and most figurative in its early stages when the two different explanations of the necessity of figure are most operative.

Language, then, depends on the figurative in at least two ways, stressed to different degrees by different writers; the efficiency of class terms requires the grouping of different things under common names, and, not entirely incompatible with this pressure, passion and inclination are important parts of what we mean to communicate in language, and we do so by the use of figures. I say not incompatible, in that observation of affinities lies behind both, the differences residing largely in the novelty or familiarity of the observation.

I pass on now to a third area of inquiry, that pertaining to the theory of knowledge strictly speaking, which brought forward questions about the presence of a 'figurative' element in the way in which the mind sees the objects of its attention. The theorized relation between objects and object-parts will help to make clear why the relational apprehension of common qualities, which we have seen to apply in the use of class terms, has about it the features of a figured representation.

The opening chapter of *Leviathan* will serve as a starting point. Here, Hobbes rather breathlessly delivers an account of the particle or atom theory of the transmission of sense data by motion, from object to subject. Man's thoughts, or ideas, are

every one a *representation* or *appearance*, of some quality, or other accident of a body without us, which is commonly called an object.

(*Works*, III, 1)

These qualities and accidents act on the sensorium, producing in it a reaction which, "because *outward*, seemeth to be some matter without. And this *seeming*, or *fancy*, is that which men call sense" (p. 2). This is important, for it makes clear that "the object is one thing, the image or fancy is another" (pp. 2–3). There is a much longer and more explicit account of the process in the *Elements of Philosophy* (*Works*, I; see especially p. 390ff.); what is most important to the argument here is that Hobbes makes it clear that we *compose* the idea of an object or substance out of an assemblage of variously received sense data transmitted to us by various qualities or accidents. This epistemology seems to have come to Locke by way of Robert Boyle, whose *The Origine of Forms and Qualities*, 2nd ed. (Oxford, 1667) goes much further in explaining the implications. Boyle's is a strong argument against the necessity of any assumption about substances, or unitary 'real' objects, to explain the workings of the senses and the mind. For

> whatever men talk in Theory of substantial Formes, yet That, upon whose account they really distinguish any one Body from others, and refer it to this or that *Species* of Bodies, is nothing but an Aggregate or convention of such Accidents, as most men do by a kind of agreement (for the thing is more arbitrary then we are aware of) think necessary or sufficient to make a portion of the Universal Matter belong to this or that determinate *Genus* or *Species* of Natural Bodies.
>
> (p. 41)

We agree, in other words, to give names to 'objects' according as they possess the particular qualities or quality agreed upon as the one(s) required to so name them. Thus "there needs no more to discriminate sufficiently any one kind of Bodies from all the Bodies in the world that are not of that kind" (p. 42). Boyle then makes the point that some qualities are ignored as we go about naming substantial forms (objects):

> But because it very seldome happens, that a Body by generation acquires no other Qualities, then just those that are absolutely *necessary* to make it belong to the *Species* that denominates it, therefore in most Bodies there are diverse other Qualities that may *be* there, or may be *missing*, without essentially changing the

Subject: as Water may be clear or muddy, odorous or stinking, and still remain Water.

(p. 60)

It is naming which determines what qualities are essential to one thing, and what to another (p. 92), and naming may in fact be an inaccurate rendering of the aggregates of different and common qualities in bodies:

> most commonly men look upon these as distinct *species* of Bodies, that have had the luck to have distinct names found out for them; though perhaps diverse of them differ much less from one another then other Bodies, which (because they have been hudled up under one name,) have been look'd upon as but one sort of Bodies.
>
> (pp. 107–8)

Names thus represent and disseminate figured forms, made up out of the "innumerable multitude of singly insensible Corpuscles" (p. 102) which constitute primary matter, according as they strike us when assembled into qualities able to impinge upon the senses.

Boyle also puts forward a clear statement of something implicit in Hobbes, and that is the difference between primary and secondary qualities (see pp. 27–32, 65). This, as we have seen already, was to be an important part of Locke's epistemology, and, like Boyle, he maintains that neither primary nor secondary qualities involve any assumptions about substance. We invent a name,

> which by inadvertancy we are apt afterward to talk of and consider as one simple *Idea*, which indeed is a complication of many *Ideas* together; Because, as I have said, not imagining how these simple *Ideas* can subsist by themselves, we accustom our selves, to suppose some *Substratum*, wherein they do subsist, and from which they do result, which therefore we call *Substance*.
>
> (*Essay*, Bk. II. ch. 23, p. 295)

The question of *how* we combine the data received through the different senses into employable wholes, and how indeed we produce a consensus about which assemblies of qualities we refer to in using specific names, is not one which, as far as I can see, Locke takes on in any 'strong' argument. It is "ordained by our Maker" that our ideas serve as efficient modes of both perception and communication,

> and are as real distinguishing Characters, whether they be only constant Effects, or else exact Resemblances of something in the things themselves: the reality lying in that steady correspondence, they have with the distinct Constitutions of real Beings.
> (Bk. II, ch. 30, p. 373)

But, if the efficiency of perception and communication be not frontally questioned, we can nevertheless see that, as with his account of the association of ideas, Locke has put forward here much material for an inquiry into the possible discontinuity in the mind's representation of the 'real', and the communication of its results to other minds. What we call 'objects' are figured forms, tending not to appear as such as long as we all figure them in the same ways. At the same time, the distinction between primary and secondary qualities brings into question the issue of which of our ideas are resemblances of qualities in objects, and which appear to us in some mediated way.[14] Schopenhauer identified the continuity between Locke and Kant as consisting in Kant's extension of this second category of ideas in Locke:

> The share of the sensation of the senses in perception was separated out by Locke under the name of *secondary qualities*, which he rightly denied to things-in-themselves. But Kant, carrying Locke's method farther, also separated out and denied to things-in-themselves what belongs to the *elaboration* of that material (the sensation of the senses) through the *brain*. The result was that included in all this was all that Locke had left to things-in-themselves as *primary* qualities, namely extension, shape, solidity, and so on, and in this way the thing-in-itself becomes with Kant a wholly unknown quantity x. . . . With Kant . . . the thing-in-itself has laid aside even all these last qualities also, because they are possible only through time, space, and causality. These latter, however, spring from our intellect (brain) just as do colours, tones, smells, and so on from the nerves of the sense-organs. With Kant the thing-in-itself has become spaceless, unextended, and incorporeal.[15]

This is a clumsy reading of Locke, in that it fails to take account of the distinction between ideas (all of which are in the mind) and qualities (all of which are in objects). But the misreading is less important than the point Schopenhauer seeks to make by perpetrating it; that between Locke and Kant, 'things-in-themselves' become mental constructs. That they always were so, as in Boyle's and Locke's remarks on substances, only strengthens the point in terms of historical continuity, even as it deprives Schopenhauer of some of his faith in novelty. There is no doubt, however, that Kant stresses the point, brings it forward more urgently, and this is what we would expect in a philosopher of the late eighteenth century. Early in the nineteenth, Goethe was to advance what Locke had called secondary qualities as our sole means of constructing the world we see and act within:

> We now assert, extraordinary as it may in some degree appear, that the eye sees no form, inasmuch as light, shade, and colour together constitute that which to our vision distinguishes object from object, and the parts of an object from each other. From these three, light, shade, and colour, we construct the visible world . . .[16]

The rationalist philosophers had, of course, by means of their adherence to form, been able to insist on the radical instability of colour. Goethe's challenge certainly does not seek to advance the disintegration of all securely shared experiences of objects; but we can see it, in a more implicit way, as part of an emphasis on the qualities or faculties which had traditionally been regarded as sources of differences between people. As they are accorded more and more of a place in the constitution of the 'real', so the question of how much people really share when they communicate becomes correspondingly more urgent. Degrees of deviance become critical. We have seen the bipartite structure of the transcendental solution at work in Coleridge's conviction that he shares with joy the unshared joys; the deviance is ascribed to the contingent, empirical part of perception (what Charles Lamb is actually seeing, or is thought to be seeing), leaving the *a priori* faculty of the mind to stand forth as the vehicle for a potential community of minds, needing only the lively recollection of a former view to set itself in action. It ceases to matter whether Charles is really seeing what Coleridge thinks he is; the aroused joy can still imagine what he *would* be feeling if he were. In Wordsworth's analysis, I have suggested that such creative introversion is not enough of a solution, and indeed is only possible in certain chosen vales or bowers. It is the element of intention in perception which Wordsworth sees as important, and it seems that the aesthetic subsists as free from intentionality only in the Schillerian sense, that is, as a briefly experienced moment between more contingent states and dispositions. Drummond argues that, whilst it is probable that all knowledge of the material world comes to us through the senses, "our particular organization, whatever it may be, will always determine the degree and nature of that knowledge":

> Every man has his peculiar organization, and, consequently, so far as the specific difference exists, the mode, in which any individual is constructed, will influence the perceptions, which he may have of external objects.[17]

It is 'as if' there is a direct intentional transfer of meaning from the mind to the world; we see what we want, or need, to see, or are in the habit of seeing.

Let me give one more example. Mill's *System of Logic* employs a distinction between "perception" (otherwise called "consciousness") and "inference" in its mode of accounting for the undeniable fact of "mal-observation" (*Works*, VIII, 782). Mistakes arise in taking the one for the other. Perception is indeed "infallible evidence of what is really perceived", but it is a very small part of the combination of sense data and mental activity which makes up the whole of what is 'seen'. Thus

> What we are said to observe is usually a compound result, of which one-tenth may be observation, and the remaining nine-tenths inference.
>
> (*ibid.*, p. 642)

The very words Mill employs, "perception" and "consciousness", seem to militate against the use he specifies for them, as strictly objective; but what is interesting is the immediate retreat from the prospect that such such 'objectivity' might afford any viable basis for consensus. The usefulness of such a percept or unit of 'consciousness' is severely compromised if it habitually provides only one tenth of what is usually called 'seeing'. Thus we cannot make the statement 'I saw my brother this morning' with any degree of sense-certainty:

> If any proposition concerning a matter of fact would commonly be said to be known by the direct testimony of the senses, this surely would be so. The truth, however, is far otherwise. I only saw a certain coloured surface; or rather I had the kind of visual sensations which are usually produced by a coloured surface; and from these as marks, known to be such by previous experience, I concluded that I saw my brother. I might have had sensations precisely similar, when my brother was not there. I might have seen some other person . . . I might have been asleep . . . or in a state of nervous disorder, which brought his image before me in a waking hallucination.
>
> (p. 642)

Mill is engaged in a logical rather than an epistemological inquiry; he is explaining the true status of an apparent matter of fact proposition rather than describing in detail any theory of mind. But we can nevertheless sense the degree of epistemological scepticism which underlies the argument. Nine tenths of 'seeing' depends on inference, and inference is vulnerable to the distortions of what Drummond had called our "peculiar organization". This in turn is a function of a series of inner and outer conditions whose exact operations and limits we can never determine, because we must always remain within them. What is 'left' to the objective world now becomes almost irrelevant, in that there seems to be no human perspective from which it may be *seen* to be objective. We can imagine two people making the same statement about having seen their brothers, in ignorance both of themselves and of each other, and in reference to two quite different situations. That cancelled stanza of Wordsworth's 'The Thorn', where the old sea captain bids the narrator to go to see the evidence for himself:

> Perhaps when you are at the place
> You something of her tale may trace
>
> (*PW*, II, 244)

becomes in this context not a prospect for a pure and dispassionate 'seeing', but a challenge to the narrator or reader about his own preoccupations or processes of inference. In addition, the context of

Wordsworth's poem suggests that it really matters, in unarguable human terms, how these processes operate and affect others. If there is "mal-observation" then Martha Ray is suffering from it. While no one in the community of superstition invoked by 'The Thorn' would appear to be consciously punishing her, yet it is clear that some level of ungenerosity is implicit in the rumours and events that are reported to us. 'Perception' is actually judgement calling itself true seeing; it is intentional perception.

Bentham, in fact, uses the word 'intention' to apply to behaviour directed at particular ends, themselves chosen according to "motives" (*Principles*, pp. 91–4). It is a term which is useful to him in establishing a theory of punishment. Such a theory would indeed be the final degree of institutionalization of conventions governing how the members of a community see each other and what they believe about that 'seeing'. Hobbes had argued that we see in figures, often not being aware of the fact. This becomes crucial when it becomes possible that we may not share those figures.

II FIGURING BY DESIRE: FICHTE, HEGEL, SCHOPENHAUER

Early in the *Critique of Practical Reason* Kant makes the following observation:

> *Life* is the faculty of being by which it acts according to the laws of the faculty of desire. The *faculty of desire* [das *Begehrungsvermögen*] is the faculty such a being has of causing, through its ideas [*Vorstellungen*], the reality of the objects of these ideas.[18]

When we have the idea that such objects or actions agree with the subjective conditions of life, then we have "pleasure". Later, in the *Critique of Judgement*, Kant refers back to this passage in the light of a complaint he has received about the definition of the faculty of desire. He tells us that he has been accused of having left unclear the difference between "desire" and "mere wishes [bloße Wünsche]" (I, 16; *Werke*, V, 246), the latter referring to situations where there is no question of the object being called into existence. In reply, Kant maintains that "this proves no more than the presence of desires in man by which he is in contradiction with himself"; man has desires, such as the desire to undo the past, which are *not* realizable.

Although our representations (*Vorstellungen*) are indeed inefficient in this respect, we still wish that they were not. Thus there remains a

> causal reference of representations to their objects — a causality which not even the consciousness of inefficiency for producing the effect can deter from straining towards it. — But why our nature should be furnished with a propensity to consciously vain desires [leeren Begehrungen] is a teleological problem of anthropology. It would seem that were we not to be determined to the exertion of our power before we had assured ourselves of the efficiency of our faculty for producing an object, our power would remain to a large extent unused. For as a rule we only first learn to know our powers by making trial of them. This deceit of vain desires is therefore only the result of a beneficient disposition in our nature.
>
> (*CJ*, I, 16–17)

So all discord is harmony not understood, and Kant invokes once again the image of the fortunate fall. But what is potentially radical here is the admission of the status of desire as able to create figured forms (representations) at the service of intention, without reference to empirical probability. To pay attention to this in any exhaustive way would clearly unsettle the assumption of a normal standard for experience on which Kant's major contribution to the theory of knowledge is based. The dissatisfaction resides in the attempt or aspiration to convert the representation into an object for empirical experience, and we remember here Kant's definition of the beautiful as able to assume universality only because it is placed beyond the contingent; the universality of art, which is itself only an assumption, has no utilitarian contribution to make to empirical experience. Any attempt to translate it must produce frustration, and the same frustration would be the result of trying to enforce a judgement of the beautiful upon one who is not already in agreement.

This leads to a relationship of contradiction between art and desire, and it is this which characterizes the aesthetic theories which developed from the *Critique of Judgement*. Translations tend to mask the fact that there is something of a change in terminology; the place which Kant gives to *das Begehrungsvermögen* is largely taken over, in Schiller and Hegel, by *die Begierde*. This seems to be a stronger term, perhaps with analogous sexual overtones; 'desire' becomes more aggressive and more disturbing. This remains the faculty which art must exist to supplant. Thus Hegel:

From the practical interest of desire, the interest of art is distinguished by the fact that it lets the object persist freely and on its own account, while desire converts it to its own use by destroying it.[19]

Art has "the capacity and the vocation to mitigate the ferocity of desires" (p. 48); it produces "wonder", which only occurs

> when man, torn free from his most immediate first connection with nature and from his most elementary, purely practical, relation to it, that of desire, stands back spiritually from nature and his own singularity and now seeks and sees things in a universal, implicit, and permanent element.
>
> (p. 315)

This itself seems to constitute an attribution of value for art; because it is antithetical to what is negative, it is itself positioned as positive. Schiller, however, had been rather more forceful in denying the very idea of 'value' as having any reference to the beautiful, properly conceived:

> beauty produces no particular result whatsoever, neither for the understanding nor for the will. It accomplishes no particular purpose, neither intellectual nor moral; it discovers no individual truth, helps us to perform no individual duty and is, in short, as unfitted to provide a firm basis for character as to enlighten the understanding.[20]

Conversely, it restores the absolute freedom of vacancy, a freedom so absolute that it is not even 'known' as such, relating to contingent experience only as an antithesis. It cannot contribute to even the most deeply held and generous among our moral and intellectual structures of belief; any relation we might seek to establish would be an infringement upon it.

The emphasis Schiller places on this disconnection between the experience of the beautiful and that of everything else is important, in that it suggests that all these other excluded elements are, actually or potentially, *divisive* of man from man. They thus ask to be assessed as the products of the very desire and inclination which the beautiful excludes. This implies a much larger place for those parts or kinds of experience which are disruptive of potential consensus than had been allowed by most of the rationalist philosophers. To a mind which is committed to a process of moving between different *determinate* relations to the world — as it was, for Schiller — the aesthetic moment must, in order to remain absolutely distinct from these relations and thus continue to provide a 'clear' space between them, be both amoral and 'useless'. The part of experience which is not composed of the beautiful, and that is of course much the largest and most familiar part, is implicitly beset by the pressures of desire.

Schiller is very close here to the formulation of the amoral imagination in Wordsworth, wherein the importance of that faculty is made to consist, not in its particular figurations at any privileged moment, but in the range of its activities held together through time; 'imagination' itself is what happens 'between' these assembled particularities. The philosopher who comes perhaps closest to Wordsworth, however, though he was almost certainly never read by him, is Fichte. Fichte actually begins his most important book by declaring that philosophy itself, in theory and method, can never hope to convince, because it is itself the product of interest and predisposition. The division in the readership, suggested by Coleridge in 'The Nightingale' and all through Wordsworth's poetry as the source of moral urgency, is here declared as a first principle to be born in mind by all those who publish. The choice of an affiliation is not the *result* of dispassionate consideration, but has been made before the moment of reading, and

> is governed by caprice [Willkür], and since even a capricious decision must have some source, it is governed by *inclination* and *interest* [*Neigung* und *Interesse*]. The ultimate basis of the difference between idealists and dogmatists is thus the difference of their interests.[21]

The philosopher seeks to "maintain and assert himself in the rational process" (p. 15), and the two types of philosophy are thus the public expressions of two major classes of people. Dogmatists, or materialists, have not yet become conscious of freedom, and can only

> find themselves in the presentation of things [im Vorstellen der Dinge]; they have only that dispersed self-consciousness which attaches to objects, and has to be gleaned from their multiplicity. Their image is reflected back at them only by things, as by a

mirror; if these were taken from them, their self would be lost as
well . . . they themselves exist only if things do.

(p. 15; *Werke*, I, 433)

There is a large class of protagonists in nineteenth-century fiction
which can be identified by this description; what is most forceful is
the suggestion that those within it cannot understand an alternative
system, idealism, because there is no basis in their *experience* for such
an understanding. Theory, in other words, has become a function of
the life process, what we might call an 'ideology'. The assumption of
a dispassionately motivated society of reasonable readers, one which
can be described by the vocabulary of the 'normal', has
disappeared. In its place we are faced with the separately figured
world views of different societies and interests; men in cities, and
men among the Lakes.

This is the point of Fichte's constant habit of discouraging the
attention of a certain kind of reader. This is not the result of mere
spleen, but is based on a conviction about the difficulty of arguing
against an intentional predisposition. To attack 'belief' is also to
attack life and behaviour, which are the causes of belief; the stakes
are too high, and the processes of mystification too complicated, for
the easy achievement or expectation of a consensus.

Having stressed the importance of these reservations on Fichte's
part, we may pass on to the details of his argument, which is far more
sophisticated than its popular reputation as an uninhibited
'Ichphilosophie' would suggest. Fichte himself is aware of this
attribution; he does not mean, he says, that "at every moment,
throughout our whole life, we are always thinking I, I, I, and never
anything else but I"; the point is rather that to "everything thought
of as occurring in consciousness, the self must necessarily be
appended in thought; in the elucidation of states of mind we may
never abstract from the self" (p. 71). This is absolutely central to the
model within which all Romantic theories of knowledge were
articulated, and it insists that there is a question to be asked about
the status of self-consciousness in all formulations of 'meaning'. The
same predicament informs Wordsworth's idea of the mind-world
relation as a mind-*made* form. Thus, within what Fichte calls the
"absolute totality of the real", the not-self is endowed with reality
(i.e. must be *thought of* as being endowed) by the carrying over of a
degree of activity *from* the self. It is thus 'active' to exactly the degree
that the self *posits* itself as passive (p. 130). This is the famous "law of

interdetermination [Wechselbestimmung]" (p. 130; *Werke*, I, 135),
and it is the centrepiece of Fichte's whole theory of knowledge,
"namely, that *the self posits itself as determining the not-self*" (p. 219).
We must remain clear, however, that no assertions are made about
the mechanical (or other) functions of a 'real' world of objects (using
the word 'real' in its material sense). This "critical idealism" is
strictly a function of thought and self-consciousness; as such, it

> runs dogmatically counter to dogmatic idealism and realism, in
> that it shows how neither does the mere activity of the self provide
> the ground of the reality of the not-self, nor the mere activity of
> the not-self the ground of passivity in the self; but, confronted
> with the question it is called upon to answer, namely, what may
> then be the ground of the interplay assumed between the two, it is
> resigned to its own ignorance, and shows us that investigation of
> this point lies beyond the bounds of theory.
>
> (p. 164)

Similarly, Wordsworth stresses the importance of the mind's
rehabilitations of its own preconstituted figures in relation to new
experiences, rather than allowing a static epistemology based in a
rigid and abstract dualism to become the focus of his inquiry. In
neither case is there a denial of the world outside thought, a 'real'
world or a world for other thoughts. Quite the opposite, and this is
why both Wordsworth and Fichte are obsessed with the *partiality* of
perception. But we can only think about those areas of attention
which are a function of thought, and even here it is clear that it is a
contradiction to posit thought as thinking 'authoritatively' about
itself, except as that authority accrues from the conviction of
performed experience, so that theory is related back to the life
process from which it came. Theory thus becomes a mode of delayed
self-affirmation.

To return to Fichte; the "ultimate ground of all reality for the
self" is thus

> an original interaction between the self and some other thing
> outside it, of which nothing more can be said, save that it must be
> utterly opposed to the self.

We can feel this opposing force, but we cannot 'apprehend' it as
such, because its appearance in consciousness must always be

related to the self and spoken of as a function of it. Moreover, even to thus reflect on the existence of this 'something else' is an act of consciousness, so that

> the independent factor again becomes a product of its own power of thought, and thus something dependent on the self, insofar as it is to exist for the self (in the concept thereof).

This is not a resolution of the traditional problem of the theory of knowledge as it specifies the mind-object relation, and it is not meant to be. On the contrary, it is a statement of the necessity of the problem's eternal recurrence. We go on and on performing this operation, imagining bigger and bigger elephants upholding others on their backs, and at each stage the independent object is posited as "further out". It is never either eliminated or apprehended. It is only ever *displaced*, so that the self is committed to the progressive repetition of a search which it is "able to extend into infinity, but can never escape" (p. 247).

Perhaps more completely than ever before, the whole status of epistemology is framed within a structure of desire — not the Hegelian *Begierde* but the pure, abstract process of seeking. In a similar way, the "soul" which generates *The Prelude* aspires with "growing faculties",

> With faculties still growing, feeling still
> That whatsoever point they gain, they still
> Have something to pursue.
>
> > (II, 339–41)

The growing never turns to the grown, and the ambiguity of the subtitle to the poem, "Growth of a Poet's Mind", asks to be resolved by a recognition that the poem as printed product is prophetic of the *growing* still to happen. Wordsworth too moves "further out" in a process of "shapeless eagerness" (IX, 11) and "regular desire" (II, 50). Fichte describes an interplay between the finite and the infinite, whereby

> the finite activity of the self relates to a *real* object, while its infinite striving is directed upon a merely *imaginary* [*eingebildetes*] object.
>
> > (p. 236; *Werke*, I, 267)

The two belong together, so that 'desire' is the condition of the possibility of all experience. The process of positing the real as "further out" is the mechanism for the production of all knowledge:

> *in relation to a possible object,* the pure self-reverting activity of the self is a *striving* [ein *Streben*]; and, as shown earlier, *an infinite striving* at that. This boundless striving, carried to infinity, is the *condition of the possibility of any object whatsoever:* no striving, no object.
>
> (p. 231; *Werke*, I, 261–2)

The real both is, and is not, the imaginary, or the figured; and because the real is always redigested by the figured, there is, at least in this world, no end to the experience of striving.

This striving, as it is the condition of all possible objects, is also the source of what is conventionally called 'personal identity'. Acting and willing are not dependent on the "system of our presentations [Vorstellungen]"; on the contrary, "our system of presentations depends on our drive and our will . . . this system introduces throughout the whole man that *unity* and *connection* which so many systems fail to provide" (p. 259; *Werke*, I, 295). As in Wordsworth, the implication is that the connecting principle in personal identity, the concept of coherent experience of self through time, is based in the presence of dissatisfaction and incompletion. Self-consciousness emerges from the fusion of active and passive, "longing [Sehnen]" and "limitation [Begrenzung]" (p. 266; *Werke*, I, 266), and these are in fact one and the same drive, motivated by an inner impulse and continuing as long as there is life. This is nothing less than a structure of desire, though Fichte does not use the word. The self experiences

> a drive towards something totally unknown, which reveals itself only through a *need* [*Bedürfniss*], a discomfort [*Misbehagen*], a void [*Leere*], which seeks satisfaction, but does not say from whence. — The self feels a longing in itself; it feels itself in want [bedürftig].
>
> (p.265; *Werke*, I, 302–3)

Longing and unfulfilment are themselves the guarantee of ongoing experience through time, and are essential to the practical side of the science of knowledge.

Fichte further incorporates the problem faced by the English philosophers about the relation of part to whole, object 'parts' with the substantial 'thing' which we might need to think of as holding them together. All action depends upon a prefiguration or conceptual anticipation of what is to "happen', and this is a function of volition. The self cannot discover itself in action "without projecting a picture [Bild]" of what it wishes "to bring about" (pp. 38–9; *Werke*, I, 464). Matter, as such, "in no way belongs to the senses, but can only be framed or thought [entworfen oder gedacht] through productive imagination [productive Einbildungskraft]" (p. 275; *Werke*, I, 315). But what is in fact an "accident" of the self is necessarily transformed into "the accident of a thing required to be external":

> That this matter [Stoff] itself may indeed be only something entirely subjective that occurs in you [in euch vorhandenes, lediglich subjectives] is a thing you should long ago have come at least to suspect; if only because, without any new feeling being added from such matter, you can straightway carry over [übertragen] to it something that by your own admission is entirely subjective (such as sweet, red etc.); and further because, without a subjective property to be transferred to it, such a matter simply does not exist for you, and is this nothing more for you than the bearer [Träger] you need for the subjective property that is to be carried over from yourself.
>
> (p. 275; *Werke*, I, 314)

Fichte here makes the existence of what Locke would have called 'secondary qualities' question the nature of the 'primary' ones; but his second point is the stronger one. Whatever level of the 'real' we might incline to think about as unavailable to us, the "*mode* and *manner*" of "presentation" are determined by the self (p. 220; *Werke*, I, 248). The word Fichte uses for this "presentation", *Vorstellung*, has latent within it the active sense of 'putting forth' of 'placing before', and the "*presentation drive* [Vorstellungstrieb]" (p. 259; *Werke*, I, 294) through which the self first becomes an intelligence operates in a way which is implicitly figurative. The conceptual image or representation on which practical experience is based is not the 'thing in itself' but a phenomenal variant which we (usefully, of course) mistake for the 'real'.

Fichte's model contains all the elements of an intentional theory of perception, and indeed moves much closer towards such a theory by emphasizing the vital place of the "presentational drive" and the cycle of incompletion which keeps it operating. But, like Kant, Fichte preserves the normative status of the faculty for presentation. In this way he can insist that the transcendental philosophy calls into question the "reality of things" as the understanding relies on them, and can speculate whether the whole assumption might not be a "deception" (p. 208); but, for the purposes of communication and consensus, this does not matter so long as we are all deceived in the same way. No reference to the 'real' is required provided that we all distort or shape it in the same way. In Fichte's words,

> how, again, do you contrive to assume an interior to the body, within the surfaces, though you do not feel it? This obviously comes about through the productive imagination. — Yet you take this matter to be something objective, and rightly so, since you all agree on its presence, and are bound to do so, since the production thereof is based on a universal law of all reason.
>
> (p. 276)

The case is saved. The "universal law of all reason" is what prevents the theory supporting the possibility of a world of private vision and incoherent languages. Fichte places his faith in the reason, not in language, and for that reason is much less anxious about the threats to consensus than is Hobbes. Moreover, he is a logician rather than a psychologist, trying to explain what must be thought about the consensus which he assumes, as a first principle, to exist. He is not therefore concerned with the mechanism or incidence of deviations from it. In this respect, and through setting himself a different task, he does not go as far as Wordsworth does in exploring the figurative activity as it divides man from man. He does not break down the 'universal' into an assembly of partial and incommensurable world views, nor redefine 'law' as ideology.

Hegel comes closer to such a formulation, though such is not apparently the aim of his method. The same issues about the status of representation (*Vorstellung*) in Fichte are dealt with again by Hegel, this time with the explicit reintroduction of the faculty of desire (*Begierde*, not Kant's *Begehrungsvermögen*). Even more significantly, Hegel's model of human development is at once diachronic and synchronic, both teleologically directed and eternally recurring. Thus the limited function which desire fulfils in the progressive evolution of mind or spirit viewed teleologically, within the career through time of an ideal subject, is posited at the same time as ever-present for those consciousnesses which are either *at* that particular moment of their development, or are (for other reasons) obliged to remain or return there. In this way we can take Hegel's analysis of desire and intention to position them as perpetually recurring threats to the evolution of absolute spirit, and it therefore takes on considerable polemical urgency.

Hegel was concerned to redirect contemporary philosophy away from the strictly mentalist end of the spectrum covered by the theory of knowledge:

> The Kantian philosophy may be most accurately described as having viewed the mind as consciousness, and as containing the propositions only of a *phenomenology* (not of a *philosophy*) of mind.[22]

'Philosophy' is thus a whole of which phenomenology is but a part, and in constructing that whole Hegel employs a kind of evolutionary psychology wherein the mind passes through a whole range of positions in a process of effort or labour. Desire and intention are thus features of an enacted empirical experience, rather than abstract threats belonging to a different part of the system, or faculty of the mind. Hegel's assumptions remain universalist in that they purport to apply to the psychology of every human subject (and, at times, more awkwardly, to the collective history of the human race), but he includes the recognition of disparity in his specification of the different stages along the way. Each (ideal) subject, as it achieves the goal of "absolute spirit", has thus briefly experienced every point within that range. This has crucial implications for any theory of deviation — for example, a theory of punishment — in that it allows the person judging such deviation no authoritative position or perspective. Every human being, actually or potentially, contains every other; all minds have within them the same range of possible experiences.

Hegel's positioning of desire (*die Begierde*) in his two major discussions of the subject, which occur in the *Phenomenology of Spirit* of 1807 and in the *Philosophy of Mind* which appeared as the third part of the *Encyclopaedia* of 1830, makes it a stage on the way to a genuinely social mode of living in the world. In each case it is a symptom of a relation to objects which is preparatory to the evolution of the master-slave relationship, which is itself the beginning of intersubjectivity. In the situation where desire is the totality of self-consciousness, where self can only apprehend itself through desire for objects, then the relation to the world is at once destructive and unfulfilling:

> Thus appetite [Begierde] in its satisfaction is always destructive, and in its content selfish: and as the satisfaction has only happened in the individual (and that is transient) the appetite is again generated in the very act of satisfaction.
>
> (*Phil. of Mind*, p. 169; *Werke*, X, 279)

It is the recognition of other subjects, other human beings, which both redeems and complicates this recurring cycle of satisfaction and desire. This recognition converts the subject from animal existence to self-consciousness. Here it becomes clear that Hegel is not writing simply from the perspective of the logical first person, as Fichte is, but presents the experience of society as an essential moment in the development of *Geist*.[23] At the same time, the argument constitutes an ethical imperative not to remain in the private world of immediate consciousness, one limited to reiterated apprehensions of disconnected objects, each arising as others are digested or annulled.

There is throughout Hegel's writings a strong animus against uncontrolled intention, which is recognized as the habit most resistant to the evolution of social conventions of behaviour and meaning. This is clear in the estimation of "feeling [*Gefühl*]":

> But the form of selfish singleness to which feeling reduces the mind is the lowest and worst vehicle it can have — one in which it is not found as a free and universal principle, but rather as subjective and private, in content and value entirely contingent. . . . If a man on any topic appeals not to the nature and notion of the thing, or at least to reasons — to the generalities of common sense [*Verstandesallgemeinheit*] — but to his feeling, the only thing to do is to let him alone, because by his behaviour he refuses to have any lot or part in common rationality, and shuts himself up in his own isolated subjectivity — his private and particular self.
>
> (*Phil. of Mind*, p. 194; *Werke*, X, 316)

What is striking here is the confession that such a preoccupation with feeling can and does arise in particular people, and that it is not subject to resolution by argument. Whatever 'theory' which is to be built upon the successful supersession of feeling will then only apply to *some* human subjects; whatever academically formulated epistemology Hegel might propose thus takes account of the prospect that there is no universal compulsion on all human subjects to engage with it. The theory of knowledge is implicitly contained within a social psychology, just as it is in Wordsworth. Human beings can become fixated, and still remain human.

The status of representations (*Vorstellungen*) remains, in Hegel as in Fichte, within the universal, but only in the ideal subject. Representations, although they are constituted by a mental or categorical faculty, are not to be confused with the operations of immediate consciousness in its lowest terms. They accrue from "recollected or inwardized intuition" as the "images" employed by the memory as it relates new intuitions to past experience (p. 201). The loss of "clarity and freshness" which the intuition undergoes in being processed by the "ideating intelligence [vorstellende Intelligenz]" (p. 203; *Werke*, X, 331) is, one supposes, implicitly a shared process, since the very categories of such ideation are the result of the development of a means of communication. Hegel is making a similar point about the "clarity and freshness" of the intuition as A. B. Johnson, for example, made about the capacity of language to describe specificity; its very existence as an efficient tool presumes that it cannot do so. Hegel incorporates the qualifications to his own system, but it remains at the first level a system directed at the production of an organic society. That it seeks to persuade, rather than pretending to 'demand' within the pseudo-authoritative conventions of abstract inquiry, may be taken as a measure of the difficulty of preserving a rôle for universal reason in the first part of the nineteenth century; the questioning of that reason is also a questioning of the consensus which it had been assumed to produce.

Hegel can then be said to both maintain and undermine the reliance on the universal evident in Kant and Fichte; it is with Schopenhauer that the undermining becomes most obviously more prominent than the maintaining. The first volume of *The World as Will and Representation* was published as early as 1819. The second, which was the more prominent source of that philosophy of pessimism which made such an impression on Thomas Hardy, among others, did not appear until the second edition of 1844. This second volume, however, is largely a development and exploration of what had been quite clearly formulated by 1819, although with little public response.

Schopenhauer's declaration of the possessive principle, "The world is my representation [Vorstellung]" (I, 3; *Werke*, I, 3), need not of itself have been shocking to those brought up on an idealist philosophy. Much more radical is the corollary of this, "The world is my will" (I, 4), where the will is defined as that which determines representation, from the subjective side, while remaining itself unapprehendable by any discourse or structure of self-consciousness. Schopenhauer thus goes to the heart of the transcendental philosophy's assumption of a normal standard of experience which it then sets itself to explain. The validity of Kant's laws, he says, begins "only after existence, the world of experience generally, is already settled and established" (I, 420). Arguing for the retention of causality alone out of Kant's twelve categories (I, 448), Schopenhauer at the same time refuses to allow the application of a retrospective causal principle to any hypothesis of an unconditioned beginning for the human reason. Brahmanism and Buddhism, for example, "neither know nor admit such assumptions, but carry on to infinity the series of phenomena that condition one another" (I, 484). In fact, causality is retained by being taken out of the control of any rational or moral faculty, and is attributed only to the "will", which is not here a faculty exercising free and conscious choice, but a primal assembly of unconscious drives. Considered in itself, the will is

devoid of knowledge, and is only a blind, irresistable urge, as we see it appear in organic and vegetable nature, and in their laws, and also in the vegetative part of our own life.

(I, 275)

The phenomenal world is the mirror of this will, and the means by which we 'know' it; but in thus seeing its representations we do not see *how* it forms them, or what it means by them. Only in action do we recognize what the will intends. The body itself is will as it is perceived by the understanding, and reason becomes radically inefficient in predicting or controlling its operations, now 'known' only after the event:

Only the carrying out stamps the resolve; till then, it is always a mere intention [Vorsatz] that can be altered; it exists only in reason, in the abstract. Only in reflection are willing and acting different; in reality they are one.

(I, 100–1; *Werke*, I, 120)

To limit the utility of prediction is clearly to threaten the rôle of conscience and moral conviction in governing experience, and to maximize the place of the uncontrollable. If experience as it happens is more authentic than experience as it is thought about, then all methods for setting the normal apart from the deviant are questioned, indeed rendered possible only as the contingent results of events outside our control and unforeseen. As the simple, integrated subject can no longer speak for others, so it has no control over itself, for it is no longer either simple or integrated:

> Even in us the same will in many ways acts blindly; as in all those functions of our body which are not guided by knowledge [Erkenntniβ], in all its vital and vegetative processes, digestion, circulation, secretion, growth, and reproduction. Not only the actions of the body, but the whole body itself, as was shown above, is phenomenon of the will, objectified will, concrete will. All that occurs in it must therefore occur through will, though here this will is not guided by knowledge, not determined according to motives [Motiven], but acts blindly according to causes, called in this case *stimuli* [Reize].
>
> (I, 115; *Werke*, I, 136-7)

What we know of ourselves, and can account for, is a poor second to what our will is effecting without our knowledge; the "intellect, like the claws and teeth, is nothing but a tool for the service of the will" (II, 398). The presence of desire and intention, which Hegel had tried to restrain within the evolutionary model of the mind, is now the dominant one, and deflects or determines all human activity:

> Every passion, in fact every inclination or disinclination, tinges the objects of knowledge with its colour. Most common of occurrence is the falsification of knowledge brought about by desire and hope, since they show us the scarcely possible in dazzling colours as probable and well-nigh certain, and render us almost incapable of comprehending what is opposed to it. Fear acts in a similar way; every preconceived opinion, every partiality, and, as I have said, every interest, every emotion, and every predilection of the will act in an analogous manner.
>
> (II, 141)

That element of fantasy admitted by Kant, whereby desire is able to create representations which it wishes to convert into empirical reality even in the face of impossibility, is here readmitted as of major significance. Here, it would seem that the mind is able to perform that conversion with no reference to any external standard of what is possible or 'true'. It quite literally makes its own world, and makes the world it wants; and the mind is itself 'made' by the will to do just that.

The connections between this passage and a large number of Wordsworth's poems will by now be apparent. Many of Wordsworth's protagonists display the misattributions consequent upon interest, predisposition or fear; it is not just Harry Gill who demonstrates the power of the imagination "to produce such changes even in our physical nature as might almost appear miraculous" (*PrW*, I, 150). Even more frequent, indeed, is the power of the imagination to produce changes in other natures, a gesture which is, as we have seen, often corrected by reference, if not to things 'in themselves', then at least to the achieved standards of other perceivers and their shared figures and convictions, which may indeed be the only 'reality' we can be sure of within the nominalistic model of experience. Wordsworth's poems demonstrate not only such moments of correction, but also their instability and their tendency to slip into further transgressions. They also suggest the strains directed at the small societies of sharers for whom such 'reality' can be supposed to function. Grasmere is besieged from within and from without; Wordsworth is deeply unsure of his own place in the vale, as the vale itself is pressured from outside by tourism and by the capitalization of the land.

Schopenhauer can be said to provide the philosophical complement to that part of Wordsworth's discourse which investigates what divides man from man. It is implicit in what he says of the will that any institution within human society can only arise and be maintained as the contingent common factor of certain unconscious interests. Describing the "defective nature of the intellect", he comments that

> Nature has produced it for the service of an individual will; therefore it is destined to know things only in so far as they serve as the motives of such a will, not to fathom them or to comprehend their true inner essence.
>
> (II, 142)

We have consensus, then, and shared experience, only in so far as our wills happen to have common directions, and we can do very little to bring it about otherwise. Wordsworth sets himself a moral as well as a descriptive purpose; having analysed what it is that divides, he argues also for the prospect of the less authoritative but nevertheless reconstituted unities of interest and feeling which he believes may be maintained within the chosen vales. Schopenhauer is less optimistic, seeing a situation where

> Every grade of the will's objectification fights for the matter, the space, and the time of another. Persistent matter must constantly change the form, since, under the guidance of causality, mechanical, physical, chemical, and organic phenomena, eagerly striving to appear, snatch the matter from one another, for each wishes to reveal its own Idea.
>
> (I, 146–7)

This describes not just the state of affairs pertaining between different life forms, or different people, but is also the inner nature of each identity, each 'person'. For, although the "will" is always spoken about in the singular, it can only be understood as a collective noun, a plurality of drives and desires competing for space and precedence. The authority and authenticity of self-consciousness is completely destroyed, in a way remarkably prophetic of Freud. We do not see ourselves as we 'are'; it is "the will that is spoken of whenever 'I' occurs in a judgement" (II, 140). Schopenhauer now actually appeals to the phenomenon of compulsive behaviour (allowed for, but discouraged, by Hegel) as evidence for this:

> To believe that knowledge really and radically determines the *will* is like believing that the lantern a man carries at night is the *primum mobile* of his steps. He who, taught by experience or by the exhortation of others, recognizes and deplores a fundamental defect in his character, firmly and honestly forms the resolution to improve himself and to get rid of the defect; but in spite of this, the defect obtains full play on the very next occasion.
>
> (II, 223)

It is not that we do not possess self-consciousness, or moral faculty; rather, what we have is useless in the face of the determining operations of the will, which can neither be described nor controlled. Thus Schopenhauer recognizes the incidence of what

Freud was to call 'repression', or something very close to it (II, 209–10), as well as the autonomous and amoral activity of the will in dream life (II, 214). That which has most influence on human behaviour and human ways of seeing is now located as firmly outside our control.

The narrative element in life, whereby we may think of our actions, both in the short term and the long term, as tending toward some end (and the analogies with Wordsworth's autobiographical poem are obvious), is also undermined by Schopenhauer's emphasis on the will. Although every separate act has a purpose or end (largely unknown to us, of course, except as it happens), "willing as a whole has no end in view" (I, 165). Life is movement, fuelled by desire, and that fact has no deeper meaning:

> Eternal becoming, endless flux [ewiges Werden, endloser Fluß], belong to the revelation of the essential nature of the will. Finally, the same thing is also seen in human endeavours and desires [Bestrebungen und Wünschen] that buoy us up with the vain hope that their fulfilment is always the final goal of willing. But as soon as they are attained, they no longer look the same . . . It is fortunate enough when something to desire and to strive for still remains, so that the game may be kept up of the constant transition from desire [Wunsch] to satisfaction [Befriedigung], and from that to a fresh desire, the rapid course of which is called happiness, the slow course sorrow, and so that this game may not come to a standstill, showing itself as a fearful, life-destroying boredom, a lifeless longing without a definite object, a deadening languor.
>
> (I, 164; *Werke*, I, 196)

The motive force behind this eternal recurrence is simply the attempt to avoid pain and to satisfy want. This attempt persists even though it can never be gratified. With Nietzsche that fact alone will come to be a redeeming one, as it had been, implicitly, with Wordsworth.

Representations, or figured forms, have then with Schopenhauer moved further from the prospect of being contained within a consensus of different human subjects than ever before. The balance of sharing and not sharing which Coleridge preserved in his 'conversation' with Charles Lamb has been inclined very much toward the unshared. It must thus seem surprising to declare that there is, for Schopenhauer, yet one sphere of activity which can be preserved from the domination of the will. That activity is art, at least when informed by genius, and his views on the operation of genius take us right back to Kant and the argument of the *Critique of Judgement*. With Nietzsche and Freud, art too will be claimed by the operations of desire and intention, and become a language of wilful misrepresentation. Schopenhauer, prophetic as he is of those later writers, has yet one foot in idealist aesthetics. Art is our only chance to raise ourselves "out of the endless stream of willing", the only medium within which attention

> considers things without interest, without subjectivity, purely objectively; it is entirely given up to them insofar as they are merely representations [Vorstellungen] and not motives [Motive].
>
> (I, 196; *Werke*, I, 231)

It is as if there is a fresh recourse to 'reality', to a world beyond the figurings of desire:

> Accordingly, genius is the capacity to remain in a state of pure perception, to lose oneself in perception, to remove from the service of the will the knowledge which originally existed only for this service. In other words, genius is the ability to leave entirely out of sight our own interest, our willing, and our aims, and consequently to discard entirely our own personality for a time, in order to remain *pure knowing subject*, the clear eye of the world.
>
> (I, 185–6)

To make this work, Schopenhauer now proposes what is in effect a 'sliding scale' for estimating the presence of genius according to the absence of intentional distortion in our representations:

> Now just as . . . in the case of decided aversion or affection, the falsification of the representation by the will is unmistakable, so it is present in a lesser degree in the case of every object that has only some remote relation to our will, in other words, to our inclination [Neigung] or disinclination. Only when the will with its interests has forsaken consciousness, and the intellect freely follows its own laws, and as pure subjects mirrors the objective world, yet from its own impulse is in the highest state of tension

and activity, goaded by no willing, only then do the colour and form of things stand out in their true and full significance. Only from such an apprehension, therefore, can genuine works of art result, whose permanent value and constantly renewed approval spring from the very fact that they alone exhibit what is purely objective.

(II, 373; *Werke*, II, 425)

It is almost as if the will, otherwise the determining force behind the whole of our existence, is in the sphere of art relegated to an unfortunate tendency which must be put aside. At the same time, the authority of self-consciousness appears to be re-established in the notion that we can *know* when we are seeing things 'as they are', rather than as they are represented and falsified by the will:

every work of art really endeavours to show us life and things as they are in reality; but these cannot be grasped directly by everyone through the mist of objective and subjective contingencies. Art takes away this mist.

(II, 407)

Here it would seem to be art which might offer the basis for a consensus which can obviously never be established through the will. Schopenhauer does not pursue this possibility, and it is indeed an extraordinary one. For Kant, it will be remembered, had insisted that the assumption of the universality of the judgement of the beautiful depended on its being completely disconnected from any aspiration toward empirical presentation; the 'reality' of art, then, cannot be an empirical one, and Kant certainly never seeks to relate it to any world of supersensible forms. Kant had no need of such a recourse, moreover, because he preserved the model of a normative experience on which consensus is based. With Schopenhauer, on the other hand, it is the sphere of ordinary experience which is radically dislocated by the machinery of the will, so that art comes to be appealed to as the repository of the 'real'. How far that 'reality' may be shared is, as far as I can see, a question which Schopenhauer cannot afford to investigate too deeply; to resolve it would have required a wholesale redirection of the historically accumulating hegemony of desire and intention as the defining functions of the human identity.

This is not to suggest, of course, that as soon as Schopenhauer wrote his book it became suddenly impossible for human beings to communicate with each other (except via 'genius'!), nor that he wrote it simply as a result of observing such a phenomenon. But yet it must seem that the specific discourse within which he writes responds to some kind of historical crisis, one which Wordsworth is also reacting to, in the social experience, the experience of what can be shared, and under what conditions. Hence poetry and art, and the 'figures' in which they express themselves, instead of being theorized as tolerated deviations from an implicitly normal experience, come to be constituted as the paradigms for all perception and communication. And, once that process has been completed, it seems that we find Schopenhauer wearing another hat and replacing the 'real' by art itself. At the same time, this must seem an unworkable substitution, in that the commonly accepted status of art as notoriously open to dispute is not properly reformulated. There is no explanation in Schopenhauer of just how we see the 'real' in art, and no indication of just who will adjudicate the disagreements. Dickens' novels will present an 'ordinary' world in which things have gone radically wrong, one dominated and determined by the figures of interest or will emanating from the master-concerns of society and its controllers. But, when he uses the privileges of art to bring about an alternative, as he does in creating small and enlightened communities based on a 'pure' seeing, an insight into what is wrong and a strong sense of what is true and right, he necessarily opens up the whole question of how far his readers can 'agree' about the solutions. Victorian readers wanted happy endings, as we know from the history of *Great Expectations*. Among the possible motives for this desire, we might suggest a belief in fiction as an alternative to life. Whatever 'art' is in this context of an unpleasant ordinary world, it is certainly not free from interest. Readers do not fight over conclusions which speak forth the implicitly shared world of the ideal, will-less knowing, "the clear eye of the world".

III METAPHOR AND SYMBOL IN AESTHETICS

I hope it will not seem that in the above discussion I have moved too far from the centre of the argument into a specialist subject, but it does appear to me that the increasing importance of desire in Romantic theory from Kant to Schopenhauer, and the sudden endowing of genius with saving potential by Schopenhauer, illuminates very directly the issues faced by the more strictly 'literary' writers in their various ways of dealing with the status of the figurative. Thus, the various pressures articulated within the formal theories of knowledge, as they tend to interpret all organized or meaningful perception as a product of the figurative faculty, are closely related to those which I have argued to be important to Wordsworth. In particular, the movement away from any faith in the universal, which reaches a culmination in Schopenhauer (when he is *not* talking about genius), bears very directly upon Wordsworth's sense of the social constitution of mind and 'reality'.

To turn to the the major discussions of the figurative in Romantic aesthetics is to be aware of a further set of strictures on the propensity of figured form either to disrupt consensus or to re-establish it on the most uncreative foundations. Despite differences of priority and vocabulary, the same ethical concerns as we have found in Wordsworth about reorganizing the given world are here rehearsed again. We must retain the generic term 'figurative', because more specific terms tend not to be used in the same ways by different writers. Coleridge, for example, makes a crucial distinction in kind between symbol and metaphor, whereas for Hegel the latter is merely a subspecies of the former.

Hegel's *Aesthetics* describes the 'symbolic' mode as typical of the early stages of the development of art, and of oriental art in particular, though of course it is likely to recur in "subsidiary productions and individual traits" (p. 303) within any period or genre. It is characterized by a relation of disequilibrium between idea and image; the idea is not at one with the image or vehicle which expresses it, and which it continues to feel as "external to itself". In this way it "corrupts and falsifies the shapes that it finds confronting it" (p. 300). In particular, metaphor, allegory and simile are typical of that stage of the symbolic when "the universal meaning comes explictly into dominion [Herrschaft] over the explanatory shape which can still only appear as a mere tribute [Attribut] [—a mistranslation, or misprint, though not an un-motivated one!] or capriciously chosen picture [Bild]" (p. 322; *Werke*, XII, 432). Since such figures belong to the "subjective art of the poet as maker" (p. 396) they should be offered only as the accessories to an artistic form, and never as its inner nature. This has its place in Hegel's general concern to limit the scope of desire and its tendency toward intentional reconstruction of the world, for the

sense and aim [Geist] of metaphorical diction in general
.... must be found in the need and power of spirit and heart
which are not content with the simple, customary, and
plain, but place themselves above it in order to move on to
something else.

Metaphor is thus the vehicle of power, or an aspiration toward
power, in its redistribution of the conventional relations between
things. Heart and passion [*Gemüth und Leidenschaft*]

strive to express their own stormy passion and their grip on all
sorts of ideas [Vorstellungen] by correspondingly transferring
them out into all sorts of cognate phenomena and by moving in
images [Bildern] of the most various kind.

(p. 406; *Werke*, XII, 537–8)

At the same time as these limitations apply, such gestures are in fact
necessary to the spirit as it comes to consciousness of itself. For the
figurative operates through "the labour of the spirit [die Arbeit des
Geistes]" (p. 411; *Werke*, XII, 544) and is therefore, like the master-
slave relation in general, an essential moment in its ongoing
evolution. Thus the recognition of the necessity of the figurative
activity coexists with an urgent sense of its dangers and drawbacks,
and this is why Hegel finds himself stressing the precedence of one
side of the mind-matter relation; metaphor must show the presence
of spirit in matter as more important than that of matter in spirit.
Metaphoric invention must then consist

first, in transferring, in an illustrative way, the phenomena,
activities, and situations of a higher sphere to the content of lower
areas and in representing meanings of this more subordinate kind
in the shape and picture of the loftier ones. The organic, e.g., is
inherently of higher worth than the inorganic, and to present
death in the form of life enhances the expression.

(p. 405)

This would cover, for example, Coleridge's criterion for the
identification of poetic genius, as (among other instances) "when a
human and intellectual life" is transferred to images "from the
poet's own spirit". In this way Shakespeare "gives a dignity and a
passion to the objects which he presents" (*Biographia*, II, 16, 17).

This vitalization of objects, which latterday critics, with other priorities in mind, have come to call the 'pathetic fallacy', was held to be of the first importance by Hegel and Coleridge, as they were anxious to preclude the human mind becoming passive before the external world. But there are two qualifications to be lodged. The first, of which Hegel is clearly aware, is the danger of excess, whereby the metaphoric becomes the vehicle for the tyrant eye to consolidate its own special view of the world. The second is perhaps obvious from Hegel's priority as expressed above; how can we be sure to signal only the presence of mind in matter, and not that of matter over mind? It is as if, in using the metaphor 'man is rock', one were to specify that the field of connotation should include only those associations which do not materialize the human. Man may have the firmness of rock, for the rock is then upgraded by being used to point up an admirable human disposition; but not apparently its roughness, deadness or immobility. Hegel seems not to confess here to the possibility that the use of metaphor is in fact double-edged, and that there is a high degree of ambiguity about whether it serves to vivify the inanimate (as he would prefer) or deanimate the human. Dickens' novels display a great deal of such deanimation as the appropriate imagery of a world gone wrong, and Wordsworth's inquiry into the figurative also stresses the ubiquity of this second and more ignoble option. The reason for this, in both cases, is that what is being investigated is the predisposition, anterior to the *use* of metaphor and determining it, to see the world in that particular way. We can see this analysis at work in the tortured retrospect of 'A slumber did my spirit seal', where the human seems to have been viewed as the material — "She seemed a thing that could not feel" (*PW*, II, 216) — in order to preclude, perhaps, the speaker's having to deal with the incoherent and difficult elements of properly envisaged *human* relations. At the end of the poem, where the 'she' is compared to, indeed made a companion of "rocks, and stones, and trees", how does the conjunction work? What is being humanized and what deanimated? Has she passed into the living world of natural forms or the sleep of death, or into a realm wherein we cannot choose between them? Similarly, if in a manner much less sharpened by the inscription of a possible guilt, the identification of the old man, the stone and the sea beast, in that famous stanza from 'Resolution and Independence' already discussed, announces quite clearly that the old man is "divested" of a proportion of the "indications of life and motion" (*PrW*, III, 33) in order to make the metaphor efficient. In both these cases, human beings are figured into things, and it seems clear that Wordsworth means to refer us to the state of mind of the speaker of each poem, and his motives for seeing in that particular way. With these examples from Wordsworth in mind, we can suspect that behind Hegel's aesthetics there lies a polemical imperative about *how* it is most generous to see the world; the figurative look is not an innocent one, and uncharitable consequences can ensue from seeing people as stones, or as things that cannot feel. In criticizing the "romantic imagination" (by which he meant principally that evident in the poetry of the East) for its overenthusiasm in expressing itself metaphorically, Hegel suggests that he is well aware of the propensity of metaphor toward narcissism:

> this poetry has nothing to do with merely presenting something definitely and visibly, for on the contrary the metaphorical use of these far-removed phenomena becomes in it an end on its own account: feeling is made the centre, it illuminates its rich environment, draws it to itself, uses it ingeniously and wittily for its own adornment, animates it, and is delighted by this roving hither and thither, this involvement and expatiation in its self-portrayal.
>
> (*Aesthetics*, pp. 1004–5)

Such metaphor is a measure of the identity of its users, and in so far as it is a public statement, it is an appeal to others to be like them. The same tendency is cited by Hegel as an explanation for the universality of all art:

> man brings himself before himself by *practical* activity, since he has the impulse, in whatever is directly given to him, in what is present to him externally, to produce himself and therein equally to recognize himself. This aim he achieves by altering external things whereon he impresses the seal of his inner being and in which he now finds again his own characteristics. Man does this in order, as a free subject, to strip the external world of its inflexible foreignness and to enjoy in the shape of things only an external realization of himself.
>
> (p. 31)

Here, art is on the edge of becoming appropriation, or at least narcissism. We can see why any discourse concerned with the

evolution of the spirit, as Hegel's certainly is, should prefer us to
animate what is otherwise dead, rather than to deaden what is alive.
And once again, the option which Hegel means here to exclude
appears as an undeniable presence in the mainstream of nineteenth-
century literature.

To turn to Coleridge's discussion of metaphor and symbol is to
encounter a different use of the terms, and a different emphasis. In
his comments on metaphor, Coleridge shows himself less concerned
with what the generation of the figure involves for the subject
employing it, than with its effect once created, both on its originator
and his community or audience. Thus he does not emphasize the
metaphoric gesture as an intentional projection of the self into the
world, but is more worried by the tendency of the already created
metaphor to insinuate itself as the real. The result of this is to tempt
the mind away from a continuing consciousness of its own creative
faculty as the true locus of the process of perception, and to incline it
to worship as 'objective' the products of its own (or another)
activity.[24] It is the persuasive aspect of metaphor, the more
persuasive as the more striking and novel, which concerns Coleridge
here, in view of the fact that the unalerted mind tends to regard
conviction as a product of mere sense reception, not of a vivifying
mental activity. He recognizes, implicitly, the same duality of mind
and world as Hegel had recognized in the metaphor, but unlike
Hegel he is ultimately concerned to establish a mode of representation which does away with this division — to by-pass, in other
words, or to construct an alternative to the consequences of the fall.
For the two aspects of the metaphoric operation separately stressed
by Hegel and Coleridge actually belong together as the two halves
of a recurring dialectic. The mind as lord and master, and the mind
as slave to the world of things or images, are in fact two identical
positions in that the experience of the one inevitably invokes the
other. Wordsworth accepted this, I think, as a fact about
experience, and came up with a method of making this ethically
acceptable through his admission of the modifying effects of time
and memory and their contribution to a continuously creating play
of representations held within the life of the subject and, ideally,
that of his community. Coleridge, however, seems to have aspired,
especially in his later writings, to the theorization of a species of
figure which does not have to do with 'standing for' or 'seeing as',
but partakes rather of an operative truth. This figure he called the
'symbol', invoking a use of the term now quite distinct from Hegel's;

and because it seeks to do away with all the problems of a dualistic epistemology it must be cast as a truth not to 'things' but to the essential identity of mind *in* things. For Coleridge, the 'symbolic' is distinguished from all other figurative modes. Symbols are "consubstantial with the truths, of which they are the *conductors*", and the individual symbol is marked by

> a translucence of the Special in the Individual or of the General in the Especial or of the Universal in the General. Above all by the translucence of the Eternal through and in the Temporal It always partakes of the Reality which it renders intelligible; and while it enunciates the whole, abides itself as a living part in that Unity, of which it is the representative.

Allegory, which includes similitude and metaphor, involves a quite different kind of representation, providing only "empty echoes which the fancy arbitrarily associates with apparitions of matter".[25] The derogatory use of the word "arbitrarily" holds the clue here, for what Coleridge is proposing is a way of seeing which is not at all informed by what we might now call the 'semeiotic'. In the symbol, the relation of signifier to signified is not arbitrary but essential, in the same way that the Christian marriage contract is "an outward Sign co-essential with that which it signifies, or a living Part of that, the whole of which it represents".[26] This effectively abolishes any tension between the act of mind and the material acted upon, and it avoids at the same time any problem of selectivity, any misappropriation of part for whole; here, the whole is implicit and active within the part, which is thus "living". There can be no anxiety attached to representation as long as the mode of seeing and communicating is a preordained harmony of that which is within and that which is without the mind.

Coleridge's theory of the symbol never becomes, it seems, a fully comprehensive answer to the problems of figured perception, and perhaps it was never meant to be. How, for example, can the example of the Christian marriage ceremony be made to apply to language, and how can we adjudicate the status of a representation which is not our own, and decide whether or not it deserves the name of a 'symbol'? Within the symbolic, the mind cannot dominate its world, nor remain rooted in passivity and idolatry; the relation of perceiver to perceived is organic and consubstantial, in the same way that the image or representation itself belongs essentially and substantially *within* what it represents. This is important, for example, in Coleridge's philosophical Trinitarianism, as it describes the relation of man to God through Christ. He became as we are, that we might become as He is; being and becoming are essentially conflated in such a formulation, in that 'to be' is a function and consequence of 'to become'. Christ is the middle term, symbolically connected both to God and to mortal men. But how can the conviction which a particular human subject might have about what is and is not symbolic be shared with others? How can something which must be performed in order to be understood — the act of will which creates (and hence co-creates) the symbol as a mental idea, which for Coleridge reconciles man's free activity with the divine — be extended to or described for other people? In fact, Coleridge's theory of conviction is quite openly and consciously placed within a frame of performance rather than one of mere inference. Those who agree will discover their agreement in the act of agreeing. This cannot apply to all, except as a *prospectus* for experience, which some will follow through as others ignore it. This is clear in the discussion of the interpretation of the Scriptures:

> as much of reality, as much of objective truth, as the Scriptures communicate to the subjective experiences of the Believer, so much of present life, of living and effective import, do these experiences give to the letter of these Scriptures.[27]

Lived experience (which may be habit, culture, prejudice, interest) not only modifies the message of the sacred texts, but actually co-creates them; they will stand as symbolic only for those whose particular state of predisposition, and/or whose innate spiritual energies, activate them into life. Hence it is that the "primal act of faith", which is what establishes the living relation of the believer to his God, is "enunciated in the word, GOD" (*Lay Sermons*, p. 18); it is the speaking forth, the performance of the word, which authenticates it as a symbol.

This of course also renders it private, for how can we know the spirit in which things are said, except by generous inference? And we have even less chance of thus verifying the nature of the written word, which comes to us without the added information provided by the tones and inflections of the human voice. Coleridge is of course aware of this, and it is why he insists on the futility of such inferential modes in the perception of the most essential truths. Those we must prove on our pulses. Accepting this, we must yet register the point that this considerably unsettles the business of communication, and the achievement of shared experience which might be its goal (even as a strong element in the Protestant mind of course denies such sharing). Johnson, as reported by Boswell, made a not unrelated point about the Methodists:

> Speaking of the *inward light*, to which some methodists pretended, he said, it was a principle utterly incompatible with social or civil security. "If a man (said he,) pretends to a principle of action of which I can know nothing, nay, not so much as that he has it, but only that he pretends to it; how can I tell what that person may be prompted to do? When a person professes to be governed by a written ascertained law, I can then know where to find him."[28]

This side of the Protestant ethos had always been thus subversive of sure social order, and in its extreme form it was to appear in the ironical selfhood theorized by Kierkegaard. But Johnson's point about the written law needs to be questioned in the light of Coleridge's comments, for that is exactly the kind of authority the Scriptures might have been thought to be. For Coleridge, these written words too are brought to life only by the correlative experience of the reader, without which they remain empty shells, either objectively authoritarian or ignored completely. No one knew better than Coleridge that that experience could be missing, and was missing in many cases. This being so, no consensus can be forthcoming:

> Without that Spirit in each true believer, whereby we know the spirit of truth and the spirit of error in all things appertaining to salvation, the consequence must be—So many men, so many minds!
>
> (*Confessions*, p. 90)

Here is Fichte's insight, restated; how can one argue against an audience which puts forward the same rights of conviction as oneself, but within an antithetical system taking its life from different interests and experiences? This question goes a long way toward explaining the care with which Coleridge constructs his theoretical reliance upon an enlightened clerisy, whereby those who are capable of active symbolical perception must communicate the *results* of those perceptions as *facts* to be taken on faith. "Non omnia possumus omnes" (*Biographia*, I, 198). This is a kind of authoritarianism, and it certainly invokes the questions one always asks about the control of the many by the few; Coleridge accepts and approves it as the best possible course of action in a world where absolutely shared experience is not seen to be possible, and where other and rival forms of hegemony are striving for attention. Thus, in so far as the control of society is in the hands of those envisaged by Coleridge, with the Bible as their agent, the result should be a gradual inclusion of those who *can* awaken their own dormant creative wills within a continually expanding subgroup, always *potentially* total, of those who can recognize the fact of the symbol. They are encouraged to move, from a contemplation of the product to a performance of the process, because the text thus contemplated (the Scriptures) itself demands an effort of elucidation and synthesis. Without effort, no understanding.

We should rather say, no understanding of the 'proper' sort. Coleridge well knew, both from his academic experience of sectarian controversy and his own lived-through movements of mind and heart, that large numbers of us will always be content with the simpler, less demanding, and hence 'inauthentic' forms of understanding. It is a fact of life that man is divided from man. It is also a fact of experience that man is divided from himself, and it is out of that division or sensed incompletion (itself an ethical desideratum) that creative interchange is generated. As with Wordsworth, the concept of identity comes to consist in the positive instability of the holding together.

We can see, then, that the element of assumption or prospectus which Kant had emphasized in the proposed universality of the aesthetic judgement of the beautiful has been understood by Coleridge to apply to the most important aspects of a theory of mind and of mind in society. Just as the sharing of joy in the song of the nightingale is open only to those who have been through an essential predisciplinary experience, so in the same way the vitalizing truths of the will and imagination will be acceded to by those who have enacted them for themselves. Coleridge describes the beautiful as intuitive in that the mind cannot but "have complacency in whatever is perceived as pre-configured to its living faculties" (*Biographia*, II, 243), but those faculties may remain dormant and unexercised by some or even many of their possessors. In the same way, with habitual consciousness, every man has knowledge of the "IMMEDIATE" even as "the original intuition, or absolute affirmation of it, . . . does not in every man rise into consciousness" (*ibid.*, I, 168).

Both Coleridge and Hegel, then, position the figurative faculty as that which, ideally, leads the mind away from its tendency to repose within fixed forms, and toward a consciousness of its own dynamic identity as *natura naturans*. They also, in so doing, allow for and explore the social function of creative representation as it qualifies the self-centredness imposed by immediate consciousness. For Hegel, the awareness of the fact of 'representation' is the beginning of a notion of personal identity and of social exchange; both self and environment are now experienced as held together through time. For Coleridge, the experience of the symbolic is the ideal principle of cohesion within a society necessarily made up of persons committed to different levels of understanding of that cohesion; what contains the seeds of freedom must appear as authority until such time as those seeds can develop.

These specifically social and cultural dimensions to the figurings of the individual mind, the exploration of which Coleridge and Hegel share with Wordsworth, are important again to Shelley, and particularly to that libertarian theory of history which is rehearsed in *A Defence of Poetry*. Shelley's leading concern is with the relation of part to whole; of the poetic part to the individual human subject and its language, and of the human subject to the larger spectrum of history and society. The principle of creativity and liberation from habit is embodied in the unstable qualities of the metaphoric mode as it continues to create new metaphors in an ongoing displacement of figures already formed. I have elsewhere gone some way towards describing the implications of this manifesto for the individual mind (see *Irony and Authority*, pp. 160–5), but it must now be stressed that Shelley means it to relate very directly to the nature of, and prospects for, historical change in society at large. Thus he saves the poetic, whose essence is vitally metaphorical, from being intentionally appropriated by the individual subject, by defining its operations as unconscious and uncontrollable. The poet, who is the medium through whom the poetic makes itself manifest, is not able to control or predict either the genesis or the effects of poetry; to describe or define it does not fall within the powers of an efficient self-consciousness. The poet *himself* is now a nightingale, knowing neither the sources and features of his own song, nor its effect on those alerted hearers, Coleridgean or otherwise, hearing into the darkness:

> A Poet is a nightingale, who sits in darkness and sings to cheer its own solitude with sweet sounds; his auditors are as men entranced by the melody of an unseen musician, who feel that they are moved and softened, yet know not whence or why.[29]

This insistence on the unavailability of what is truly poetic for the private purposes of interested individuals or factions enshrines its continuing availability for the disturbing of the habitual; for poetry is "the faculty which contains within itself the seeds at once of its own and of social renovation" (p. 124). As the poetic is incorporated within particular historical configurations — as Shakespeare, for example, has been made both the upholder of order and the apostle of anarchy — so it always resists ultimate incorporation into ideology by supplying more images and delights than can be held within any single, purposive view of the world:

> after one person and one age has exhausted all its divine effluence which their peculiar relations enable them to share, another and yet another succeeds, and new relations are ever developed, the source of an unforeseen and an unconceived delight.
>
> (p. 131)

We look to history, and to literature, in other words, for companionable forms, but in so far as we are dealing with the poetic, we receive rather more than we are asking for. What is difficult about Shelley, as indeed it is with Hegel in his notorious comments on the contemporary Prussian state, is that he can be read as suggesting that such historical progress and experience of new relations derives from an underlying and implicit whole, a kind of universal idea.[30] When Shelley says of poetry, however, that it unveils "the permanent analogy of things by images which participate in the life of truth", and that it is "universal, and contains within itself the germs of a relation to whatever motives or actions have place in the possible varieties of human nature" (p. 115), I do not take him to be encouraging any gesturing toward a final product, a once and for all social condition in which all that is uncreative will disappear. On the contrary, his history of civilization clearly recognizes the cyclic nature of growth and decay (the seed in the soil is the image of this) and the inexorable fact that poetry has disappeared and doubtless will again under pressure from utilitarian and materialistic demands. In this sense "that great poem, which all poets, like the co-operating thoughts of one great mind, have built up since the beginning of the world" (p. 124) can only be understood as something which is continually *being* created and refracted through different forms — literature, art, social institutions, and so forth. That poetry "reproduces the common Universe of which we are portions and percipients" (p. 137), reading us into a relation to ourselves and to others which is very closely akin to that intimated in Coleridge's description of the symbolic, is not to be taken as suggesting a reliance upon a stable set of values and perceived relations, which is exactly that which deadens and decays, but must demand a continually recurring validation of the unapprehended and the new, a selective revitalization of discourse and society wherein "a single word even may be a spark of inextinguishable thought" (p. 116). It is the habit of reading, and its wider ancillary practices in the construction of a culture, that we take such sparks to be the product of what is 'in' that word, instead of the combustion possible only because of its coincidence with the igniting functions of our own minds.

There is in Shelley's *A Defence of Poetry* a remarkably complete theory of culture and history, from the perspective of an imperative to maximize the poetic, which becomes even more of an imperative as the writer points out all that threatens it. Shelley recognizes the presence and power of interest and intention as a principle of selectivity, and the poetic is that element of language which survives and subverts such appropriation. The figured form, the impermanent, is what we *call* 'reality'; whereas what is most real is what lies within the transition between such forms, the imagination as a principle of creative change. We deduce from this manifesto both the licence to build culture with forms produced by interest and by partial perception of relations — for this must always happen — and also the veto on any attempt to inhibit the evolution of other, future forms by the consolidation of our own. Shelley does not, then, go as far as Nietzsche will go in maintaining that

life itself is *essentially* appropriation, injury, overpowering of what is alien and weaker; suppression, hardness, imposition of one's own forms, incorporation and at least, at its mildest, exploitation.[31]

Like Schopenhauer, he is concerned and feels able to preserve that which belongs to 'genius' and 'poetry' as a lifeline guaranteeing ongoing social and individual development.

In fact, with the shift toward an insistence on the total hegemony of intention evident here in Nietzsche, we have reached something of a watershed in nineteenth-century speculation. Dickens, for example, preserves a faith in the potential of a sentimental education to direct at least small portions of humanity out of the kind of world which Nietzsche intimates as the natural one. This faith is imaged in the presence of uncorruptible personalities, those who are beyond the figurings of false consciousnesses imposed by personal or external interests. With Conrad, on the other hand, the prospects become darker. Here, the figure is again omniscient, at least for the men; there is always the MacWhirr way of life, an uncritical immersion in the details of function and routine, but whatever saving potential this has for the individual concerned is to be set against the fact that he remains an obedient ghost in someone else's machine, like all good company men. In Wordsworthian terms, such figures never experience the fall into consciousness and its fortunate corollaries of authentic self-constitution and responsible social exchange. Alternatively, there is the fixation of the ideal, perhaps differing only from the habitual in the sophistication of its corruption, and its capacity to represent as imagination and moral law what is often nothing more than the disguised operation of interest and ambition. Thus the copula connecting hitherto unrelated things in Conrad's world is as often as not a sublimated figuring of trade.

This is, however, to anticipate an argument which I have not space to mount here. We have seen that Wordsworth, Shelley and Coleridge, and indeed the specialist theories of knowledge in whose historical context they operate, consciously or otherwise, all take into account the inevitability and indeed the creativity of the figurative. They share also a sense of the problems to which it must give rise if it is once allowed to stand outside the control of time and change. As a means of preventing this, all these writers emphasize the ethic of the polymorphous, both within the individual psyche and within the social contract as it tries to take account of different interests and dispositions. The more that the 'real' is recognized as the 'figured', the more important it becomes to keep in play as many figurings as possible. In the following chapter I shall discuss the importance of polymorphous perception in nineteenth-century ethics and aesthetics, and also try to give some sense of the pressures that were felt to be operative upon it.

3 Societies of Figures

There is *only* a perspective seeing, *only* a perspective "knowing"; and the *more* affects we allow to speak about one thing, the *more* eyes, different eyes, we can use to observe one thing, the more complete will our "concept" of this thing, our "objectivity", be. But to eliminate the will altogether, to suspend each and every affect, supposing we were capable of this — what would that mean but to *castrate* the intellect? —
Nietzsche, *The Genealogy of Morals*, III, 12

I THE MANY AND THE ONE

At the end of chapter 1, it was suggested that Wordsworth's writings demonstrate an acceptance and a making virtue of the necessity of figurative attribution as the mechanism of human perception and communication. Conditions are imposed which make clear that some versions of this process are to be preferred to others; the attribution should be in the mind rather than materialized as a monument, unless it is the result of an authentic and potentially communal relation to place, in which case monumentality may be sanctioned. As far as possible, the emblems employed or created should be recognized as vehicles of changing states of mind or heart, at the same time as they serve to hold together such variables into a working identity. Their integrity, in other words, depends on their holding together of the polymorphous or antithetical predications of passion without reducing the play of that polymorphousness. The whole subordinates the parts only in so far as the parts would be meaningless without the whole.

This model of the 'one in many' and 'many in one' is a dominant paradigm in Romantic thought. It constitutes a way of maximizing the creative aspects of the mind conceived as a structure of desire, a way of accepting the intentional dispositions of particular representations by making sure that no one of them becomes endowed with the status of fixity. Movement and experiment, at best perhaps a radically experimental science and culture, are the features of the ideal mind in which the aspirations of desire, as in Fichte's theory of knowledge, serve to counter and displace the momentary appeal of and investment in fixed forms, realized figures.

This model of mental and social health is presented with an urgency which certainly relates to the observation of a great deal in the historical environment which must have seemed to threaten such an ideal. We have seen this already in Wordsworth's description of what happens in cities, where disconnection and incoherence rule over and determine the activities (or passivities) of the mind. Conversely, the polymorphous ideal of the perfect interaction of the many and the one underlies a great many Romantic positives. Wordsworth sees Grasmere as

> A Whole without dependence or defect,
> Made for itself and happy in itself,
> Perfect Contentment, Unity entire.
> *(Home at Grasmere, p. 48)*

To use a favourite Romantic metaphor, centre and circumference are held together in perfect balance, with the centrifugal force exactly setting off the centripetal. There is no tension between part and whole, the many and the one:

> Society is here:
> The true community, the noblest Frame
> Of many into one incorporate.
> *(Ibid., p. 90)*

Here there can be no problem of selection or 'representation', nothing is made to 'stand for' anything else, nothing is disjoined from membership of the whole. All is "without dependence or defect". This model of society, as we have seen, is based on the co-existence of small groups of independent and yet mutually support-ive owner-occupiers. The same paradigm appears again in Wordsworth's aesthetic response to a favourite epitaph:

> This composition is a perfect whole; there is nothing arbitrary or mechanical, but it is an organised body of which the members are bound together by a common life and are all justly proportioned.
> *(PrW, II, 89)*

Similarly, Coleridge's ideal poem is to be identified by its "proposing to itself such delight from the *whole*, as is compatible with a distinct gratification from each component *part*" (*Biographia*, II, 10); and the perception of beauty, to take another example, is "that in which the *many*, still seen as many, becomes one" (*ibid.*, p. 232). The mind which can recognize this principle of "Multeity in Unity" must itself be constituted in a correlative way; it will be the polymorphous psyche whose variety and range is exercised in the creation and dissolution of form and figure. Hence that balance or identity of creative mind and created form which characterizes the 'whole' which is Shakespeare, and becomes for Coleridge a yardstick of excellence in art:

> In all his various characters, we still feel ourselves communing with the same human nature, which is every where present as the vegetable sap in the branches, sprays, leaves, buds, blossoms, and fruits, their shapes, tastes, and odours. Speaking of the effect, i.e. his works themselves, we may define the excellence of *their* method as consisting in that just proportion, that union and interpenetration of the universal and the particular, which must ever pervade all works of decided genius and true science.
>
> (*The Friend*, I, 457)

Every character (part) signifies the whole of that which it stands within (human nature), and there is no redundancy of the particular when that whole is perceived by means of it. This is clearly a 'symbolic' species of art, as Coleridge seeks to theorize it, and it is not accidental that the obvious image for Shakespeare in his works is that of God in his creation. For the symbolic is, I think, a concept central to Coleridgean theology, and one difficult to apply with equal conviction to the fallen media. This helps to explain why Coleridge, as I shall suggest, seems to misunderstand much of Wordsworth's poetry as it works out the implications of dislocation and division.

Another manifestation of the trope of 'many in one' appears in the solution to the problem of objects and object parts which we saw to be implicit in the account of primary and secondary qualities. Once again, it is a socio-aesthetic idea of the mind which has Wordsworth casting the infant as

> prompt and watchful, eager to combine
> In one appearance, all the elements
> And parts of the same object, else detach'd
> And loth to coalesce.
>
> (*The Prelude*, II, 247–50)

The mind synthesizes the data taken in by the different senses into a unity, a single representation which it calls a 'thing'.

But it is in the theory of the imagination, as we might expect, that the unity of the many and the one is most insistently spoken for. Kant had described its workings in the aesthetic idea as bound up with the polymorphous dislocation of the sufficiency of the concept:

> In a word, the aesthetic idea is a representation of the imagination, annexed to a given concept, with which, in the free employment of imagination, such a multiplicity of partial representations are bound up, that no expression indicating a definite concept can be found for it — one which on that account allows a concept to be supplemented in thought by much that is undefinable in words.
>
> (*CJ*, I, 179)

Poetry, of all the arts, is the most productive of this oversupply of thought to concept. It allows the mind to operate on nature and beyond it, becoming thereby "a sort of schema" for the "supersensible":

> It plays with semblance [Schein], which it produces at will [nach Belieben], but not as an instrument of deception; for its avowed pursuit is merely one of play, which, however, understanding may turn to good account and employ for its own purpose.
>
> (*ibid.*, p. 192; *Werke*, V, 403)

Kant's formulation here is marked by a confidence in the simply positive effects of the imagination, in a way which sets it off from the more complicated and paradoxical insights of his successors; but even here it is clear that the imagination operates antithetically on what is 'given' to it, producing representations for 'play' which are not directed at the constitution of a world for ordinary, utilitarian activity. Wordsworth takes this disruptive potential further, just as he heightens the problems which accompany it, in seeing the "imagination" as delighting in nothing more than the activity of

> consolidating numbers into unity, and dissolving and separating unity into number,—alternations proceeding from, and governed by, a sublime consciousness of the soul in her own mighty and almost divine powers.
>
> (*PrW*, III, 33)

Similarly, Coleridge calls the imagination "esemplastic" because of its ability to "shape into one" (*Biographia*, I, 107), and this is its most common and important function in a world where the 'given' tends to be a plurality of disconnected sensations. The "secondary imagination" (which must be understood, I think, as a *symbol* of the primary, in the strictest Coleridgean sense)

> dissolves, diffuses, dissipates, in order to recreate; or where this process is rendered impossible, yet still at all events it struggles to idealize and to unify. It is essentially *vital*, even as all objects (*as* objects) are essentially fixed and dead.
>
> (*Biographia*, I, 202)

Only by operating on what is given, we may infer, does it come to consciousness of itself as a vital and creative faculty; so that, if the given form be already a unity, it must be dissolved and dissipated for re-creation.

Wordsworth, I have suggested, did not have Coleridge's ideal faith in a symbolic mode — even for Coleridge, it is certainly an ideal — so that, seeing the question of representation much more immediately in terms of human consensus and the 'society' of perceivers it might produce, he necessarily commits himself to a less uniformly optimistic investigation of the figurative faculty. This may help to explain some of the negative estimations of crucial aspects of Wordsworth's poetry to which Coleridge gives voice. For example, under the rubric of an objection to "the INCONSTANCY of the *style*", what Coleridge really seems to be talking about is the disruption of organic form which Wordsworth's poems effect:

> There is something unpleasant in the being thus obliged to alternate states of feeling so dissimilar, and this too in a species of

writing, the pleasure from which is in part derived from the preparation and previous expectation of the reader.

(*ibid.*, II, 97–8)

That this non-gratification experienced by the reader might have a dramatic purpose and a thematic importance does not seem to exercise Coleridge here. In the same way he records as a fault the disjunctions occasioned by the "laborious minuteness and fidelity in the representation of objects, and their positions, as they appeared to the poet himself", and by the "insertion of accidental circumstances, in order to the full explanation of his living characters, their dispositions and actions" (p. 101), without seeming to want to entertain the possibility that accidentality, minuteness and special perspective might be constitutive of the 'truths' being investigated. Coleridge's emphasis is toward the universal and the symbolic, and its analogue in organic form, whereas Wordsworth, I think, remains more concerned with the particular and the more contentious aspects of the figurative. The process of which Coleridge complains, that

> We first look at one part, and then at another, then join and dove-tail them; and when the successive acts of attention have been completed, there is a retrogressive effort of mind to behold it as a whole
>
> (p. 102)

can in fact be read as an exact anatomy of the Wordsworth poem as it is conceived to be exploring the coherence, epistemological status and ethical import of figured forms. In the same light, we can evaluate Coleridge's complaints about "an undue predilection for the *dramatic* form", an "occasional prolixity, repetition, and an eddying, instead of progression, of thought", and a "disproportion of thought to the circumstance or occasion" (p. 109). Coleridge is employing the traditional habits of *a priori* criticism in assuming that he can upbraid Wordsworth for what he *does* effect because he is in possession of the truth about what he is *trying* to effect. The assertion of the nature of another's thoughts and feelings, explored so tentatively in Coleridge's own poetry in terms of the transcendental model, is here simply announced as a universal principle of poetic excellence. The precision of Coleridge's objections, however, is such that we can infer from them a directly antithetical reading of 'purpose' according to which Wordsworth becomes a poet using the dramatic form as a *means* of articulating the disjunctions about which he is so urgently curious, for all the reasons put forward in the first chapter of this book.

Wordsworth's concern to maintain the integrity of the whole of experience, a whole wherein each part, however unpleasant or incoherent it may seem when seen alone, is yet an irreducible component of the life process, is evident once more in his description of the ideal childhood. We do not find a "Therefore all seasons shall be sweet to thee", but the prospect of

> A race of real children, not too wise,
> Too learned, or too good; but wanton, fresh,
> And bandied up and down by love and hate,
> Fierce, moody, patient, venturous, modest, shy;
> Mad at their sports like wither'd leaves in winds;
> Though doing wrong, and suffering, and full oft
> Bending beneath our life's mysterious weight
> Of pain and fear; yet still in happiness
> Not yielding to the happiest upon earth.
>
> (*The Prelude*, V, 436–44)

This is an oxymoronic model of the personality, where love and hate and error and recognition are integrally connected into the energy of ongoing experience. Even pain and fear have their place as forces acting against habit, preoccupation and standardization; they operate by surprise, and thus upset what is elsewhere called "that most dreadful enemy to our pleasures, our own pre-established codes of decision" (*PrW*, I, 116). We cannot avoid pain without avoiding pleasure also, because the two are organically related and exist in a mutually defining tension. For

> as the mind grows serious from the weight of life, the range of its passions is contracted accordingly; and its sympathies become so exclusive, that many species of high excellence wholly escape, or but languidly excite, its notice.
>
> (*PrW*, III, 64)

This is true, for example, of those who read with "religious or moral inclinations", and we are reminded again of that deep-seated

Romantic preoccupation, evident also in Schiller and in Shelley, and worked out very fully by Wordsworth, with preserving the amorality of the aesthetic. Kant, as so often, is eloquent on this subject:

> The changing free play of sensations (which do not follow any preconceived plan) is always a source of gratification, because it promotes the feeling of health; and it is immaterial whether or not we experience delight in the object of this play or even in the gratification itself when estimated in the light of reason . . . the affections of hope, fear, joy, anger, and derision here engage in play, as every moment they change their parts, and are so lively that, as by an internal motion, the whole vital function of the body seems to be furthered by the process — as is proved by a vivacity of the mind produced — although no one comes by anything in the way of profit or instruction.
>
> (*CJ*, I, 197–8)

This is a description of what we commonly call 'play' in the simplest sense, but we can see the connection with Wordsworth's ideal infant personality. In the face of the problems posed by a developing intentionalist psychology, and the context of social repression and the struggle of interests which was seen to accompany or determine it, the aesthetic (which Shelley calls 'poetry') is anxiously maintained as the one drive which is undirected and irrepressible. It is thus always available to clear the way for something 'new', even as the new itself slips forward into habit and preoccupation, rising to vanish in the face of further and different novelties.

It is Schiller who works out most fully the implications of Kant's positioning of the aesthetic, at least at the level of theoretical discourse — for it is implicit in a great deal of what Wordsworth wrote, and in almost everything of Blake's. Schiller's model of the psyche, and of the ideal macrocosm corresponding to it in the social order, is one organized around a series of dualisms between whose extremes there is continuing dialectical oscillation. Man has moral instincts, operating through "reason", and aesthetic ones, through "nature". Each must serve to hold the other in check, the domination of either being undesirable:

> Consequently, whenever Reason starts to introduce the unity of the moral law into any actually existing society, she must beware

of damaging the variety of Nature. And whenever Nature
endeavours to maintain her variety within the moral framework
of society, moral unity must not suffer any infringement thereby.
Removed alike from uniformity and from confusion, there abides
the triumph of form.

(Aesthetic Education, pp. 21–3)

The gap between the "ethical" and the "dynamic" is bridged by
the "aesthetic"; properly defined, the aesthetic is that which
"consummates the will of the whole through the nature of the
individual":

> All other forms of communication divide society, because they
> relate exclusively either to the private receptivity or to the private
> proficiency of its individual members, hence to that which
> distinguishes man from man; only the aesthetic mode of com-
> munication unites society, because it relates to that which is
> common to all.

(p. 215)

As such, it cannot tolerate "privilege" or "autocracy"; but we
should not be misled by these highly charged terms into a
misunderstanding of the operations of the aesthetic in society. As we
have seen, it must remain interest-free, and undirected at
particular, contingent ends. Beauty, which is its centrepiece, is itself
a function of the co-operation of two antithetical principles or
drives, the formal and the material, combined in the play-drive. Its
highest manifestation must therefore be an "equilibrium" which

> remains no more than an Idea [Idee], which can never be fully
> realized in actuality. For in actuality we shall always be left with
> a preponderance of one element over the other, and the utmost
> that experience can achieve will consist of an *oscillation*
> [*Schwankung*] between the two principles, in which now reality,
> now form, will predominate. Beauty as Idea, therefore, can never
> be other than one and indivisible, since there can never be more
> than one point of equilibrium; whereas beauty in experience will
> be eternally twofold, because oscillation can disturb the equilib-
> rium in twofold fashion, inclining it now to the one side, now to
> the other.

(p. 111)

This is very much in the spirit of Wordsworth's insistence on the totality of experience as a system which makes the unavoidable operations of the figurative less power-fraught than they would otherwise be. For it is the *un*achievable nature of the equilibrium, coexisting with its presence as an ideal in consciousness, which is the source of the creative imagination, which it thus defines as being rooted in desire. Hegel makes the same point in relating the model of the one and the many (*Eins und Vieles*) to the deduction of matter and being:

> It is an ancient proposition that the one is the many and especially that the many are one. We may repeat here the observation that the truth of the one and the many expressed in propositions appears in an inappropriate form, that this truth is to be grasped only as a becoming, as a process, a repulsion and attraction—not as being, which in a proposition has the character of a stable unity.[1]

There is, we may infer, no end to the process, and in a similar way the aesthetic idea exists in society and in the individual mind as an idea never to be *realized*; it is this very quality which enables it to function as the organ of a continually creative and adaptive practice. Arnold, who takes over exactly this principle of dynamic adjustment in his own theory of culture, makes much the same point in his famous distinction between Hebraism and Hellenism. Roughly speaking, and in the terms of the argument I am making, the former corresponds to obsessional attachment to a single form or value (the adherence, that is to say, to a single 'figure' as authoritative) and the latter to flexibility and polymorphous response. The times call for a concentration on this second, Shelleyan extreme:

> Now, and for us, it is a time to Hellenise, and to praise knowing; for we have Hebraised too much, and have over-valued doing. But the habits and discipline received from Hebraism remain for our race an eternal possession; and, as humanity is constituted, one must never assign to them the second rank to-day, without being prepared to restore them to the first rank to-morrow.[2]

Doing requires momentary suspension of the full field of generous possibilities, as Arnold realizes; but for particular doings to remain creative, they must accept the necessity of their own revaluations or modifications. They must be placed back into the context of possible alternatives. *The Prelude* had been built around this oscillation, or something very close to it. The poem moves between the free play of undirected energies, ever about to be, and the goal-seeking inclinations of specific intentions. The prospect of absolute freedom and perpetual novelty,

> The earth is all before me: with a heart
> Joyous, nor scar'd at its own liberty,
> I look about
>
> (I, 15–17)

coexists and interacts with the tendency toward "steady choice" (I, 171). The Miltonic quotation tells us that both options are contained within the spectrum offered to postlapsarian man, and each indeed defines the other in the ideal case. Without the steadiness of choice, free play turns into idleness and indifference, but it is only free play which keeps that steadiness away from bigotry or blindness. Through time, the mind is variously

> sportive and alert
> And watchful, as a Kitten when at play
>
> (VII, 470–1)

and given to high seriousness, to themes "Single and of determined bounds" (I, 669).

II ECONOMIES OF MIND

As a description of the evolution through time of the ideal human subject, Wordsworth's model of the mind as holding together the many and the one is an affirmative one. We have seen, however, that as applied to the whole of society at any *one* time, and to the different interests within it, no such affirmation emerges from Wordsworth's writings. The ideal individual economy of the psyche is seen to be more and more adversely affected by developments in the national economy. The mind in London is not to be described in the same terms as the mind in Grasmere. By contrast, the classical liberal response to the question is framed within the terms of the organic metaphor, and the idea behind Kant's definition of the organism is at the heart of it:

> In such a natural product as this every part is thought as *owing* its presence to the *agency* of all the remaining parts, and also as existing *for the sake of the others* and of the whole, that is as an instrument, or organ . . . the part must be an organ *producing* the other parts—each, consequently, reciprocally producing the others.
>
> (*CJ*, II, 21–2)

Applied to social organization, as it is, for example, by Arnold, the organic ideal aims at a "*general* perfection, developing all parts of our society",wherein "if one member suffer, the other members must suffer with it" (*Culture and Anarchy*, p. 11). Durkheim's later and more sophisticated theory was to rely on the same fundamental model, this time envisaged as operating through the corporate bonding of various previously bonded groups (divided, perhaps, in the first instance, from each other) in a perfectly evolving harmony of many and one:

> In a group formed of numerous and varied elements, new combinations are always being produced. There would then be nothing rigid about such an organization, and it would consequently find itself in harmony with the mobile equilibrium of needs and ideas . . . A group is not only a moral authority which dominates the life of its members; it is also a source of life *sui generis*. From it comes a warmth which animates its members, making them intensely human, destroying their egotisms.[3]

This is, crudely speaking, the 'liberal' social theory which conceives of the tolerant coexistence of different interests. Marx would have defied it for its ignoring of the fact and laws of capital, and the construction or reproduction of society as we find it in for example, Dickens is certainly not of this sort. Dickens' world is not one where the suffering of one produces a reciprocal suffering in others, and if such prospects do emerge then they do so only by the flouting of the privileges of fiction. But even before Marx and Dickens, the ideal balance of the many and the one as a viable model for describing social interaction had been tested and qualified, and not just by the theorists of the division of labour. Wordsworth briefly perceived a moment in history when the question could be put aside:

> How bright a face is worn when joy of one
> Is joy of tens of millions.
>
> (*The Prelude*, VI, 359–60)

The early stages of the French Revolution seemed to offer the prospects of a larger community bonded by a common interest, and one committed to re-evaluating and modifying that interest through time. But this was not, as we have seen, what he found in his native land. The continuation of a passage which has already been cited is significant in this context. Unpublished, it describes Grasmere:

> Society is here:
> The true community, the noblest Frame
> Of many into one incorporate;
> That must be looked for here; paternal sway,
> One Household under God for high and low,
> One family and one mansion; to themselves
> Appropriate and divided from the world
> As if it were a cave, a multitude
> Human and brute, possessors undisturbed
> Of this recess, their legislative Hall,
> Their Temple, and their glorious dwelling-place.
>
> (*Home at Grasmere*, p. 90)

Wordsworth does not, we assume, mean to invoke the presence of a conventional landlord, maintained by his tenants; it is the church which is the proper "mansion" and "legislative Hall", and it exhorts the democratic interaction of the lakeland owner-occupiers. And it is the *whole* of the chosen vale, or "recess", which is syntactically pressured into identification with the legislative hall; the part which traditionally operates as the fount of decision within the whole which it governs is thus here made one with that larger whole, the "dwelling place" which is itself a composite form made up of people, animals and physical objects. This is an organic or (in Coleridge's sense) symbolic relation of part to whole; each stands within the other, and no hierarchy is established. The passage is explained by an account of how the Lakes had been settled "till within the last sixty years":

Towards the head of these Dales was found a perfect Republic of Shepherds and Agriculturists, among whom the plough of each man was confined to the maintenance of his own family, or to the occasional accommodation of his neighbour. Two or three cows furnished each family with milk and cheese. The chapel was the only edifice that presided over these dwellings, the supreme head of this pure Commonwealth; the members of which existed in the midst of a powerful empire, like an ideal society or an organized community, whose constitution had been imposed and regulated by the mountains which protected it. Neither high-born nobleman, knight, nor esquire, was here; but many of these humble sons of the hills had a consciousness that the land, which they walked over and tilled, had for more than five hundred years been possessed by men of their name and blood.

(PrW, II, 206)

This is what the Ewbanks are robbed of in 'The Brothers' by the developing capitalization of the land; but we note also, in the prose as in the verse passage, that the pure commonwealth governed by no lord and based in co-operative independence is maintained by virtue of the small size of the community, and by its being geographically cut off from the wider world as if "it were a cave" (once before, as we have seen, the locus of an ideal mode of perception for Wordsworth). Ferguson had made a similar point about size and cohesion in 1767:

In proportion as territory is extended, its parts lose their relative importance to the whole. Its inhabitants cease to perceive their connection with the state, and are seldom united in the execution of any national, or even of any factious, designs. Distance from the seats of administration, and indifference to the persons who contend for preferment, teach the majority to consider themselves as the subjects of a sovereignty, not as the members of a political body. It is even remarkable, that enlargement of territory, by rendering the individual of less consequence to the public, and less able to intrude with his counsel, actually tends to reduce national affairs within a narrower compass, as well as to diminish the numbers who are consulted in legislation, or in other matters of government.[4]

Thus writes a Scotsman, and one conscious of the irony whereby even organized dissent is rendered difficult by distance from the seat of government and of consequently critical intervention. The smaller the society, the more chance there is that its parts will cohere as a whole without sacrificing the integrity and independence of any among those parts. In small societies there is less need for *representation*, less need for the selecting out of some privileged figures as the emblems of others and the guardians of their interests. Nothing 'stands for' anything else, no one speaks on behalf of another — as the English, perhaps, had been speaking for the Scots, since the Act of Union.

It is understood by Ferguson that there are different interests within a society, and the more so the larger it is or becomes. This tension was heightened for Wordsworth by his intuition that life in the city actually produces a different *mind*, or a different set of preoccupations and capacities in the mind, from that which is nurtured inside the cave, and with the leisure for the second look.

In larger societies, it seems, the gesture of representation must inevitably inscribe a division of interest. Schopenhauer was providing the materials for a theory of mind which postulated something very close to a struggle of each against all, the one against the many in a competition for preferential use of available resources. Any model of social interaction to come out of such a theory must be divisive and tragical, a conflict of interest in which the interested parties may not even be aware of what their interests are. For this, we look to Hardy's novels. Leaving aside the blinding demands of the unconscious, however, as a principle of absolute division of man from man, and from woman, there are significant instances in earlier Romantic theory of an insight into the forces threatening the ideal social equilibrium of the many and the one. In Godwin, for example, the paradigm fails to apply because of the fundamentally self-interested nature of institutions and their tendency, not to tolerate alternatives, but to impose upon them their own ways of seeing. The consequent repression is both synchronic and diachronic; it inhibits the full development of the individual personality at any one moment, and as a result the general possibility of creative historical change. Godwin holds it to be axiomatic

> That institutions calculated to give perpetuity to any particular mode of thinking, or condition of existence, are pernicious.[5]

Where man is naturally "in a state of perpetual mutation" (and there is a political ethic as well as a theory of mind behind this statement), then by "its very nature positive institution has a tendency to suspend the elasticity and progress of mind" (I, 245–6). The "genuine and wholesome state of mind" is "to be unloosed from shackles, and to expand every fibre of its frame, according to the independent and individual impressions of truth upon that mind" (II, 202). This is a mode of naturalism closely related to Shelley's stress upon poetry in its function of reintroducing the independent and the individual within whatever collective or patterned representation we might, individually or culturally, be working. In this sense, he had defined 'poetry' as that which is resistant to complete incorporation within such representations. Government is to Godwin what memory and reason are for Shelley, or habit for Wordsworth, that which

> fixes the mercurialness of man to an assigned station. We can no longer enquire or think; for enquiry and thought are uncertain in their direction, and unshackled in their termination.
>
> (II, 216)

This mercurialness is what saves us from the deadening repetition of familiar figured forms and the specific intentions which they support. It is the equivalent and corollary, at the social level, of what imagination is for the individual mind. Consequently it will resist party and association, as that which tends to "make a part stand for the whole" (I, 286), in just the way that imagination refuses to allow such modes of representation to solidify into a 'reality' instead of remaining moments within a process:

> Party has a more powerful tendency, than perhaps any other circumstance in human affairs, to render the mind quiescent and stationary. Instead of making each man an individual, which the interest of the whole requires, it resolves all understandings into one common mass, and subtracts from each the varieties, that could alone distinguish him from a brute machine. Having learned the creed of our party, we have no longer any employment for those faculties, which might lead us to detect its errors.
>
> (I, 289)

Unlike what we find in Durkheim, there is here no attempt to impose an organic or 'symbolic' model on the separate factions which make up society; they do not give identity to their members, but take away that which is there already. Individuality is threatened as representation (of many by few) becomes necessary to efficient social organization. A truly free and organic relation, to self as to society, can be preserved only within a specifically formulated economic situation, one very close to that which Wordsworth invokes:

> If every man could with perfect facility obtain the necessaries of life, and, obtaining them, feel no uneasy craving after its superfluities, temptation would lose its power. Private interest would visibly accord with public good; and civil society become what poetry has feigned of the golden age.
>
> (I, 15)

Elsewhere, Godwin makes it clear that such a society would operate according to the harmony, through time, of separately disjoined states within a single life experience, of the sort that we have seen outlined in the account of the operations of the 'spots of time':

> The situation which the wise man would desire, for himself, and for those in whose welfare he was interested, would be a situation of alternate labour and relaxation, labour that should not exhaust the frame, and relaxation that was in no danger of degenerating into indolence. Thus industry and activity would be cherished, the frame preserved in a healthful tone, and the mind accustomed to meditation and improvement. But this would be the situation of the whole human species, if the supply of our wants were fairly distributed. Can any system be more worthy of disapprobation, than that which converts nineteen-twentieths of them into beasts of burden, annihilates so much thought, renders impossible so much virtue, and extirpates so much happiness?
>
> (II, 110–11)

Wordsworth's ideally postulated oscillation between activity and passivity, joy and pain, in the individual mind is here related to a specific condition of society, one which also bears comparison with Schiller's idea of the aesthetic mode as alternately tensing and relaxing. Very clearly to the front here is the statement about the elements of the status quo which inhibit such possibilities. Wordsworth differs from Godwin, I think, in that he locates the optimum community not in a vanished golden age, but on the margins of what exists in the present. It is a sterner version of the ideal, because it suggests that the very high proportion of work to relaxation made necessary by the sheer difficulty of surviving in the landscape of the English Lakes is what saves the mind from losing control of the alternation. He implies, in other words, that if the land really were as rich and compliant as the golden age would have it be, then the temptations into indolence and perhaps the growth of capital might be irresistible for the human mind, which is always in Wordsworth positioned as on the edge of transgression, moving indeed between the two sides of that edge, and recalled from the one position by the prospect of the other. It is the fact that nature refuses to smile, or rather to keep on smiling, that keeps man from sliding back into unconsciousness, for it is only the consciousness of continual self-correction which maintains society as a generous institution respectful of those within it.

We may see this at work in 'Michael' (*PW*, II, 80–94). Here, the shepherd's household is engaged in full-time work, "endless industry" (l. 97), even in the evenings after the day's work is done. The proportion of the waking life taken up with the tasks required for subsistence is a very high one. But any hardship which there might otherwise be in this exigent condition is mitigated by the fact that Michael and his family work for themselves; he owns the land he works. Wordsworth tells us of the effect this has on his mind:

> Which, like a book, preserved the memory
> Of the dumb animals, whom he had saved,
> Had fed or sheltered, linking to such acts
> The certainty of honourable gain;
> Those fields, those hills — what could they less? had laid
> Strong hold on his affections, were to him
> A pleasurable feeling of blind love,
> The pleasure which there is in life itself.
>
> (ll. 70–77)

Work and pleasure are interactive, not distinct, so that even the love of gain takes on an authentic cast. This is possible for the owner-occupier who is working for himself, and in a letter to Charles James Fox (14 January 1801), lamenting the threats which modern developments were posing to the "domestic affections" among this class, Wordsworth observes that

Their little tract of land serves as a kind of permanent rallying point for their domestic feelings, as a tablet upon which they are written which makes them objects of memory in a thousand instances when they would otherwise be forgotten.[6]

The deepest affections are here in harmony with the basic economic needs of the material life. Wordsworth does not invoke any primitive communism here, and is quite ready to confess to the place that "honourable gain" plays in life. This is the difference, indeed, between life on the land and the life of the town, to which Luke is consigned in an attempt to rescue the family fortunes. In the town, there is no organic relation between work and place, between affections and the love of gain. As Luke leaves the "fond correction" (l. 173) exercised by his father and by his way of life as a whole, he leaves the place where discipline and deviation, work and pleasure, can be held together within a satisfying way of life. Luke is sent forth in his "best garments" (l. 279), and more of such are *bought* for him; he is sent forth to cut a figure, in a world of figures. The parents are both hopeful and uneasy at letting him go, and in this way Wordsworth puts over with great subtlety the feelings of people pressured by forces which they suspect but cannot quite apprehend. Luke is going from a rural to a commercial economy, from a place where the objects of work are real and living — "the profit they bring is not put off to a distant time, & falls in according to the wants of the house by commodious detail" (*PrW*, II, 311) — to one where distancing and desire govern the energy of endeavour.

'Michael' ends with the disappearance of this sternly pleasurable way of living, in a movement which validates the written record of the poem itself as a substitute for the book-like but unwritten memory of Michael the man, now dead. But in the urgency of this disappearance we can sense, as we sense in the letter to Fox, a plea for the recognition and preservation of a threatened way of life. Wordsworth misses nothing of, and perhaps even emphasizes, the necessity of a near full-time labour. Here he differs markedly from Godwin, who has a much rosier prospect for man freed from the surplus economy and the problems it generates:

If superfluity were banished, the necessity of the greater part of the manual industry of mankind would be superseded; and the rest, being amicably shared among the active and vigorous members of the community, would be burthensome to none.

(II, 460)

A state of equality would require so little effort that it would rather "assume the guise of agreeable relaxation and gentle exercise, than of labour". It is the "unnecessary employments" which currently occupy the time of the great mass of mankind (II, 482). This is a considerable difference of emphasis from that we find in Wordsworth, even though the aim of abolishing the distinction between work and pleasure is held in common. Godwin does not stress the essentially creative nature of work; it remains "agreeable relaxation" rather than imaginative participation in the landscape and its community. It may be that

> The mathematician, the poet and the philosopher, will derive a new stock of chearfulness and energy, from the recurring labour that makes them feel they are men.
>
> (II, 482)

But they do not show the fullest employment of their faculties in the activity of work itself; fullness here is composed of the various different things they do at different times. Wordsworth, on the contrary, implies that every moment of the day contains its own fullness; each is symbolically related to every other. And Wordsworth, as I have said, has a much stronger sense of the need for nature's severer interventions, and of the amount of time which must be spent to achieve subsistence. He has, in fact, a more fully dialectical sense of the relation of pleasure to pain.

Wordsworth combines, then, I think, a Protestant recognition of the dangerous elements at work in the individual mind (operative, as we have seen, through 'figuring') with a historical sense of the specific problems faced by the mind in his own generation, and in particular places. What needs to be stressed is that the two are held together; we can infer from Wordsworth's writings that, however firm and universal a metaphysic it might be that the human mind is prone to acts of transgression in its modes of representation, there are yet specific contexts in which that tendency will be encouraged or discouraged. This complexity of insight and response makes it possible, I think, to place Wordsworth at the head of a consistent tradition in the nineteenth century which explores the situation of the imagination in the *context* of the demands made by particular social configurations. The ideal of polymorphous humanity voiced in that famous passage in *The German Ideology*, for example, stands very firmly within the vocabulary of Romantic theory. In a communist society, where nobody has one exclusive sphere of activity but each can become accomplished in any branch he wishes, society regulates the general production and thus makes it possible for me to do one thing today and another tomorrow, to hunt in the morning, fish in the afternoon, rear cattle in the evening, criticise after dinner, just as I have a mind, without ever becoming hunter, fisherman, shepherd or critic.[7]

It is the model of the many and the one, applied both to the operations of the imagination and to the coexistence of distinct factions or interests within society, which stands as the important element in the vocabulary of common concern connecting the two, and positions them as interdetermining functions. The incidence of the division of labour and interest in society is the analogue of the presence of different and perhaps antithetical faculties and dispositions in the mind. The nature of the relation between imagination and society, and the question of whether the individual imagination be conceived of as universal or particular, is what tends to divide those who commented on the subject. Most famously, it divides Hegel from Marx, and the terms of that division mark out the watershed between 'idealism', as we might usefully describe it, and the renewed sense of historical complexity which replaced it, and which we may see rehearsed and indeed worked out in Wordsworth.

In Hegel, the predicament of alienation is a constructive negative, a necessary stage in the evolution of the spirit toward self-consciousness. As all human subjects go through it, so all may prospectively emerge on the other side as reconstituted personalities, all the better for the experience:

for the self that has an absolute significance in its *immediate* existence, i.e. without having alienated itself from itself, is without substance.

(*Phenomenology*, p. 295)

We notice the vocabulary of self-instigation, and the priority it gives to the process of perception itself, as a universal, in the account of the division. The 'substance' thus constituted takes the form of "culture [die Bildung]", and it prescribes a universally subjective origin for the body of representations known as reality:

The process in which the individuality moulds itself by culture [Die Bewegung der sich bildenden Individualität] is, therefore, at the same time the development of it as the universal, objective essence, i.e. the development of the actual world [der wirklichen Welt]. Although this world has come into being through individuality, it is for self-consciousness immediately an alienated world [ein unmittelbar Entfremdetes] which has the form of a fixed and solid reality over against it. But at the same time, certain that this world is its substance, it sets about making it its own. It gains this power over it through culture [Bildung] which, looked at from this aspect, has the appearance of self-consciousness making itself conform to reality, and doing so to the extent that the energy of its original character and talent permits.

(p. 299; *Werke*, II, 378–9)

As an efficient explanation, this idea would clearly require the suspension of certain external influences and pressures. It theorizes the isolation of the single subject, which can work through in an undisturbed way the demands of the (universal) mind and its relation to the world; or, what amounts to the same thing, the universality of the process of constructing culture, so that all minds are doing the same thing at all times, albeit at different stages of self-consciousness. Within this schema, and when he treats the master-slave relation again in the *Encyclopaedia*, Hegel is thus able to suggest that the experience of slavery is more conducive to self-discovery than that of mastery:

This quaking of the single, isolated will, the feeling of the worthlessness of egotism, the habit of obedience, is a necessary moment in the education of all men. Without having experienced the discipline which breaks self-will, no one becomes free, rational, and capable of command.

(*Philosophy of Mind*, p. 175)

It is as if the individual subject is organically determined, so that having experienced slavery it is at once on the way to the assumption of command; the many facets of experience are contained within and constitutive of the one identity as it passes through time. All Hegel's discussions of alienation have to be seen from this perspective. In a similar way "wealth" is described as something whose identity consists in circulation rather than its being fixed and possessed by the members of a faction; at the same time as being

> something passive, something devoid of inner worth, it is equally
> the perpetually produced result of the labour and activity of all,
> just as it is dissipated again in the enjoyment of all.
>
> *(Phenomenology,* p. 301)

And again, language is presented not as a tool for social control, whereby a vested interest might impose its view of the world through a publication of its special figures, but as the affirmative admission into universality for the language-using subject (pp. 308ff.). It is only for the "perverted, and perverting and distracted, self of the world of culture" (p. 395), historically related to Rameau's Nephew and to the period prior to the Enlightenment, that it embodies an alienated identity. That alienation is real, to be sure, but it is a reality which is implicitly being transcended as soon as it is recognized, as if the mere fact of recognition is enough, in this mind-made world, to remove the threat and create a new reality.

Marx's objection to this aspect of Hegelian philosophy, whereby "only *mind* is the *true* essence of man" (*Works*, III, 382), is well known, and need not be documented at length here. He saw, and theoretically accounted for, an arresting of the process of development in this ideal human subject, and a force appearing at the collective level which was not simply a product of the arithmetical aggregate of the individuals involved. Language is only one among other media of exchange, and exchange (which includes, of course, what would usually be called 'imagination' in its capacity to perceive and communicate relations between things) is governed by material rather than ideal contingencies. Like Wordsworth, Marx recognizes figurative attribution, or the endowing of images with life and value, as of the essence of human communication, but the laws of capital are such as to prevent such attributions being reassessed and reprocessed through time. On the contrary, they impose a limited series of figures as 'real' in order to inhibit the development of others. This takes the determination or 'creation' of a society firmly out of the hands of most of its subjects, so that "Our *mutual* value is for us the *value* of our mutual objects":

> The only intelligible language in which we converse with one
> another consists of our objects in relation to each other. We would

not understand a human language and it would remain without effect . . . We are to such an extent estranged from man's essential nature that the direct language of this essential nature seems to us a *violation of human dignity*, whereas the estranged language of material values seems to us to be the well-justified assertion of human dignity that is self-confident and conscious of itself.

(*Works*, III, 227)

To use the terms of Coleridge's concerned critique of metaphor, the mind has come to worship the products of mind as real things external to it and having authority over it; or simply to recognize nothing else as 'real'. Where Coleridge feared this eventuality as a tendency in the individual mind, however, Marx places it in an intersubjective context where some minds are handed down the products of other minds, those products or figures having themselves the capacity to redetermine what the many see as reality.

Marx was not the first to point to the problems raised by the materialization of humanity. Schiller saw developing a world in which "material needs reign supreme and bend a degraded humanity beneath their tyrannical yoke" (*Aesthetic Education*, p. 7), and a social life wherein each person is a disconnected part of a whole which never quite comes into being:

one has to go the rounds from one individual to another in order to be able to piece together a complete image of the species . . . the various faculties appear as separate in practice as they are distinguished by the psychologist in theory, and we see not merely individuals, but whole classes of men, developing but one part of their potentialities, while of the rest, as in stunted growths, only vestigial traces remain.

(p. 33)

This disruption of "the inner unity of human nature" is related directly to the "more rigorous separation of ranks and occupations" in the state (p. 33), and this involves not just a social hierarchy but more specifically the division of labour, which has indeed assisted the progress of the "species as a whole" (p. 39) but only by accomplishing also the alienation of the individual. As "enjoyment" has been divorced from "labour", so man has become "nothing more than the imprint of his occupation or of his specialized knowledge" (p. 35). Shelley also commented on the situation whereby "man, having enslaved the elements, remains himself a slave". The discoveries which have been made for "abridging and combining labour" have, instead of assisting the pleasure potential in human life, "added a weight to the curse imposed on Adam" (*Works*, VII, 134). The weighting of the mind-world relation toward the material side is related to the influence of interest; from an "excess of the selfish and calculating principle, the accumulation of the materials of external life exceed the quantity of the power of assimilating them to the internal laws of human nature" (p. 135).[8] This is just what Wordsworth found in London, and it makes clear once again the urgency of his sense of the pressures operating upon creative figuration:

> For a multitude of causes unknown to former times are now acting with a combined force to blunt the discriminating powers of the mind, and unfitting it for all voluntary exertion to reduce it to a state of almost savage torpor. The most effective of these causes are the great national events which are daily taking place, and the encreasing accumulation of men in cities, where the uniformity of their occupations produces a craving for extraordinary incident which the rapid communication of intelligence hourly gratifies. To this tendency of life and manners the literature and theatrical exhibitions of the country have conformed themselves.
>
> (*PrW*, I, 128)

This is the analogue, in the critical prose, of the case which has already been made for Wordsworth's theory of self-consciousness and social relation, and for the different versions of the figurative which are available to city dwellers and to those who live on the margins of 'civilization'. We notice his emphasis on the negative results of the speed of communication, wherein there is no time for the 'second look' and for the mind's dissolution and reconstruction of what is given to it; and also his stress on the monotony of occupation inflicted upon the worker in the urban, factory-modelled economy. As labour is divided, so work becomes monotonous, and disconnected from the pleasures which compensate for it. Wildly pursued, such pleasures are a mere semblance no longer founded in the deeper creative instincts. As they are the products of a divided society, so they reproduce a divided self.

Representation as the individual act of figuring forth, both for self-intelligibility and for communication with others, can now be seen to have both microcosmic and macrocosmic resonances. There are forces at work in the larger social and historical context which are seen effectively to determine the scope of the subjective imagination, even in its most private meditations. Wordsworth's case for the essential differences between town and country life can be seen within the spectrum of a whole range of contemporary debates about population, agriculture and manufacture, commerce and luxury, and of course the division of labour. These large-scale questions came more and more to be seen as critically affecting the mind's intrinsic organization.

They are indeed hard to discuss separately, since in many cases they were seen as parts of a cycle, each moment of which predetermines the others. Before trying to give a sense of this synopsis, I shall however emphasize the importance of the arguments about the division of labour as perhaps the primary among all these controversies. It is, of course, a phenomenon completely antithetical to the ideal Wordsworthian paradigm of polymorphous work-and-pleasure in a variable and testing career and landscape. Michael and his family, as we have seen, met all their needs themselves. They were not tempted into combination, division and the production of surplus; or, more sternly, they were never offered the chance to develop this kind of economic organization, since the land they lived upon was not rich enough to produce more than the bare necessities, and these only with the greatest efforts. For Wordsworth, this kind of deprivation turns out to be a saving grace. Just as they are not given the chance to produce a surplus for exchange, so they are not presented with any extraneous or unnecessary objects which they might desire. There is thus no point to an exchange, for there is nothing that they 'want' beyond what they already have. They are thus completely closed off from the problems and temptations of a commercial economy.

It is this exigent natural landscape which pre-empts the division of labour, which is always the result of men combining together to produce a surplus (strangely, it is almost never theorized as a rational mode of producing necessities, but is always implicated in a cycle of exchange). It is striking that there is almost nothing in the English tradition which corresponds to Hegel's ideal cyclic model of the master-slave relation and the progressive universality of every single human being. Adam Smith touches on a similar ideal, but as we shall see he has a more complicated sense of its viability. Commonly, alienation is firmly defined as the result of the domination of one class by another, which is seen to arise from the division of labour. Here is a passage from Ferguson's *Essay on the History of Civil Society:*

> Even in manufacture, the genius of the master, perhaps, is cultivated, while that of the inferior workman lies waste. The statesman may have a wide comprehension of human affairs, while the tools he employs are ignorant of the system in which they are themselves combined. The general officer may be a great proficient in the knowledge of war, while the soldier is confined to a few motions of the hand and the foot. The former may have gained, what the latter has lost; and being occupied in the conduct of disciplined armies, may practise on a larger scale, all the arts of preservation, of deception, and of stratagem, which the savage exerts in leading a small party, or merely in defending himself.
>
> (p. 183)

This is the necessary feature of a society wherein "the exaltation of a few must depress the many" (p. 186), so that society as a whole consists in "parts, of which none is animated with the spirit of society itself" (p. 218). The many are subordinated to the interests of the few, and the reification of social flexibility and free exchange which thus sets in is duplicated in the effects on the individual psyche which is theorized, as we have seen, as most healthy when most polymorphous.

John Millar, in his analysis of the social consequences of the division of labour, had seen a similar threat to the psychic balance and potential for independent thought among the labouring class:

> As their employment requires constant attention to an object which can afford no variety of occupation to their minds, they are apt to acquire an habitual vacancy of thought, unenlivened by any prospects, but such as are derived from the future wages of their labour, or from the grateful returns of bodily repose and sleep. They become, like machines, actuated by a regular weight, and performing certain movements with great celerity and exactness, but of small compass, and unfitted for any other use.[9]

This is the means of a widening rift within society, between those who thus work and those who profit from their work. The former

> are likely, in proportion as the rest of the community advance in knowledge and literature, to be involved in a thicker cloud of ignorance and prejudice. Is there not reason to apprehend, that the common people, instead of sharing the advantages of national prosperity, are thus in danger of losing their importance, of becoming the dupes of their superiors, and of being degraded from the rank which they held in the scale of society?
>
> (p. 381)

Similarly Steuart had seen a problem in the introduction of machines, requiring the presence of a benevolent controlling statesman,

> so as to prevent the vicissitudes of manners, and innovations, by their natural and immediate effects or consequences, from hurting any interest within the commonwealth.[10]

There was then a significant body of opinion — and more could be invoked — in the writings on political economy relating to the concerns expressed by Wordsworth, Shelley and Schiller about the figuring of human beings into mechanical functions. The paradox noted by Schiller, whereby the progress of the 'species' is effected at the expense of the happiness of many or even most of the individuals who make up the species, appears again as an apparently unpointed tension in that classic apology for the natural necessity of divided labour, Adam Smith's *The Wealth of Nations*. Smith has this to say on the relative consequences of rural and mechanical labour, in a voice which Wordsworth would certainly have endorsed:

> Not only the art of the farmer, the general direction of the operations of husbandry, but many inferior branches of country labour require much more skill and experience than the greater part of mechanick trades. The man who works upon brass and iron, works with instruments and upon materials of which the temper is always the same, or very nearly the same. But the man who ploughs the ground with a team of horses or oxen, works with instruments of which the health, strength, and temper, are very different upon different occasions. The condition of the materials

which he works upon too is as variable as that of the instruments which he works with, and both require to be managed with much judgment and discretion. The common ploughman, though generally regarded as the pattern of stupidity and ignorance, is seldom defective in this judgment and discretion. He is less accustomed, indeed, to social intercourse than the mechanick who lives in a town. His voice and language are more uncouth and more difficult to be understood by those who are not used to them. His understanding, however, being accustomed to consider a greater variety of objects, is generally much superior to that of the other, whose whole attention from morning till night is commonly occupied in performing one or two very simple operations. How much the lower ranks of people are really superior to those of the town, is well known to every man whom either business or curiosity has led to converse much with both.[11]

Wordsworth would have gone on to specify that the variety be not too great, but the emphasis is the same; what sets apart the rural labourer is that he is used to applying himself to different tasks and contexts, and also to being responsible for the whole of whatever task he is engaged upon. He is more intelligent and flexible, and therefore happier in his work and in himself. He is obliged to create and react to a world of changing figures in exactly the way most calculated to produce a healthy mind. In an earlier passage in the same book, however, Smith had spoken of the rural worker in a completely different way:

> The habit of sauntering and of indolent careless application, which is naturally, or rather necessarily acquired by every country workman who is obliged to change his work and his tools every half hour, and to apply his hand in twenty different ways almost every day of his life; renders him almost always slothful and lazy, and incapable of any vigorous application even on the most pressing occasions. Independent, therefore, of his deficiency in point of dexterity, this cause alone must always reduce considerably the quantity of work which he is capable of performing.
>
> (p. 19)

It seems that the exact qualities and circumstances which make the rural labourer happier in himself, more intelligent, and more adaptable, are those which make him least useful to the factory owner. The need to transfer from one kind of work to another induces the habit of pausing during working time, of "sauntering", and the experience and expectation of a multitude of tasks reduces the concentration and exclusive perfection of any one of them. He works more slowly, in fact, because he is used to thinking as he works, and about what he is doing.

As far as I can see, Smith never discusses this paradox in an integral way; the one perspective sees the labourer in and for himself, the other regards him as 'for others', and specifically for the factory employer. In the system of divided labour, it is in fact quite clear that only those who are outside the labour process itself, like Ferguson's masters, statesmen and officers, can preserve the flexibility of mind which enables them to enjoy themselves, and to remain continually creative and inventive. Thus, for Smith, those who *make* machines are "often capable of combining together the powers of the most distant and dissimilar objects" (p. 21). This is exactly the process of relational apprehension which appears in the classical definitions of metaphor, whether they be approving or disapproving, seeing a yoking together of the heterogenous by violence, or a creative establishment of new connection and analogy. Here, then, it is the inventors of machines who remain able to think 'metaphorically', indeed whose very function it is to do so, whereas the users of those inventions are compelled to pay homage to the *products* of those apprehensions. The ideal subjectivity within which so many Romantic theories of perception are phrased — though many of them do imply or insist on a division of interest — is here quite overtly dislocated by a recognition of the consequences of divided labour and the capitalization of the economy. Wordsworth saw not just a difference of priority or inclination between the city and the country, but a difference of *mind*, and the supporting evidence for this insight can be traced through contemporary discussions of the effects of the division of labour.

Adam Smith's presentation of the issue is worth looking at in further detail, since it demonstrates very clearly the Romantic aesthetic of continual creation and the organic interdependence of part and whole, applied to a social and economic situation whose darker possibilities it seeks to turn to the good. In this way it also questions the credibility of that aesthetic.

Division of labour is, at best, not division of interest, and in this respect Smith's theory, at least in the ideal prospectus it holds out, differs from those of Millar and Ferguson. There are points at which Smith does see negative implications; the monotony of working at "a few simple operations" can debilitate both body and mind, leaving the labourer "as stupid and ignorant as it is possible for a human creature to become" (*Wealth of Nations*, p. 782). At such moments government must consider some form of intervention, and in particular it must look to the requirements of primary education. This is not, however, the dominant emphasis of the argument, and one could even suggest that the adverse effects of the division of labour are to some degree (though only I think to a degree) the results of society's failure to remove the restrictions Smith criticizes. For his ideal commercial society is characterized by uninhibited recirculation and exchange, a continual responsiveness of part to whole, both nationally and internationally. Combination is prompted by an ongoing assessment of needs and market forces, which naturally determine productive energies. The division of labour is thus self-elected as first described, every man seeking to better himself by assisting others. There is, in the famous pin factory (pp. 14ff.), no 'capitalist' in the sense that we now tend to use the term, no figure whose interest inclines him to exploit the workers. Masters do indeed combine in surreptitious ways (pp. 83–4), but in general they should see it as in their interest to treat their employees well. Workmen require rest and relaxation, and he who works "so moderately, as to be able to work constantly, not only preserves his health the longest, but, in the course of the year, executes the greatest quantity of work" (p. 100). Such wealth as accrues from the division of labour does not, in a "well-governed society" (p. 22), tend to a few possessors, but recirculates through the entire commonwealth as it is supposed to do in Hegel's model. A similar relation of complementarity should obtain between town and country (pp. 141–2) — this issue was a traditional source of outrage in writers like Cowper and Goldsmith, critical of Whig ideology — and the model of uninhibited circulation informs also Smith's comments on the free movement of labour (p. 470) and of commodities between different countries, who should never (at least in times of peace) see themselves as anything but sharers in commercial prosperity (pp. 494–5). There is no need for government interference in the balance of trade. The market adjusts production, so that supply never exceeds demand:

> If ten people only want a certain commodity, the manufacture of it will never be so divided as if a thousand wanted it.[12]

As the market changes, labour and investment change with it, and the cycle begins again.

This is very much the best of possible worlds, however, and the qualifiers Smith himself introduces suggest the threats to such a harmony of interests. The perfect balance of the one and the many is upset by the regulation of commerce, which governments introduce out of a mistaken belief in its necessity. On the contrary,

> The natural effort of every individual to better his own condition, when suffered to exert itself with freedom and security, is so powerful a principle, that it is alone, and without any assistance, not only capable of carrying on the society to wealth and prosperity, but of surmounting a hundred impertinent obstructions with which the folly of human laws too often incumbers its operations; though the effect of these obstructions is always more or less either to encroach upon its freedom, or to diminish its security.
>
> (*Wealth of Nations*, p. 540)

They may also, as we shall see, interfere with the operation of a "natural effort" by enervating the mind. Another threat to harmony is the growth of monopoly, which is the result of the above species of restrictive legislation. Monopoly always places the interests of the producer above those of the consumer, and thus represents an improper relation of part to whole, one to many. Godwin was to see monopoly as the inevitable consequence of the division of labour, itself the "offspring of avarice" (*Enquiry*, II, 513). Smith, conversely, regards it as resulting from governmental interference encouraging a high rate of profit for "the owners of the great mercantile capitals" (p. 612). This is bad, and it encourages in them a predilection for luxury and waste. The model of behaviour which the 'leaders and conductors" of industry do indeed hold out to their workers then becomes a negative one; frugality and moderation are destroyed as worthwhile ideals.

Smith's description of what happens to those who profit from the disturbance of the 'natural' progress of the division of labour, and its effects on those who look up to them as models, brings us to the point where the cyclic relation between economic and wider social developments must be accounted for. I am not qualified to be at all authoritative on this subject, but I do mean to try to bring out the centrality of Wordsworth's ideas as they relate to contemporary writings on political economy. This is one more way of emphasizing the importance of his polemic in historical terms.[13]

The argument about population will serve as a starting point. In *An Essay upon the Ways and Means of Supplying the War* (1695), Charles D'Avenant had argued that

> People are the real strength and riches of a country; . . . Where there are but few inhabitants, and a large territory, there is nothing but sloth and poverty; but when great numbers are confined to a narrow compass of ground, necessity puts them upon invention, frugality and industry; which, in a nation, are always recompensed with power and riches . . . Where countries are thinly inhabited, the people always grow proud, poor, lazy and effeminate; qualities which never fail to prepare a nation for foreign subjection.[14]

In thus putting forward a prospectus almost exactly contrary to that which is implicit in Wordsworth, D'Avenant is of course wearing his heart upon his sleeve. He is concerned to fill the ranks with redcoats, and the more the merrier. And the inferences and assumptions he makes reveal a direction not often echoed in the later and more major writers on civil society. Smith's model of the manufacturing economy based on the division of labour does not suggest that a dense population produces emulation and invention among all men; once division has taken place this becomes the privilege of the masters and inventors only. It is the rural workers in the more sparsely populated areas who have more chance to remain inventive and adaptable. Nor is it the case that a concentration of people was generally thought to entail the encouragement of frugality, which was more often seen as a feature of societies closed to commerce. Surplus production creates the opportunity for the satisfaction of needs beyond mere necessities, and this is the point at which desire and fantasy enter into the economic cycle.

The question of population is rejoined once again by Paley, whose *The Principles of Moral and Political Philosophy* had reached its twentieth edition by 1814. Paley notes "the tendency of nature, in the human species, to a continual increase of its numbers",[15] and sets out to examine the factors inhibiting or assisting this tendency. Among the latter he points out the desirability of tillage over pasture as able to support more people:

tillage, as an object of national care and encouragement, is universally preferable to pasturage, because the kind of provision which it yields, goes much further in the sustentation of human life. Tillage is also recommended by this additional advantage, that it affords employment to a much more numerous peasantry. Indeed, pasturage seems to be the art of a nation, either imperfectly civilised . . . or . . . declining from its summit by luxury and inactivity.

(II, 362–3)

Again, we see the clear contrast with Wordsworth, who is much more concerned with the changes in ownership brought about by the conversion of pasture to tillage, and not at all interested in stimulating a denser population, which would threaten the well-being of the mind as he describes it by providing too many prefigured forms in narrower limits of space and time. Moreover, the life of Wordsworth's mountain shepherds is strenuous, frugal and precariously balanced. It is town life which produces the ills Paley describes, "luxury and inactivity".

Like Adam Smith, Paley remains a defender of the primacy of agriculture over commerce and industry. Land is the ultimate source of all wealth, and its status must be maintained by a balance between the different interests in the national economy. Thus:

I believe it is true that agriculture never arrives at any considerable, much less at its highest, degree of perfection, where it is not connected with trade, that is, where the demand for the produce is not increased by the consumption of trading cities.

(II, 376)

The "whole system of commerce, vast and various as it is, hath no other public importance than its subserviency to this end" (p. 377). The argument again hinges on Paley's assumption of surplus production. More people can be maintained by the land than need to work on it, which is noticeably not the case in the marginal economy Wordsworth describes. Those who are not agricultural workers must

provide articles which, by tempting the desires, may stimulate the industry, and call forth the activity, of those upon the exertion of whose industry, and the application of whose faculties, the production of human provision depends.

(p. 373)

He goes on:

> It appears also, that it signifies nothing, as to the main purpose of trade, how superfluous the articles which it furnishes are; whether the want of them be real or imaginary; whether it be founded in nature or in opinion, in fashion, habit, or emulation: it is enough that they be actually desires and sought after.

(p. 374)

This introduction of the pattern of desire into the rural economy would have horrified Wordsworth. The superfluity of such articles and their subservience to fashion and emulation makes sure that 'possession' of what it is that they are thought to provide can never be ultimately attained. Fashion is unstable because it creates a self-image which is embodied in emblems rather than in authentic inner consciousness. Such emblems are functions of division, as we have seen with Wordsworth's surplice, and they encourage their bearers to derive their identity from how they are seen by others. They become 'figures', alienated from their own creative faculties, fixated on the products of prior figurings. And, in pursuit of these imaginary and unsubstantial gratifications, real effort is expended. As Coleridge argued, the "true advantages of Commerce consist in debauching the field Labourer with improportionable toil by exciting in him artificial Wants";[16] and that last word may be registered as a pun.

A sense of the interaction between commerce, luxury and the structure of desire is presented by Adam Smith as basic to human psychology. In *The Theory of Moral Sentiments* he places the need for approbation at the heart of the social contract. The primary social bond is our need to be approved of by others; fear of censure is the fundamental communal discipline. A problem suggests itself, however, in that one of the things we do in order to be approved of is to pursue wealth, and Smith indeed goes on to describe how it is that an intended principle of sympathy can so dominate an individual's behaviour as to disrupt his organic relation to society, and also his own peace of mind. Greatness (embodied by wealth) is envied by others even though it may become a destructive and restraining condition for the person experiencing it.[17] That person is then divided against himself, doing something for the sake of approbation which is contrary to authentic self-interest, so that the social bond actually sets in motion a process of alienation. Driven by an imagined self-image as "most in the view of general sympathy and attention", he behaves in a way which disrupts any positive relation between part and whole:

> And thus, place, that great object which divides the wives of aldermen, is the end of half the labours of human life; and is the cause of all the tumult and bustle, all the rapine and injustice, which avarice and ambition have introduced into this world.
>
> (p. 57)

At this point, Smith is close to defining a structure of desire at work in man's relation to society. He is impelled by a drive which pushes him further and further from the goal of authentic satisfaction to which it purports to be leading him. The goal is preserved as a focus of imagined gratification, even as actual experience moves further and further from it, backwards. "Power and riches" are

> ready every moment to burst into pieces, and to crush in their ruins their unfortunate possessor. They are immense fabrics, which it requires the labour of a life to raise, which threaten every moment to overwhelm the person that dwells in them, and which while they stand, though they may save him from some smaller inconveniences, can protect him from none of the severer inclemencies of the season. They keep off the summer shower, not the winter storm, but leave him always as much, and sometimes more exposed than before, to anxiety, to fear, and to sorrow; to diseases, to danger, and to death.
>
> (p. 183)

Smith does, indeed, manage to find something positive in this. The "deception" we preserve about the nature of power and riches, enforced as it is by the imagined approbation they will bring us, is what "rouses and keeps in continual motion the industry of mankind":

> It is this which first prompted them to cultivate the ground, to build houses, to found cities and commonwealths, and to invent

and improve all the sciences and arts, which ennoble and embellish human life; which have entirely changed the whole face of the globe, have turned the rude forests of nature into agreeable and fertile plains, and made the trackless and barren ocean a new fund of subsistence, and the great high road of communication to the different nations of the earth.

(pp. 183–4)

'Civilization', in other words, is a function of desire, of an impulse whose defining characteristic is that it is incapable of fulfilment. The same impulse operates in the arguments of *The Wealth of Nations*. We desire and search for gold in the face of the obvious fact that its value is based on its scarcity, which will almost certainly mean that we are wasting our time (p. 563). It is desire for what is forbidden, or made scarce by the interests of monopoly, which produces drunkenness; Englishmen are seldom drunk on ale, Frenchmen never on wine (pp. 492–3). Only the cultivation of desire leads to excess.

More positively, it is desire which comes athwart the cycle of circulation and exchange (and thus, implicitly, athwart one part of Smith's argument) by imposing frugality:

But the principle which prompts to save, is the desire of bettering our condition, a desire which, though generally calm and dispassionate, comes with us from the womb, and never leaves us till we go into the grave. In the whole interval which separates those two moments, there is scarce perhaps a single instant in which any man is so perfectly and completely satisfied with his situation, as to be without any wish of alteration or improvement, of any kind.

(p. 341)

The habit of frugality is also reinforced by the pressures of the need for approbation. Because others do not share the immediacy of our present wants, they tend to approve of our putting them aside for the sake of some future, promised end:

Hence arises that eminent esteem with which all men naturally regard a steady perseverance in the practice of frugality, industry, and application, though directed to no other purpose than the acquisition of fortune.

(*Moral Sentiments*, pp. 189–90)

In so doing, we do not threaten the equanimity of others by behaving in ways with which they cannot sympathize. Everyone respects everyone else's self-interest, and in fact this is the only thing which makes possible such frugal behaviour, since if it were not for the need to be approved of, no deferred future restoration would substitute for the urgency of present inclinations.

This might seem to put a stop to the compulsion toward expense and display. In fact, it is implicated with it in a cyclic way. As far as I can see, there are two mutually cancelling moments in Smith's explanation of the economic structure of the mind. The need for approbation (appealing to the self-interest of others) and our own long-term ambitions for wealth, encourage us to save, to defer spending. However, as we amass wealth we are also pressured to cut a figure, to spend on ornaments and attributes in order to display ourselves and to receive the respect of those who wish to be like us. This may be disastrous for a nation if, for example, the monarch, who is the most 'visible' of all objects of attention, thus expends his wealth. If a war should arise, the monarch will not then possess the capital to finance it, and he will be driven to call upon his subjects. In this way a national debt or sinking fund is set up, and such an innovation did in fact appear as a fact of life in the late seventeenth century. Because it introduced *credit* into the economy in a big way, it was widely seen as the institutional embodying of what I have called 'desire'. Credit encourages the perpetual deferral of one's returns, and Pocock (*The Machiavellian Moment*) has argued very convincingly that the national debt was seen as a real threat to the citizen in his attempt to uphold civic virtue and independent judgement, qualities dependent on frugality and immediate reciprocity in exchange. As exchange comes to be dominated by credit, so the present is mortgaged to an always deferred future. In *The Wealth of Nations* Smith opines that "a sinking fund, though instituted for the payment of old, facilitates very much the contracting of new debts" (p. 916).

The national debt, the deferral of all 'realization' to an ever-receding future, is in this way the macrocosmic image of a process Smith identifies as dangerously implicit within the human psyche. Paley too saw a threat to self-sufficiency in the communal effects of luxury. As soon as attributes are seen as essences, accessories as necessities, figures as realities, then each man feels obliged

to comply with the example of his equals, and to maintain that appearance which the custom of society requires. This obligation

creates such a demand upon his income, and withal adds so much
to the cost and burden of a family, as to put it out of his power to
marry, with the prospect of continuing his habits, or of maintaining his place and situation in the world. We see, in this
description, the cause which induces men to waste their lives in a
barren celibacy; and this cause, which impairs the very source of
population, is justly placed to the account of luxury.

(II, 358)

Here, procreative energies are literally deadened, converted to the
pursuit of lifeless things. The mind becomes, to use a prophetic
word, 'fetishized'. Whether the result of luxury be celibacy, as here,
or some other form of dissolution or deactivation, such as happens to
Luke in Wordsworth's 'Michael' when he goes to the town, the
destructive effect is the same.

As has been said, the possibility of commerce, out of which desire
for luxury may be generated, was seen to be the result of surplus
production. Agricultural workers are driven by the desire for
luxuries to produce more than they need, so that it may be
exchanged for manufactured commodities. This basic principle of
contemporary economic theory emphasizes the point of
Wordsworth's stress on the virtues of subsistence farming, with no
surplus produced — or at least, only enough to help out the odd
needy neighbour. As long as there is nothing to exchange or sell,
then the dangerous object-displacements fuelled by desire cannot
take place. The harsher the climate and the landscape, the less time
there is for wasted speculation over what others possess, and the
more sequestered and cut off from the world the landscape is, the
more it is a 'cave', the less exposure there is to the alternative
commercial life of those others. That is why going to the town can be
a disaster. The place of desire in Smith's theory of the mind may
indicate the extent to which Wordsworth thought it a threat, all too
natural to the psyche in any but the most stringent and unremitting
environments. The unbalancing or fixation of the process of
figurative attribution is always a risk, even for the healthiest mind in
the most perfect surroundings. The career of Martha Ray shows this
happening as a result of severe emotional upset, and the minor
transgressions of the speaking 'I' of Wordsworth's meditative poems
intimate a tendency to disequilibrium in all imaginative or figurative consciousness. Those risks are magnified many times when
the mind is removed from the sources of creative external discipline.

Surplus production is itself most obviously a consequence of divided labour. Twelve men combined make many more pins in a day than twelve men separately carrying through every part of the process. No division, then the less chance of surplus, and trade, and the mental instabilities that go with the pursuit of luxuries. Thus Steuart, like Wordsworth, looks to a small social group (where there is less incentive to divide) as a paradigm for the positive exclusion of commerce in commending the Spartan constitution. Lycurgus, he says,

> was no stranger to the seducing influence of luxury; and plainly foresaw, that the consequences of industry, which procures to mankind a great variety of new objects of desire, and a wonderful facility in satisfying them, would easily root out the principles he had endeavoured to instil into his countrymen, if the state of simplicity should ever come to be corrupted by foreign communications.
>
> (*Works*, I, 341)

The censoring of the foreign could be applied to countries — as Johnson expressed a fear of foreign trade corrupting the language by the introduction of new terms — or to divisions within a state, such as the tension between town and country. Thus the chosen vale is veiled, obscure, protected, like a cave.

There were many debates about social organization which were implicated in the evaluation of the effects of commerce and of the division of labour. For example, the respective advantages of militias and standing armies were urgently debated (as by Paley, *Principles*, II, 429–36). Surplus wealth in the hands of the head of state enabled him to finance a standing army. This might indeed be a more efficient defence against foreign invasion (divided labour being generally more efficient) but it also provided a force which could be used against the people. Moreover, just as this directly erodes political independence, it was also felt by some to be an attack on individual civic virtue, that "self-dependent power" to which Johnson adverted in providing the closing lines of Goldsmith's 'The Deserted Village'. The occasional bearing of arms in a militia was in this sense seen as an important element in the polymorphous personality of the complete man. It was, of course, a militia which had challenged the British in America, and one which fought because it cared rather than because it was being paid. We can see again the model of the many in the one, the ideal person who can be hunter, farmer, philosopher and poet, threatened by divided labour and the production of wealth, itself used to further divide man from man, and from himself.

We can now estimate the full range and coherence of Wordsworth's case for the positive benefits of life among lakes and mountains. I have described at length in the earlier parts of the book the importance he attached to the mind's having time to operate upon what it is given, adapting itself to existing figures and refiguring them anew. There must be time for the 'second look', and space so that mind and eye shall not be too pressured by distractions. This is the basic psychological model with which Wordsworth operates. It involves, I have tried to show, definite political and economic policies, implicit and explicit. Owner-occupiers in small societies are able to live with the minimum amount of corporate organization, and thus with the minimum of *representation*, thus avoiding the problems Godwin specified as arising when identity is transferred from individual to "party". This kind of political autonomy can of course be causally implicated with the ideal epistemological model described above; without the one, the other will not be possible — we will start to perceive passively, and merely receive the figurings of others as our preconstituted reality. Further, the Godwinian perspective is supplemented and further realized by an economic conviction which seals this model of the perfect incorporation of the many and the one. Owner-occupiers in marginal areas, with testing climates and sparse resources, will not produce a surplus. This has two immediate consequences. First, they will remain a small society, since the land is not rich enough to support a larger number of people; and second, they will not experience the temptations consequent upon trade, since they have nothing to exchange or sell.

This is a stern vision, perhaps even a punishing one. We should never forget the image of labour as the primal curse and the consequence of disobedience, its basic implication in the mythology of transgression. But, if Wordsworth invokes something of this mythology, he provides also a mode by which pain is converted to pleasure, the two indeed becoming inseparable in the properly creative life cycle. And the integrity and coherence of his vision is, I hope, clear. As the individual mind is described in its experiences of figuring and refiguring, so that mind is contextualized by a wider range of situations in politics and society. I hope it will now be apparent that the analysis of the figurative, both in epistemology and aesthetics, as it was facing the problems posed by a potentially (or actually) intentionalist psychology, appears to relate very closely to the arguments in political economy around the theorized implications and observed realities of commercial societies. As metaphor threatens to encode one person's figure as another's reality, dislocating any potential social contract based on shared perceptions and values, so divided labour disturbs that contract by eroding individual flexibility of mind, and (Smith's ideal paradigm excepted) by producing a movement of wealth from the many to the few, who are thus engaged in reproducing among the many the very habits of mind which will keep them in their positions of inferiority. The 'figures' of the few form the 'reality' for the many:

> The man of rank and distinction . . . is observed by all the world. Every body is eager to look at him, and to conceive, at least by sympathy, that joy and exultation with which his circumstances naturally inspire him. His actions are the objects of the public care.

> > (*Moral Sentiments*, p. 51)

So compulsive is this principle of sympathy, that even tyrants inspire affection and respect, and are removed by their subjects only after the most extreme transgressions (p. 53). Smith accounts, in fact, both for the presence of divided interest and the efficiency of mystification, implications not at all foreseen by the pin-maker ' collective. The rulers and the ruled are posited each by the other in the imaginary gratifications of approbation.

As the worker ceases to be encouraged or allowed to use his imagination for the deconstruction and reunification of what is put before him, and to validate and modify for himself the 'figures' which others have created as their own, motivated, companionable forms, so he becomes himself a part of that figured view, reduced in himself from whole to part. Thus Marx:

> a worker who performs the same simple operation for the whole of his life converts his body into the automatic, one-sided implement of that operation.

> > (*Capital*, p. 458)

Such figures dominate the pages of Dickens' novels. Not all of them are factory workers, of course, for they speak for an even later stage of one-dimensionality, whereby it has become the moral and cultural standard of excellence and condition of survival for the whole of society. At this point the interaction of the many and the one has almost come to a halt. Hartley had earlier described the destructive consequences of this for the individual mind:

> The perpetual Recurrency of particular Ideas and Terms makes the Vibrations belonging thereto become more than ordinarily vivid, converts feeble Associations into strong ones, and enhances the secondary Ideas of Dignity and Esteem, which adhere to them, at the same time that all these things are diminished in respect of other Ideas and Terms, that are kept out of View; and which, if they were to recur in due Proportion, would oppose and correct many Associations in the particular Study, which are made not according to the reality of things, and keep down our exorbitant Opinions of its Importance.[18]

He touches also on the mode of operation of mystification and false consciousness; as the field which defines 'reality' is contracted, and as identity itself comes to be dependent upon fewer and fewer, or even a single idea or image, so that image becomes the image of dignity and the focus of esteem. Whether the process be self-incurred or the product of external forces such as employment, the worrying implication is that the mind so affected can come to worship the very terms of its own repression. Although the corrective influence of alternative figures has been removed, the same energies can go into what is left, and the mind, if it be active at all, now actively miscreates, by omission.

With all these preoccupations now in mind, it is worth looking finally at another passage from *The Prelude*, that describing the fair beneath Helvellyn, which stands as a sort of antiphonal contrast to the experience of Bartholomew fair, in the city. This scene shows forth the ideal interpenetration of man and natural environment, and consequently of man with man. Godwin had criticized the dense grouping of men in an exactly Wordsworthian spirit:

> It is accumulation, that forms men into one common mass, and makes them fit to be played upon like a brute machine. Were this stumbling-block removed, each man would be united to his

neighbour, in love and mutual kindness, a thousand times more
than now: but each man would think and judge for himself.

(*Enquiry*, II, 466)

Conversely, at Helvellyn fair, sparseness and singleness are the
order of the day:

> Crowd seems it, solitary Hill! to thee,
> Though but a little Family of Men,
> Twice twenty, with their Children and their Wives,
> And here and there a Stranger interspers'd.

(VIII, 6–9)

Strangers are occasional, not disruptive and certainly not constitutive of this society. Bargaining and even selling goes on, but it is
neither highly developed nor unchallenged:

> The Heifer lows uneasy at the voice
> Of a new Master, bleat the flocks aloud.

(ll. 23–4)

Even inarticulate nature participates in the protest against
exchange, such is the sympathy developed between authentically
related created forms. The "sweet lass of the Valley" (l. 37), who is
indeed selling the produce of her father's orchard, does so only once
a year, "On that day only to such office *stooping*" (l. 40); the italics
are mine. As a result, she never becomes habituated to what she is
doing,

> and walks round
> Among the crowd, half pleas'd with, half ashamed
> Of her new calling, blushing restlessly.

(ll. 41–3)

The whole society, which is thus *internally* untainted by commercial
relations and the problems of luxury, since exchange by selling
always remains innocent and incipient — "blushing restlessly" —
and since there is little to waste money on anyway — "Booths there
are none" (l. 25) — is also framed as a whole by the immanent
discipline of natural forms:

                                    Immense
              Is the Recess, the circumambient World
              Magnificent, by which they are embraced.
              They move about upon the soft green field:
              How little They, they and their doings seem,
              Their herds and flocks about them, they themselves,
              And all that they can further or obstruct!

                                                    (ll. 46–52)

The purity of this commonwealth is thus determined twice over, by
its internal economy having no surplus and spawning no luxury,
and by the larger environment which is so dominant as to seem
largely untouchable by whatever human deviations might create in
the way of furtherings or obstructions.

   This society is on the margins of civilization, so called, protected
by its chosen vale, and thus as a prototype of the whole it is of
marginal conviction. Wordsworth later notes that

                              the rural ways
              And manners which it was my chance to see
              In childhood were severe and unadorn'd,
              The unluxuriant produce of a life
              Intent on little but substantial needs,
              Yet beautiful, and beauty that was felt.

                                                    (ll. 205–10)

It is not that the society thus described is being corrupted of itself
and from within; rather, it is being destroyed by the adverse
alternative, by the world wherein man is no longer the 'symbol' of
his species, but a dispensable element in some mechanical process
controlled by others among his fellows. It is divided labour which
maintains the commercial economy which generates luxury, as it
also erodes the minds and bodies of those finding employment
within it. Ferguson, like Schiller in fact, argued for the necessity of
putting aside individual interest when the survival or integrity of the
whole might be at stake, and in doing so he conflated the two
dominant classes of images which, then as now, were used to
describe or insinuate the nature of the individual's relation to that
whole:

   He is only part of a whole; and the praise which we think due to
   his virtue, is but a branch of that more general commendation we

bestow on the member of a body, on the part of a fabric or engine, for being well fitted to occupy its place, and to produce its effect.

(Essay, p. 57–8)

This conflation conceals a crucial difference of policy. If the hand or foot be disabled, we do not cut it off, except as a last resort, but try to bring it back to health. We do so because it is alive, and its presence is organically related to the body of which it is a part. It is, in other words, a 'symbol' in the Coleridgean sense. If, however, we break a light bulb or lose a screw in a "fabric or engine", we replace the part without any concern for the specificity of what is discarded. To think of human beings in either of these two separate ways is to make a decision bringing with it obvious and important ethical consequences. Is a criminal, for example, or a worker, considered as a part of a body to be nurtured and restored to health if possible, or as a part of an engine, to be replaced as soon as judged deficient? Is the individual concerned a 'symbol', essentially related to what he represents in the body politic? Or is he a metonym, a mere attribute or function standing at a distance from what he represents, and therefore replaceable without negative consequences for the ulterior 'whole'?

The enduring significance of this decision, its place in political and social rhetoric now as then, will be obvious. The figurative operations which I have specified historically in Wordsworth may be seen as the foundation of a cultural epistemology whose essential features have not yet become a thing of the past. The question of the degree to which we are figured or figure ourselves remains very much an open one, indeed it is the theatre of our differences. For the Romantics, the process of figuring constitutes an alternative to the possibility of passive perception. The essentially creative nature of the mind means that without it, moreover, there would be mere vacancy. Shelley, or his narrator, addresses Mont Blanc at the end of the poem which takes its name:

> And what were thou, and earth, and stars, and sea,
> If to the human mind's imaginings
> Silence and solitude were vacancy?[19]

The question recurs because it remains unanswered, thus ensuring the likelihood of future restorations by its readers. But the celebration of companionable forms as alternatives to nothingness or materialism is not a sufficient characterization of the Romantic insight into the workings of the figurative. In Wordsworth above all, and I think in Blake, we find a complicated recognition of the difficulties which conspire to convert the figured into the real, and thus to divert the mind's most promising resources for renovation into prefigured channels. We can see here the beginnings of an analysis of what was later to be called 'ideology', appearing in the play Wordsworth establishes between the exhilaration of new perceptions and their incipient conversion into socially divisive, or orthodox or habitual, ways of seeing. This is the spirit in which Nietzsche was to observe that some answers seem final in the construction of the real:

> A morality, a mode of living tried and *proved* by long experience and testing, at length enters consciousness as a law, as *dominating* — And therewith the entire group of related values and states enters into it: it becomes venerable, unassailable, holy, true; it is part of its development that its origin should be forgotten — That is a sign it has become master.[20]

The mystification of origins follows the mastery of signs. There is no more dissolving and dissipating in order to create anew; the mind perceives products instead of enacting processes.

Which figures have achieved mastery, and which of them are still open to regeneration by innocent perception and the second look? Nietzsche tells us that the ones which rule us we cannot know, and the fact that we never do quite agree about our authority for making the choices which decide this problem of fence-sitting may itself indicate that we live as the parts of a fabric or engine, rather than as the members of a body. Ambivalence itself may be the sure sign of a mastery hidden, or made hidden, from our view. If the hand should rebel, should the stomach tell it what to do? Who belongs with the stomach and who with the hand? There are two epigraphs standing on the title-page of this book. In one, Blake offers an explanation of seeing determined by being which is both an analysis of individual limitations and an expression of revolutionary potential in the human imagination. In the other, we see Polonius obligingly changing his mind under pressure from Hamlet's comparisons. Mocked as he certainly is, and confused by Hamlet's madness (whether for real or not), there is yet something of an excuse for his behaviour. Hamlet is the figure of power, and as such may determine how things are to be seen; those around him find it opportune to comply, rather than to insist on figuring for themselves. The masters make the rules, and even wise men may be carried with them. If the 'real' is a figured thing, the product of a selective and motivated perception, can we also figure it out, reaching back to a point of innocence and a new beginning? About this aspect of the human mind's imaginings Wordsworth had much to say. Because he is writing a literature of complicity, wherein understanding must precede outrage, he also had much to say on which of us are prisoners, which of us are guards, and which of us are both.

Notes

INTRODUCTION

1. See my account of the poem in *Irony and Authority in Romantic Poetry* (London: Macmillan, 1979), pp. 103–8. I have on occasions referred the reader to discussions carried out in that book, but have tried to make sure that the argument here is intelligible without such reference outside.
2. *The Poetical Works of William Wordsworth*, ed. E. de Selincourt, 5 vols (Oxford: Clarendon Press, 1940–9), II, 248. This edition is henceforth cited as *PW*.
3. *The Prelude*, ed. E. de Selincourt, 2nd ed. rev. Helen Darbishire (Oxford: Clarendon Press, 1959). All references are to the 1805 text, by book and line number, unless otherwise stated.
4. On this subject see Georg Lukács, *History and Class Consciousness: Studies in Marxist Dialectics*, trans. Rodney Livingstone (Cambridge, Mass: MIT Press, 1971), p. 134f.
5. *An Introduction to the Principles of Morals and Legislation* (New York: Hafner Publishing Co., 1948), pp. 299–300.
6. See *Irony and Authority*, pp. 42–6.
7. *Preliminary Discourse on the Positive Spirit* (1844), trans. W.M.W. Call (London: The Positivist Library, 1883), pp. 27–8.
8. *The Complete Works of William Hazlitt*, ed. P. P. Howe, 21 vols (London & Toronto: J. M. Dent, 1930–34), IV, 122.
9. See, for example, Keith Tribe, *Land, Labour and Economic Discourse* (London: Routledge & Kegan Paul, 1978), chapter one.
10. *On the Constitution of the Church and State*, ed. John Colmer (London and Princeton: Routledge & Kegan Paul and Princeton Univ. Press, 1978), p. 20.
11. See *The Encyclopaedia of Philosophy*, ed. Paul Edwards (London and New York: Macmillan and The Free Press, 1967), article on 'Intentionality' (IV, 201–4).

CHAPTER I

1. *Coleridge: Poetical Works*, ed. E. H. Coleridge (Oxford, London, New York: Oxford Univ. Press, 1969), pp. 178–81.
2. Thomas Reid, *Essays on the Intellectual Powers of Man* (Cambridge, Mass., and London: MIT Press, 1969), p. 792.
3. Stephen Prickett, *Coleridge and Wordsworth: The Poetry of Growth* (Cambridge: Cambridge Univ. Press, 1970), pp. 102–8, makes a case for Coleridge's use of the word 'joy' as invoking a specifically religious experience.
4. Could Coleridge have read Kant's book before writing his poem? The

evidence argues against this, though it is not conclusive. Elinor S. Shaffer, *'Kubla Khan' and 'The Fall of Jerusalem'* (Cambridge: Cambridge Univ. Press, 1975), pp. 30, 48, has pointed out the potential importance of Coleridge's acquaintance with Beddoes, who indeed wrote in to the editors of *The Monthly Magazine* appealing for an English translation of Kant, and offering a specimen of his own translation of a passage from the third *Critique*; not, it must be said, a passage of central significance for my particular problem here. The letter appeared in vol. 4 (May 1796), 265–7. In a letter to Thomas Poole of that very month, Coleridge claims to be studying German, with the idea of making a translation of "all the works of Schiller". See *Collected Letters of Samuel Taylor Coleridge*, ed. Earl Leslie Griggs, 6 vols (Oxford: Clarendon Press, 1956–71), I, 209. Coleridge might have learned something of Kant from reading or talking about Schiller, or Kant, with Beddoes. Or he might not, and the conjunctions I am arguing for could be the result of a coincidence. Coleridge's acquaintance with associationism goes some way, as I have said, toward accounting for the sequence of events in the poem. It is the recollection of former pleasures which 'associates' delight both with what the ramblers might be feeling and with the imperceptibly accumulating sensations of the immediate physical environment, the bower. Further, when Coleridge invokes "the soul" (l. 66) he is touching a chord not to be found in Kant's remarks on the aesthetic, which have no theological context. But, in the movement of attention away from the contingent objects and towards the faculty behind the experience of joy, there is certainly an emphasis analogous to that found in *The Critique of Judgement* as it investigates what can be shared of the aesthetic. My own sense is that the force of this analogy suggests a response to a commonly held historical preoccupation with the status of consensus among users of the imagination.

5. *The Critique of Judgement*, trans. James Creed Meredith, 2 vols in one (1928; rpt. Oxford: Clarendon Press, 1952, 1973), I, 43. Parentheses of the German are taken from *Immanuel Kants Werke*, ed. E. Cassirer, 11 vols (Hildesheim: H. A. Gerstenberg, 1973), V, 273.
6. In this context, however, "will" may ask to be glossed in a lower, less self-conscious sense, as synonymous with "pleasures"; thus remaining closer to "volition".
7. *The Excursion*, III, 538; in *PW*, V, 92.
8. *The Prose Works of William Wordsworth*, ed. W. J. B. Owen and Jane Worthington Smyser, 3 vols (Oxford: Clarendon Press, 1974), III, 26. Henceforth cited as *PrW*.
9. *Home at Grasmere*, ed. Beth Darlington, The Cornell Wordsworth (Ithaca, N.Y. and Hassocks, Sussex: Cornell Univ. Press and Harvester Press, 1977), pp. 60–2 (ms. B, ll. 381–97).
10. Frances Ferguson, *Wordsworth: Language as Counter-Spirit* (New Haven and London: Yale Univ. Press, 1977), pp. 53–68. There is much in this book which anticipates my own argument about Wordsworth's ethical discriminations between various kinds of figurative activity; see, for example, the reading of 'A Morning Exercise' (pp. 56–61).
11. One of the most notable adumbrations of this question by Wordsworth himself is perhaps in the letter describing the 'With Ships the Sea' sonnet, which I have discussed in *Irony and Authority in Romantic Poetry*, pp. 135–7.

12. *An Essay Concerning Human Understanding*, ed. Peter H. Nidditch, corr. ed. (Oxford: Clarendon Press, 1979), Bk. II, ch. 8, p. 137.

13. Similarly, the fourth of the 'Poems on the Naming of Places' chronicles the exchange between two different 'uses' of nature, one for fantasy and one for subsistence. Again, see *Irony and Authority in Romantic Poetry*, pp. 72–6, for an extended account of this poem.

14. Frances Ferguson, in an account of this poem (pp. 42–53) which again I find so complementary to my own, thinks that Leonard is "reading the signs of change in nature quite properly" (p. 47). There may, however, be no action or situation except as feeling makes it; and whatever the 'real' may be, what is selected for attention may still be specifically motivated. Leonard was indeed driven from his native valley by a change in the economic organization of the locale, and this could in fact have wrought real changes in the landscape; but this does not seem to be what he notices.

15. That it may not be wild nature, but a grove of trees planted by man, is suggested by l. 34, and adds another level of irony to the situation.

16. G. W. F. Hegel, *Early Theological Writings*, trans. T. M. Knox (1948; rpt. Philadelphia: Univ. of Pennsylvania Press, 1971), p. 275.

17. The sea appears again in conjunction with death in a sonnet probably written in 1828, 'A Tradition of Oker Hill in Darley Dale, Derbyshire' (*PW*, III, 49). The two brothers who set off in different directions, having planted trees as the emblems of their affection, never meet again,

> Until their spirits mingled in the sea
> That to itself takes all, Eternity.

Similarly, the churchyard is compared to the shore of a smooth sea (*PrW*, II, 63–4), though one ruffled by a sense of the unquiet forms beneath.

18. Ben Ross Schneider Jnr., *Wordsworth's Cambridge Education* (Cambridge: Cambridge Univ. Press, 1957), p. 23, gives details of the required dress of the late eighteenth-century student, who was indeed a veritable clothes-screen. Things haven't changed so much.

CHAPTER 2

1. *The Whole Art of Rhetoric*, in *The English Works of Thomas Hobbes*, ed. Sir William Molesworth, 11 vols (London, 1839–45), VI, 496.

2. James Burnet, Lord Monboddo, *Of the Origin and Progress of Language*, 6 vols (London, 1773–92), III, 41.

3. *The Friend*, ed. Barbara E. Rooke, 2 vols (London and Princeton: Routledge & Kegan Paul and Princeton Univ. Press, 1969), I, 455.

4. Alexander Bryan Johnson, *A Treatise on Language* (1836), ed. David Rynin (Berkeley and Los Angeles: Univ. of California Press, 1947), pp. 56–7.

5. At least, such seems to be the argument from *Leviathan*, from which I quote. The *De Homine* has a significant difference of emphasis:

Thus the first man by his own will imposed names on just a few animals, namely, the ones that God led before him to look at; then on other things, as one or another species of things offered itself to his senses; these names, having been accepted, were handed down from fathers to their sons, who also devised others.

See *Man and Citizen: Thomas Hobbes' 'De Homine' and 'De Cive'*, trans. Charles T. Wood, T. S. K. Scott-Craig, Bernard Gert, ed. Bernard Gert (1972; rpt. New York and Hassocks, Sussex: Humanities Press and Harvester Press, 1978), p. 38.
6. *The Collected Works of Dugald Stewart*, ed. Sir William Hamilton, 11 vols (Edinburgh: Constable, 1854), V, 185.
7. Hugh Blair, *Lectures on Rhetoric and Belles Lettres*, 13th ed., 2 vols (London, 1819), I, 292.
8. *Johnson: Poetry and Prose*, ed. Mona Wilson, 2nd ed. (London: Rupert Hart-Davis, 1957), p. 314.
9. See, for example, the article on metaphor in the *Encyclopédie, ou dictionnaire raisonné des sciences, des arts, et des métiers* (Paris, 1751–7), X, 436–40.
10. *Collected Works of John Stuart Mill*, general ed. F. E. L. Priestley, in progress (Toronto and London: Univ. of Toronto Press and Routledge & Kegan Paul, 1963–), VIII, 644.
11. *On the Origin of Language: Jean Jacques Rousseau, 'Essay on the Origin of Languages', Johann Gottfried Herder, 'Essay on the Origin of Language'*, trans. John H. Moran and Alexander Gode (New York: Frederick Ungar, 1966), p. 12.
12. For a very useful account, see James H. Stam, *Inquiries into the Origin of Language: The Fate of a Question* (New York, Hagerstown, San Francisco, London: Harper & Row, 1976), pp. 80–2, 88–93.
13. *Biographia Literaria*, ed. J. Shawcross, 2 vols, corr. rpt. (London &c.: Oxford Univ. Press, 1954), II, 115–16.
14. On primary and secondary qualities, see also Ralph Cudworth, *The True Intellectual System of the Universe* (1678), trans. John Harrison, 3 vols (London, 1845), I, 85–6. Edwin A. Burtt, *The Metaphysical Foundations of Modern Physical Science*, rev. ed. (London: Routledge & Kegan Paul, 1932), pp. 73–80, shows that Galileo's *Il Saggiatore* uses the distinction in a way which does insist on the subjectivity of secondary qualities, thus going further than Locke, who preserves a model of qualities determining ideas by powers.
15. Arthur Schopenhauer, *The World as Will and Representation*, trans. E. F. J. Payne, 2 vols (1958; rpt. New York: Dover Publications, 1966), II, 19–20. Where I have parenthesized Schopenhauer's German, I cite from *Sämtliche Werke*, ed. P. Deussen and E. Hochstetter, 10 vols (Munich, 1911–13).
16. *Goethe's Theory of Colours*, trans. Charles Lock Eastlake (1840; rpt. London: Frank Cass & Co., 1967), pp. xxxviii–ix.
17. Rt. Hon. William Drummond, *Academical Questions, Volume One* (London, 1805), pp. 90, 375.
18. *Critique of Practical Reason*, trans. Lewis White Beck (Indianapolis and New York: Bobbs-Merrill, 1956), p. 9; *Werke*, V, 9.
19. *Aesthetics: Lectures on Fine Art*, trans. T. M. Knox, 2 vols continuously paginated (Oxford: Clarendon Press, 1975), p. 38. Any citations of Hegel's German will be from *Sämtliche Werke*, Jubiläumsausgabe, facs. newly ed. H. Glockner, 25 vols. (Stuttgart, 1935–71).

20. *On the Aesthetic Education of Man*, trans. Elizabeth M. Wilkinson and L. A. Willoughby (Oxford: Clarendon Press, 1967), p. 147; see also p. 183.
21. *Science of Knowledge*, trans. Peter Heath and John Lachs (New York: Meredith Corporation, 1970), pp. 14–15. German citations are from *Johann Gottlieb Fichtes sämmtliche Werke*, ed. I. H. Fichte, 8 vols (Berlin, 1845); here, I, 433.
22. *Hegel's Philosophy of Mind*, trans. William Wallace and A. V. Miller (Oxford: Clarendon Press, 1971), p. 156.
23. Compare, for example, *Phenomenology of Spirit*, trans. A. V. Miller (Oxford: Clarendon Press, 1977), pp. 109–11.
24. See *Irony and Authority in Romantic Poetry*, pp. 143–50.
25. *Lay Sermons*, ed. R. J. White (London and Princeton: Routledge & Kegan Paul and Princeton Univ. Press, 1972), pp. 29–30. See also pp. 73, 79, and *On the Constitution of the Church and State*, p. 120.
26. *Aids to Reflection, in the Formation of a Manly Character on the several grounds of Prudence, Morality and Religion*, ed. Thomas Fenby (Liverpool: Edward Howell, 1883), p. 45. See also pp. 181–2, 229.
27. *Confessions of an Inquiring Spirit*, ed. H. N. Coleridge (London, 1840), p. 94.
28. *Life of Johnson*, ed. R. W. Chapman, corr. ed. J. D. Fleeman (Oxford, London, New York: Oxford Univ. Press, 1970), p. 443.
29. *The Complete Works of Shelley*, ed. Roger Ingpen and Walter E. Peck, 10 vols (1926; rpt. New York and London: Gordian Press, 1965), VII, 116.
30. I do not mean to take up the issue of Shelley's platonism here; a very useful statement of the terms of the debate is to be found in John W. Wright, *Shelley's Myth of Metaphor* (Athens, Ga.: Univ. of Georgia Press, 1970). My comments here are very much in the spirit of Wright's argument.
31. *Basic Writings of Nietzsche*, trans. and ed. Walter Kaufmann (New York: Random House, 1968), p. 393.

CHAPTER 3

1. *Hegel's Science of Logic*, trans. A. V. Miller (London and New York: George Allen & Unwin and Humanities Press, 1969), p. 172; *Werke*, IV, 203. The whole account of attraction and repulsion (pp. 164–84), each posited by the other in mutual subsistence, is an application of the model of 'many in one' to the theory of the physical world.
2. *Culture and Anarchy*, ed. J. Dover Wilson, corr. ed. (Cambridge, London, New York, Melbourne: Cambridge Univ. Press, 1935), p. 37.
3. Emile Durkheim, *The Division of Labor in Society*, trans. George Simpson (New York and London: Macmillan, 1933), p. 26.
4. Adam Ferguson, *An Essay on the History of Civil Society*, ed. Duncan Forbes (Edinburgh: Edinburgh Univ. Press, 1966), pp. 271–2.
5. *Enquiry Concerning Political Justice and its Influence on Morals and Happiness*, facs. of the 3rd ed., corr., ed. F. E. L. Priestley, 3 vols (Toronto: Univ. of Toronto Press, 1946), I, xxvi.
6. *The Letters of William and Dorothy Wordsworth: The Early Years, 1787–1805*, ed. E. de Selincourt, 2nd ed. rev. Chester L. Shaver (Oxford: Clarendon Press, 1967), pp. 314–15.

7. Karl Marx, Friedrich Engels, *Collected Works*, in progress (London: Lawrence & Wishart, 1975—), V, 47.

8. Compare *Capital. Volume One*, trans. Ben Fowkes (New York: Random House, 1977), p. 548:

> Factory work exhausts the nervous system to the uttermost; at the same time, it does away with the many-sided play of the muscles, and confiscates every atom of freedom, both in bodily and in intellectual activity. Even the lightening of the labour becomes an instrument of torture, since the machine does not free the worker from the work, but rather deprives the work itself of all content.

9. *John Millar of Glasgow, 1735–1801. His Life and Thought and his Contribution to Sociological Analysis*, ed. William C. Lehmann (Cambridge: Cambridge Univ. Press, 1960), p. 380.

10. Sir James Steuart, *Works Political, Metaphysical, and Chronological*, ed. Sir James Steuart the younger, 6 vols (London, 1805), I, 161.

11. Adam Smith, *An Inquiry into the Nature and Causes of the Wealth of Nations*, ed. R. H. Campbell, A. S. Skinner, W. B. Todd, 2 vols continuously paginated (Oxford: Clarendon Press, 1976), pp. 143–4.

12. *Lectures on Jurisprudence*, ed. R. L. Meek, D. D. Raphael, P. G. Stein (Oxford: Clarendon Press, 1978), p. 494. See also p. 355.

13. There is no more stimulating and comprehensive starting point than J. G. A. Pocock's work on this subject. See, especially, *Politics, Language, and Time: Essays on Political Thought and History* (London: Methuen, 1972), chs. 3 and 4 (pp. 80–147); and, yet more centrally, *The Machiavellian Moment: Florentine Political Thought and the Atlantic Republican Tradition* (Princeton: Princeton Univ. Press, 1975), chs. 13 and 14 (pp. 423–505). Pocock's account has informed, as his conclusions relate to, everything I have to say in the rest of this chapter. See also John Sekora, *Luxury: The Concept in Western Thought, Eden to Smollett* (Baltimore and London: The John Hopkins Univ. Press, 1977), especially chs 2 and 3 (pp. 63–131).

14. *The Political and Commercial Works of that celebrated writer Charles D'Avenant, LL.D.*, ed. Sir Charles Whitworth, 5 vols (London, 1771), I, 73–4.

15. William Paley, *The Principles of Moral and Political Philosophy*, 20th ed., 2 vols (London, 1814), II, 349.

16. *Lectures 1795 on Politics and Religion*, ed. Lewis Patton and Peter Mann (London and Princeton: Routledge & Kegan Paul and Princeton Univ. Press, 1971), p. 223.

17. *The Theory of Moral Sentiments*, ed. D. D. Raphael and A. L. Macfie (Oxford: Clarendon Press, 1976), pp. 50–1.

18. David Hartley, *Observations on Man, his Frame, his Duty, and his Expectations*, 2 vols (London: 1749), I, 397.

19. *Poetical Works*, ed. Thomas Hutchinson, corr. ed. G. M. Matthews (London, Oxford, New York: Oxford Univ. Press, 1970), p. 535.

20. *The Will to Power*, trans. Walter Kaufmann and R. J. Hollingdale (New York: Random House, 1968), pp. 277–8.

Bibliography

Arnold, Matthew, *Culture and Anarchy*, ed. John Dover Wilson. Corr. ed. Cambridge, London, New York, Melbourne: Cambridge Univ. Press, 1935.

Bentham, Jeremy, *An Introduction to the Principles of Morals and Legislation*, New York: Hafner Publishing Co, 1948.

Blair, Hugh, *Lectures on Rhetoric and Belles Lettres*, 13th ed., 2 vols, London, 1819.

Boswell, James, *Life of Johnson*, ed. R. W. Chapman, corr. ed. J. D. Fleeman, Oxford, London, New York: Oxford Univ. Press, 1970.

Boyle, Robert, *The Origine of Forms and Qualities*, 2nd ed. Oxford, 1667.

Burtt, Edwin A., *The Metaphysical Foundations of Modern Physical Science*, rev. ed. London: Routledge & Kegan Paul, 1932.

Coleridge, Samuel Taylor, *Aids to Reflection, in the Formation of a Manly Character on the several grounds of Prudence, Morality and Religion*, ed. Thomas Fenby, Liverpool: Edward Howell, 1883.

—— *Biographia Literaria*, ed. J. Shawcross. Corr. rpt, 2 vols, London, & c.: Oxford Univ. Press, 1954.

—— *Collected Letters of Samuel Taylor Coleridge*, ed. Earl Leslie Griggs, 6 vols. Oxford: Clarendon Press, 1956–71.

—— *Coleridge: Poetical Works*, ed. E. H. Coleridge, Oxford, London, New York: Oxford Univ. Press, 1969.

—— *The Collected Works of Samuel Taylor Coleridge*, ed. Kathleen Coburn (with Bart Winer), 16 vols (in progress). London and Princeton: Routledge & Kegan Paul and Princeton Univ. Press, 1969—

Vol. IV, *The Friend*, ed. Barbara E. Rooke, 2 vols, 1969.

Vol. I, *Lectures 1795 on Politics and Religion*, ed. Lewis Patton and Peter Mann, 1971.

Vol. VI, *Lay Sermons*, ed. R. J. White, 1972.

Vol. X, *On the Constitution of the Church and State*, ed. John Colmer, 1976.

—— *Confessions of an Inquiring Spirit*, ed. H. N. Coleridge, 1840; facsimile rpt, Menston: Scolar Press, 1971.

Comte, Auguste, *Preliminary Discourse on the Positive Spirit*, trans. W. M. W. Call, London: The Positivist Library, 1883.

Cudworth, Ralph, *The True Intellectual System of the Universe*, trans. John Harrison, 3 vols, London, 1845.

D'Avenant, Charles, *The Political and Commercial Works of that Celebrated Writer Charles D'Avenant*, ed. Sir Charles Whitworth, 5 vols, London, 1771.

Drummond, Rt. Hon. William, *Academical Questions, Volume One*, London, 1805.

Durkheim, Emile, *The Division of Labor in Society*, trans. George Simpson, New York and London: Macmillan, 1933.

Edwards, Paul, ed., *The Encyclopedia of Philosophy*, London and New York: Collier-Macmillan and The Free Press, 1967.

Encyclopédie, ou dictionnaire raisonné des sciences, des arts, et des métiers, ed. Diderot and D'Alembert, 17 vols, Paris, 1751–7.

Ferguson, Adam, *An Essay on the History of Civil Society*, ed. Duncan Forbes, Edinburgh: Edinburgh Univ. Press, 1966.

Ferguson, Frances, *Wordsworth: Language as Counter-Spirit*, New Haven and London: Yale Univ. Press, 1977.

Fichte, J. G., *Johann Gottlieb Fichtes sämmtliche Werke*, ed. I. H. Fichte, 8 vols, Berlin, 1845.

—— *Science of Knowledge*, trans. Peter Heath and John Lachs, New York: Meredith Corporation, 1970.

Godwin, William, *Enquiry Concerning Political Justice and its Influence on Morals and Happiness*, facs. of the 3rd ed., corr., ed. F. E. L. Priestley, 3 vols, Toronto: Univ. of Toronto Press, 1946.

Goethe, J. W. von, *Goethe's Theory of Colours*, trans. Charles Lock Eastlake, 1840; rpt. London: Frank Cass & Co., 1967.

Hartley, David, *Observations on Man, his Frame, his Duty, and his Expectations*, 2 vols, London, 1749.

Hazlitt, William, *The Complete Works of William Hazlitt*, 'The Centenary Edition,' ed. P. P. Howe, 21 vols, London and Toronto: J. M. Dent, 1930–34.

Hegel, G. W. F., *Sämtliche Werke*, Jubiläumsausgabe. Facs. newly ed. H. Glockner, 25 vols, Stuttgart, 1935–71.

—— *Hegel's Science of Logic*, trans. A. V. Miller, London and New York: George Allen & Unwin and Humanities Press, 1969.

—— *Early Theological Writings*, trans. T. M. Knox, 1948; rpt. Philadelphia: Univ. of Pennsylvania Press, 1971.

—— *Hegel's Philosophy of Mind*, trans. William Wallace and A. V. Miller, Oxford: Clarendon Press, 1971.

—— *Aesthetics: Lectures on Fine Art*, trans. T. M. knox, 2 vols, continuously paginated, Oxford: Clarendon Press, 1975.

—— *Phenomenology of Spirit*, trans. A. V. Miller, Oxford: Clarendon Press, 1977.

Hobbes, Thomas, *The English Works of Thomas Hobbes*, ed. Sir William Molesworth, 11 vols, London, 1839–45.

—— *Man and Citizen: Thomas Hobbes' 'De Homine' and 'De Cive'*, trans. Charles T. Wood, T. S. K. Scott-Craig, Bernard Gert, ed. Bernard Gert, 1972; rpt. New York and Hassocks, Sussex: Humanities Press and Harvester Press, 1978.

Johnson, Alexander Bryan, *A Treatise on Language*, ed. David Rynin, Berkeley and Los Angeles: Univ. of California Press, 1947.

Johnson, Samuel, *Johnson: Poetry and Prose*, ed. Mona Wilson, 2nd ed. London: Rupert Hart-Davis, 1957.

Kant, Immanuel, *Critique of Practical Reason*, trans. Lewis White Beck, Indianapolis and New York: Bobbs-Merrill, 1956.

—— *Immanuel Kants Werke*, ed. E. Cassirer, 11 vols, Hildesheim: H. A. Gerstenberg, 1973.

—— *Critique of Judgement*, trans. James Creed Meredith, 2 vols, in one, 1928; rpt Oxford: Clarendon Press, 1952, 1973.

Locke, John, *An Essay Concerning Human Understanding*, ed. Peter H. Nidditch, corr. ed. Oxford: Clarendon Press, 1979.

Lukács, Georg, *History and Class Consciousness: Studies in Marxist Dialectics*, trans. Rodney Livingstone, Cambridge, Mass.: MIT Press, 1971.

Marx, Karl, *Capital. Volume One*, trans. Ben Fowkes, New York: Random House, 1977.

Marx, Karl and Engels, Friedrich, *Collected Works*, in progress, London: Lawrence and Wishart, 1975—.

—— *Marx, Engels: On Literature and Art*, Moscow: Progress Publishers, 1976.

Mill, J. S., *Collected Works of John Stuart Mill*, ed. F. E. L. Priestley, in progress, Toronto and London: Univ. of Toronto Press and Routledge & Kegan Paul, 1963—.

Millar, John, *John Millar of Glasgow, 1735–1801. His Life and Thought and his Contribution to Sociological Analysis*, ed. William C. Lehmann, Cambridge: Cambridge Univ. Press, 1960.

Monboddo, James Burnett, Lord, *Of the Origin and Progress of Language*, 6 vols, London, 1773–92.

Nietzsche, Friedrich, *Basic Writings of Nietzsche*, trans. and ed. Walter Kaufmann, New York: Random House, 1968.

—— *The Will to Power*, trans. Walter Kaufmann and R. J. Hollingdale, New York: Random House, 1968.

Paley, William, *The Principles of Moral and Political Philosophy*, 20th ed., 2 vols, London, 1814.

Pocock, J. G. A., *Politics, Language, and Time: Essays on Political Thought and History*, London: Methuen, 1972.

—— *The Machiavellian Moment: Florentine Political Thought and the Atlantic Republican Tradition*, Princeton: Princeton Univ. Press, 1975.

Prickett, Stephen, *Coleridge and Wordsworth: The Poetry of Growth*, Cambridge: Cambridge Univ. Press, 1970.

Reid, Thomas, *Essays on the Intellectual Powers of Man*, Cambridge, Mass., and London: MIT Press, 1969.

Rousseau, Jean Jacques, 'Essay on the Origin of Languages', *On the Origin of Language: Jean Jacques Rousseau, 'Essay on the Origin of Languages', Johann Gottfried Herder, 'Essay on the Origin of Language'*, trans. John H. Moran and Alexander Gode. New York: Frederick Ungar, 1966.

Schiller, J. C. F. von, *On the Aesthetic Education of Man*, trans. Elizabeth M. Wilkinson and L. A. Willoughby, Oxford: Clarendon Press, 1967.

Schneider, Ben Ross Jnr, *Wordsworth's Cambridge Education*, Cambridge: Cambridge Univ. Press, 1957.

Schopenhauer, Arthur, *Sämtliche Werke*, ed. P. Deussen and E. Hochstetter, 10 vols, Munich, 1911–13.

—— *The World as Will and Representation*, trans. E. F. J. Payne, 2 vols, 1958; rpt New York: Dover Publications, 1966.

Sekora, John, *Luxury: The Concept in Western Thought, Eden to Smollett*, Baltimore and London: The Johns Hopkins Univ. Press, 1977.

Shaffer, E. S., *'Kubla Khan' and 'The Fall of Jerusalem'*, Cambridge: Cambridge Univ. Press, 1975.

Shelley, P. B., *The Complete Works of Shelley*, ed. Roger Ingpen and Walter E. Peck, 10 vols, 1926; rpt New York and London: Gordian Press and Ernest Benn Ltd, 1965.

—— *Poetical Works*, ed. Thomas Hutchinson, corr. ed. G. M. Matthews, London, Oxford, New York: Oxford Univ. Press, 1970.

Simpson, David, *Irony and Authority in Romantic Poetry*, London: Macmillan, 1979.

Smith, Adam, *The Glasgow Edition of the Works and Correspondence of Adam Smith*, in progress, Oxford; Clarendon Press, 1976—
—— Vol. I, *The Theory of Moral Sentiments*, ed. D. D. Raphael and A. L. Macfie, 1976.
—— Vol. II, *An Inquiry into the Nature and Causes of the Wealth of Nations*, ed. R. H. Campbell, A. S. Skinner, W. B. Todd, 2 vols, continuously paginated, 1976.
—— Vol. V, *Lectures on Jurisprudence*, ed. R. L. Meek, D. D. Raphael, P. G. Stein, 1978.
Stam, James H., *Inquiries into the Origin of Language: The Fate of a Question*, New York, Hagerstown, San Francisco, London: Harper & Row, 1796.
Steuart, Sir James, *Works Political, Metaphysical, and Chronological*, ed. Sir James Steuart the younger, 6 vols, London, 1805.
Stewart, Dugald, *The Collected Works of Dugald Stewart*, ed. Sir William Hamilton, 11 vols, Edinburgh: Constable, 1854.
Tribe, Keith, *Land, Labour and Economic Discourse*, London, Henley, and Boston: Routledge & Kegan Paul, 1978.
Wordsworth, William, *The Poetical Works of William Wordsworth*, ed. E. de Selincourt, 5 vols, Oxford: Clarendon Press, 1940–9.
—— *The Prelude*, ed. E. de. Selincourt, 2nd ed. rev. Helen Darbishire, Oxford: Clarendon Press, 1959.
—— *The Letters of William and Dorothy Wordsworth: The Early Years, 1787–1805*, ed. E. de Selincourt, 2nd ed. rev. Chester L. Shaver, Oxford: Clarendon Press, 1967.
—— *The Prose Works of William Wordsworth*, ed. W. J. B. Owen and Jane Worthington Smyser, 3 vols, Oxford: Clarendon Press, 1974.
—— *Home at Grasmere*, ed. Beth Darlington, The Cornell Wordsworth, Ithaca, N. Y., and Hassocks, Sussex: Cornell Univ. Press and Harvester Press, 1977.
Wright, John W., *Shelley's Myth of Metaphor*, Athens, Ga.: Univ. of Georgia Press, 1970.

Index